The Literature of Work

*Short Stories, Essays, and Poems
by Men and Women of Business*

THE Literature OF WORK

Short Stories, Essays, and Poems by Men and Women of Business

Edited by:

Sheila E. Murphy
John G. Sperling
John D. Murphy

University of Phoenix Press
Phoenix ✵ 1991

For information on availability, special discounts, bulk purchases,
or other details, contact:

University of Phoenix Press
4615 East Elwood Street
P.O. Box 52069
Phoenix, AZ 85072-2069

ISBN 1-880708-00-0
Library of Congress Catalog Card Number: 91-67284

First Edition

Printed in Hong Kong

Acknowledgements

THE UNIVERSITY OF Phoenix Press crystallized in March of 1991, with the decision to publish an anthology of creative writing by men and women of business. Calls for submissions were placed, generating a high volume of quality literary manuscripts as well as media coverage. The publication of this anthology in December, 1991, represents a major accomplishment for the University of Phoenix Press.

The editors express their sincere thanks to the following individuals who devoted time, energy, and creativity to make *The Literature of Work* a reality.

Harry O'Donnell and Anita Adams, for joining the editors in reading manuscripts submitted for consideration.

Laurie Easley, for masterminding the production, design, and marketing of the anthology.

Jeanne Ross Winograd and Kerry O'Neill, for their efforts in marketing the anthology.

Michelle White, for designing the cover and contents of the anthology.

Janice McKisson, for logging all manuscripts submitted and orchestrating contact with authors.

Pat Moore and Kathy Buchanan, for supervising the word processing of all contents of the anthology.

Kathy Hepworth, Barbara Marsalla, Pauline Templeton, and Diane Carpenter, for typing and proofreading of the manuscript.

Janice Melvin, Carol Broeder, Holly Wolseth, Kelly Pierce, Diane Lekberg, Sharon Stevens, Erlinda Cabrera, Sherri Kerr, and Donna Luke-Roman for proofreading of the manuscript.

Melony Henshaw, for typing of marketing materials.

Dedication

To the men and women in business
whose richness of life and profession are an enduring
inspiration for this literary genre.

Table of Contents

Essays

Poems

Editors' Foreword

ASSOCIATE THE WORD literature with business, and it typically suggests autobiographies of successful entrepreneurs or the latest in boutique management theory. Rarely does it apply the artistic endeavors of men and women of business responding creatively to the world in which they spend most of their lives.

To the best of our knowledge, *The Literature of Work: Short Stories, Essays, and Poems by Men and Women of Business*, marks the emergence of a new genre of American letters—creative writing about business by persons employed in business. The works contained in this edition, we believe, will help establish the legitimacy of this new genre by adding meaningfully to the culture of the workplace and the larger society.

Four influences resulted in the preparation of *The Literature of Work*. First, the article "These Poets Know the Bottom Line" in *FORTUNE* demonstrated an engagement of business persons with the art of writing. The article reinforced our belief that there must be hundreds of individuals leading lives as serious business professionals and as writers. Second, the insightful anthology of Japanese "Business Novels," *Made in Japan*, translated by Tamae K. Prindle, revealed a highly evolved literary genre with which we were unfamiliar. Third, our desire to publish an unique body of creative work on the uncommon literary topic of business served to inaugurate the University of Phoenix Press.

Finally, the unifying spirit of educational innovation exemplified by the University of Phoenix led naturally to the development of this anthology. As the first accredited for-profit university in the United States, the University of Phoenix has achieved a union of business and academe. It has done so by applying business efficiency and a commitment to educational innovation to the design and delivery of quality academic products and services to a specific market—the working adult student.

Is it possible to capture the romance and human drama of business and soften the image of business men and women as Babbitts and unlettered Philistines? Yes. We did it by choosing works that demonstrate an engagement with business—good and bad, excitement and boredom, nobility and rascality. We believe this anthology will help to temper the estrangement of business and *belle lettres*.

Our most difficult choices involved essays where creativity was sacrificed to analysis or the exposition of academic case studies. In choosing poetry and fiction, we faced another problem—how to decide when good writing dwelled on the private or personal rather than on the human side of business with all its rich but often pedestrian appearing complexity.

We excluded—in the main—the "I hate my job," "I'm the only human being in the place," and depictions of the business world from a brutally existential perspective. In making our selections, we emphasized accessibility with the intention of presenting a collection that meets critical standards. We hope both the business audience and the inveterate readers of *belle lettres* will find our selections enjoyable, informative, thought provoking, and maybe even unsettling.

With few conscious exceptions, the authors represented in our anthology are actively engaged in business-related careers. The exceptions are writers who have retired, left business to write full-time, or who penetratingly observe the business world from non-management positions.

Sheila E. Murphy
John G. Sperling
John D. Murphy

Introduction

FRANKLY, I HAVE dreaded writing this introduction. I agreed to do it, yes, because I wanted to believe that this anthology could debunk, once and for all, the notion that businesspeople don't have the sensitivities or the talent to be writers and poets, and that writers and poets don't have the good solid sense to be businesspeople.

But as the deadline drew near, I could not help reflecting on my personal situation and on how lonely I have felt from time to time as a businessman/poet (the typical news media description of me).

As my book, *Love and Profit*, hit the stores and the media tour began, I always faced the same questions. Some talk-show host would challenge: "Tell us, Mr. Autry, don't your business associates think it rather strange that you write poetry?" Or, "Is it *really* possible to be a poet and still be a boss?"

Clearly, the media people somehow could not accept the possibility that "bosses" or "businesspeople" were not all like the popular stereotypes we see in the movies or on TV: Short-tempered, abrasive, blunt, bullying bastards.

Yet there I was talking about the emotions of business and expressing those in prose and poetry. The reporters' and TV hosts' incredulity was almost contagious; even I began to wonder if my perceptions were distorted.

Of course I had corresponded with a few poets who were also businesspeople, and I knew there was an informal network, yet when the University of Phoenix Press contacted me, I was not at all sure there would be enough good material for the kind of landmark work which could withstand rigorous critique.

Please understand that I claim no superior literary skills; still, I know that none of us would want a collection of well-intended but not-well-done work about which some critics I know might snidely observe, "Isn't it nice that the businesspeople have taken an interest in the language?"

So I have dreaded writing this introduction because my fears got the best of me; I simply became afraid of what I might be introducing.

Oh me of little faith!

Now, reading through the hundreds of submissions making their way toward becoming a final manuscript, I am ashamed of my doubts. And I am excited by the potential of this book.

Here is ample demonstration that people in business are worthy stewards of a literary heritage which for centuries has examined and honored the connection between people and their work. Rather than an examination from the outside looking in, this intensely personal work comes from the heart of the enterprise as well as from the hearts of the writers.

This book also furthers the literature of work by its particularly late 20th century focus. This is not the stuff of the farmer's rhythmical husbandry of land and animals or the laborer's gritty connection of muscle and machine. Rather, the reader will find here the subtle dances of the executive suite, the richness of image and imagination a computer systems analyst brings to a seemingly sterile office, the sexual tension between a young saleswoman and her graying boss on a business trip.

This is the work of businesspeople who have become poets and poets who have become businesspeople, both situations out of necessity, I suspect, one economic and the other spiritual. There are many examples, but I was particularly struck by David Alpaugh's poem, "A California Ad Man Celebrates His Art." Advertising takes a rather bum rap these days, yet here is a poet and teacher by education who "drifted into advertising," finding in it and expressing its link with "The Great Tradition."

I was taken with Tina Quinn Durham's description of "My Work," a sense of what's real in her world of defense contracts, missiles, and her "elegant stacks of small truth."

I was also happy to find here some work by the undisputed best and most accomplished among us, Dana Gioia who, almost single-handedly, has established the literary legitimacy of the present day businessperson/poet.

Is all the writing here uniformly good? Of course not. Nor is that true of any anthology. But all the writing here is important, if not so much for the artfulness of it then for the very fact of it.

I commend this book to any reader who would understand better the emotional, psychological, and spiritual connections between businesspeople and their work, and who would in that process be enriched by this surprising literary achievement.

James A. Autry

The Literature of Work

Short Stories, Essays, and Poems
by Men and Women of Business

Business and Poetry

It's not easy to be a modern businessman
And also a writer of modern poetry,
And find in either profession a receptive coterie.
For though rhyme and meter can gracefully expand—
And at the same time frame—the world's infinite contents,
Only under a blue moon will poetry merge
IBM with AT&T, or even urge
A public buyout, or more rarely pay the rent.
And though an all-night corporate annual review
Will not sing a body into something electric,
Or change an unfaithful wife into an epic,
Or from a red wheelbarrow spawn a stanza or two,
Just one profitable week at the office
Will offset a recent manuscript's rejection
And white-out bad press in the *Book Review* section
By granting almost every temporal wish.
And on days when faithful clients ignore your call,
When a slumping stock becomes more than an omen,
When you stagger home wasted as Willy Loman,
How easy to write a line and damn them all.

Kate Bertrand

Racing With the Wolves

She never thought of power as her sport
until one night, over a business drink,
the sporting urge emerged. She played the flirt
to lure her lean, grey boss. And in a wink
the race was on. She hurdled past his wiles—
created charming lies, gazed in his eyes.
Of course he wrote no memo for the files,
describing nylon foot on flannel thigh
or trysts at noon. But someone did, and though
the wolf was quick, he fell behind. The race
was hers, the corner office, teak desk. No
more rendezvous—with him. The faster pace
agreed with her. The hungry young run fast,
until their youth and hunger fade, at last.

Starting Gun

James Castle Furlong

D<small>AVID</small> L<small>INK</small> B<small>EGAN</small> the semi-panicky dawn search that had become routine in recent months. With a heightened sense of touch, he could detect the strands of loose hair by running a hand over the warm contours of his pillow.

They registered as a slight feeling of graininess under his fingertips.

A five-minute search turned up six of them. You could add at least three for what he missed in the dark. He didn't want to turn on the light and awaken Tatiana. As usual, she had stayed up late reading.

It looked like a tough day ahead. He and Tatiana were to load up the Toyota station wagon and a U-Haul trailer and drive from Cambridge to central Massachusetts to spend a semester in the town of Adamston.

God, wasn't this the way baldness started? The first tentative flurries of hair falling onto the pillow thicken into a blizzard. Then the skies clear and you are as smooth and shiny up top as Kojak.

He couldn't really gauge his net hair loss. And the doctor had said only, "Medicine can't predict accurately whether you'll be bald. If it's in the genes, you will be. But the genes aren't ready to show their hand yet. I have a question for you: does it really matter that much?"

David now felt a twinge in his right eye tooth. Irv, his dentist, had x-rayed it last week and found nothing. "Let's watch it," said Irv. "Right now, there's just nothing to go on. I would violate the most important command of the Hippocratic writings if I went in there with a drill."

"What's that?"

"'First, do no harm.' Are you enjoying your life?" Irv had replied. "You like teaching at the Management School?"

It was hard to judge this Friday morning if the tooth really hurt. Was there any real distinction between mental and physical pain, he wondered. The mind can produce real physical symptoms—the blush and the ulcer, for example.

"Die, Hypochondriac Bastard," muttered David. He popped out of the bed and padded into the bathroom. He shaved, brushed his teeth and slipped into a jogging suit that Tatiana had bought him for his 30th birthday a week ago. He drove to the Beacon Hill section of Boston, parked on Brimmer Street, crossed Storrow Drive on an elevated sidewalk and, in the cool early September morning, took what he figured would be his last five-mile run along the Charles for five months. He would have to map out a course in Adamston. He needed to run to buy himself time.

* * *

They set out at 10:30 a.m. Tatiana grabbed her grey felt fedora by the brim as David started the car, whirled it twice over her head and shouted, "Westward the wagons! Westward, ho!"

They hooted, hollered and laughed for about a minute. When they stopped, she asked, "What does 'ho' mean, David?" Tatiana, daughter of a professor of Slavic literature at Harvard, had absorbed Russian from her parents before she learned English in school. She had an intense curiosity about her adopted language.

He thought, then answered like a dictionary. "1. Uttered three times in a row, 'ho' is an onomatopoeic representation of laughter, particularly that of the children's folk hero Santa Claus. 2. An interjection used in seafaring movies by scurvy actors when sighting land after a long voyage. As in 'Land, ho!' 3. Capitalized, the name of the late Vietnamese leader, Ho Chi Minh."

Tatiana, with her high cheek bones, slight overbite, blonde hair and lush body, was looking particularly fine to him today. She laughed dutifully, but he could tell she didn't really find his attempt at Cambridge-style humor authentic.

The Adamston adventure had been inspired by Dean Emery Fisher of Cambridge's renowned Graduate School of Management, the M-School, where David taught industrial relations. Fisher, fed up with charges that the school turned out theoretically oriented numbers-crunchers rather than business executives, had ordered all instructors to spend a semester in an actual manufacturing or service industry. The intellectuals were to work the fields, with the M-School paying their wages.

David looked on his forthcoming semester more as an opportunity to teach than learn. That's why he had chosen the isolated town of Adamston over Silicon Valley or Route 128. Adamston needed his outside points of view, the rational analysis he could bring to the human side of production. And if the truth were known, David wanted to be somewhere he felt needed.

Soon after arriving from Carleton College in Minnesota eight years ago, he'd begun wondering why Cambridge needed yet another bright young man, and his doubts had never really disappeared. He remained proud of his main work—a paper called "West German Worker Co-Determination at the level of Betriebsrat and Aufsichtsrat, Considered in Light of Maslow's Hierarchy of Needs; Empirical Measures of Worker Satisfaction, a Cross-Cultural Approach." He could see now, two years after writing the paper, that the title was an unintended parody of Cambridge academic style by an awed, transplanted Midwesterner. But the paper had been solid; the subject important.

* * *

"Let's stop and get Egg McBiscuits," said Tatiana, as they approached a roadside eatery.

"God, Tatiana. Those things are cholesterol bombs."

"I want one anyway," she said, with a look of amused defiance. "You should have one, too. Live a little. It's later than you think."

They had been married two years. He was a self-confessed health nut. She smoked, stayed up late reading Jane Austen, science fiction, E.L. Doctorow, *Time*, and even the *M-School Review* if nothing else was at hand. As she read, she sipped weak spritzers made with cheap red wine. She liked junk food, and she wasn't neat.

He loved her. Disorganized though she was in small matters, she had a firm sense of direction. She wanted David; two children; time for friends; and a career in high school teaching once the second child was in fourth grade. Tatiana was 24. David, six years older, wondered at how she'd been able to map her course so quickly.

It took two hours to reach Adamston, located 10 miles south of New Hampshire and roughly equidistant from the eastern and western ends of Massachusetts. Adamston was cradled in a broad valley along the Mentors River.

After entering the town, they cruised down a long hill, passing the Collins Regional High School, Adamston General Hospital, a sign for the Bear Hollow Custom Slaughtering Farm and a long-abandoned cloth-weaving factory.

Halfway down the hill, the big houses of funeral directors and executives of the town's tool and furniture companies gave way to wooden apartment houses for workers.

When David and Tatiana reached the bottom of the hill, they saw a store-front saloon called The Mentor and a sign pointing across the river to Adamston Precision Instruments Inc. API was where David would report to work Monday. It was lunch hour. Men and women talked, sipped beer and ate sandwiches in the September sunshine outside the saloon. They had sober looks and sober clothes, grey and tan chino trousers, blue shirts and plain-toed brown or black shoes with thick rubber soles. Many wore glasses.

"These people look steady. They imitate the machines they run, maybe," said David.

"I hope they're more fun than they look," said Tatiana.

As David and Tatiana rolled through town toward their rented house, they seemed to go backwards in time. Most buildings in the central business district appeared to have been constructed between 1880 and 1930. They had limestone facades on the ground floor, fancy raised brickwork above, arched windows and ample copper-covered eaves that were supported by tightly spaced cornices. Stone plaques, embedded just above the main entrances, named and dated the buildings.

A sign on an old movie marquee read: "Bingo Tonight. Triple Pot."

"Shall we go for it?" asked Tatiana. "We need to meet people. And we could use the money. I know I'm not going to like the curtains that come with the house." For some reason, curtains were important to Tatiana, who otherwise cared little about interior decoration.

"Tonight, I'd prefer to stay in," said David. "My agenda must be ready when I meet Dan Stark."

Tatiana frowned. "Maybe I can go myself. I'm not going to live here in isolation for five months."

"Fine," said David, whose natural reserve was reinforced by his professional need to spend long hours alone reading and writing. This had become a sore point, along with the question of children.

* * *

It was 8:30 that night, and David was writing after washing dishes. Tatiana had shopped in the afternoon. She improbably found a wok in the kitchen and prepared them stir-fried chicken with peanuts, David having sworn off red meat six months earlier. The only way Tatiana could stand the healthful foods he ate was by spicing them hot, and she heated up the chicken with red peppers fried black. She washed the chicken down with a glass of what she called "rot-gut Liebfraumilch" purchased from the local liquor store. He drank bottled water. After dinner, she had gone out to play Bingo, leaving David to clean the kitchen. The phone rang.

"Is this Dave?" demanded the caller.

"This is David Link," he replied.

"Dan Stark here. Glad I caught you. Meet me at the Personnel Office tomorrow morning at 6:15, Dave. We're working around the clock right now, and I'd like to introduce myself and show you the plant at a time when I won't be bothered by phone calls. After that, we'll take a short plane ride so you can get an overview of this neck of Worcester County."

"Mr. Stark, I thought we'd planned on my reporting at 9 a.m. Monday. Does this tour really need to be done tomorrow? I'm supposed to help my wife shop tomorrow."

"Call me Dan, Dave. Women like to shop alone. Believe me. I have more time for you tomorrow than I will for five months."

"I'll talk to my wife . . ."

"Does she have a veto over all your plans?"

"No, but . . ."

"This isn't too early for you, I hope. I'm not sure what time you people get up in Cambridge, but out here we're running for our lives with the Japanese, Koreans, Taiwanese and Filipinos in hot pursuit. See you at 6:15 a.m. sharp. Wear jeans or chinos, sneakers and a warm jacket, but you've got to look neat for our people on the floor," said Stark.

"'Our people?'" repeated David, dubiously.

"Not yours. API's. Mine. The work force. See you at the Personnel Office."

David put the phone down angrily. Stark might own a good part of this town, but he did not own David. Daniel Allison Stark, great grandson of the founder of Adamston Precision, had to learn that David (repeat David) Caughey Link, great grandson of a Danish-born Minnesota farmer, didn't like to be pushed and belittled.

David worked on his agenda another hour and a half. His core idea was to form joint labor-management shopfloor committees at Adamston Precision. At first, they would concern themselves with quality control and later take on other responsibilities like workers' schedules, discipline and investment of pension monies. The object would be to break down the "us-and-them" mentality that poisoned labor-management relations in the U.S.

Tatiana got home at 10 p.m.

"Vas I on roll!" she said, with a mock Russian accent. "I won $100. But I gave $50 of it to a fund for buying new equipment for the high school football team. I sat next to the wife of the API personnel director, John Foley, in the Bingo salon."

"Guess what? She invited us over for a drink at 5 Sunday afternoon."

"Dammit, Tatiana, may I please have a vote on social engagements? I have to work Sunday afternoon."

"You can work tomorrow morning, David. I'll shop for curtains myself."

"Fine, except that I have to visit the factory tomorrow morning starting at 6:15." He told her about Stark's call.

"This guy doesn't waste any time, does he?" she said.

"You mean getting me to see the factory?"

"Yes, that, and Martha Foley told me Stark is only 35."

"Sure, I knew that. He took over five years ago when his father had a stroke. It's not as if he moved up through the ranks."

"No, what I meant was Martha told me Stark and his wife have five children."

"That I didn't know. That's a real Malthusian nightmare. Reckless reproduction. Runaway replication. It will be the death of us all, if we're not annihilated first by Latin American debt," said David, smiling. "I've got to get to bed."

"Sometimes I don't like your jokes. You use them to avoid thinking."

"You mean the children thing?"

"Yes, David. The children thing. We have to get started. We won't live forever, you know. We are perishable goods. 'Breath's a ware that will not keep.'"

"We can wait until I get better settled. You're only 24."

"I could wait if I knew that you really wanted a family. But I'm beginning to wonder."

"Let's talk tomorrow."

* * *

In the grey September morning, David crossed the bridge over Mentors River to get to API's main building on the north bank. Immediately upriver from the bridge was a 20-foot dam with brown-green water pouring over the top. On the south bank was a small building, with 16-foot high windows, housing a company power station that took in water above the dam and channeled it down over turbines that pirouetted as it passed. This was a dirty, ugly workhorse of a river.

The oldest parts of the century-old plant were of clapboard, now covered by neat white vinyl siding. The main building, three stories high and made of brick, dated back to 1904, according to a plaque on the side. The walls of the newer buildings were of corrugated metal. Walkways connected the separate buildings.

David pulled open the outer door marked "Personnel" and mounted well-worn wooden stairs to a waiting room on the second floor. He pressed a button on the wall to announce his presence. While he waited, his eye fell on a framed sign on one wall.

He walked to the sign and read:

> Man is a Tool-using Animal. Weak in himself, and of small stature, he stands on a basis of some half-square foot; has to straddle out his legs, lest the very winds supplant him. Nevertheless he can use Tools, can devise Tools: with these, the granite mountain melts into light dust before him; seas are his smooth highway, winds and fire his unwearying steeds. Nowhere do you find him without Tools; without Tools he is nothing, with Tools he is all.
> —Excerpts from Thomas Carlyle (1795-1881)

9

David was about to sit down as a door opened. A short, burly man carrying a mug of coffee walked out and said:

"OK, I waited until you had read the sign. Those are words we live by, even though I found them in a booklet put out by the L.S. Starrett Company, one of our competitors upriver. I'm Dan Stark." They shook hands.

"How did you know I'd been reading it?" asked David.

"I watched you over the building security television system."

"That's a little intrusive, isn't it?" asked David.

"Yes, I intrude everywhere," said Stark, smiling broadly. Stark had a bull neck and his eyes bulged slightly, as if from internal pressure. David, the taller of the two, could see that Stark had a bald spot about the size of a silver dollar on top of his head. "This is kind of early for you Cambridge types, I know," said Stark. "How about a coffee. You take it black or regular?"

"Not really that early, and thanks, no, I had a tea at home." David heard himself sounding stiff and standoffish, but he was having a hard time with Stark's pushiness and forced familiarity.

"Tea in the morning," said Stark. "That's not strong enough for me. What kind of tea do you drink—Lipton, Earl Grey?"

"Actually, it was herbal tea," said David, who was trying it out for health reasons.

"OK," said Stark, "but that kind of stuff can lead to a chronic and debilitating caffeine deficiency. Now let's have a look around. The factory is running full tilt right now. Manufacturing companies are booming domestically and in many of our overseas markets. We are making hay while the sun shines."

"Why does manufacturing activity mean more business for you specifically?" asked David, who had yet to work out API's microeconomics.

"OK, we make precise measuring instruments, right? You can't build anything without being able to measure parts and products. You need hook rules, dividers, micrometer and vernier calipers, protractors. You familiar with what I'm talking about?"

"Somewhat. I took mechanical drawing in high school," said David.

"Well, that's Square 1 type stuff. We're at Square 57. You know what an inch is?"

"Most people do have a pretty good idea, don't they?"

"Do most people know that an inch is 42,016.807 wave lengths of monochromatic light from Krypton-86 gas?"

"Well . . ."

"We start there. Do you know how to measure the depth of a slot? You do it with one of our micrometer depth gauges. And you measure the angle of a screw thread with one of our screw-pitch indicators. You check the interior diameter of a pipe with one of our telescoping, graduated sticks. If you need to measure it, we have the ruler."

David wondered idly if API could measure the advance of baldness.

"We do get into other things," said Dan. "We also make carpenter's tools. Not the Third World crap you buy in your local supermarket, but expensive tools that will last a carpenter a lifetime."

He looked at David. "OK, I know it's like trying to drink from a fire hose. Let's just walk around."

Stark and David crossed a covered walkway one story above the ground and entered a big manufacturing area. David found himself on a catwalk built along the walls of a two-story room. Morning light filtered in through big dirty windows next to the catwalk, supplementing the glow of fluorescent fixtures suspended by long cords from the ceiling. In the room below, a man was using a forklift to mount big spools of steel onto spindles.

"We make saw blades here," said Stark. "That machine hardens 17 ribbons of steel simultaneously and hauls them past diamond-tipped cutters that notch teeth into them."

"What's the purpose of this catwalk?"

"So management can see what's going on down there. It prevents people from goofing off."

"The Hawthorne Effect."

"The what?" asked Stark.

"The Hawthorne Effect. Workers do better when they think they're being observed. It brings out the performer in them."

"Maybe," said Stark.

"Raymond," he shouted down at a young man handling the spools. The man stopped the lift so he could hear better. "What did you say, Mr. Stark?"

"Raymond, goddammit, you put one of those spools on backwards. The steel will feed out from the wrong side."

"Yes, Sir, I've discovered that the machine can handle it, and it saves time."

"Hold everything, Raymond. I'm coming down."

"Let's go," said Stark to David. Stark clambered down a set of steel steps to the main floor and walked quickly over to Raymond. David followed.

"Ray," said Stark, "this machine no way will tolerate a reversed spool. I know because I designed the machine."

Raymond, about David's age, was sweating and pale. He protested, "Yes, but I've done it before."

Stark opened a large notebook that he carried in a leather pouch slung from his shoulder by a strap. He looked carefully at a computer printout in the notebook.

"OK, Ray, I agree you have done it. And I'll tell you when. It was on Aug. 29, Sept. 3 and Sept. 7."

"That sounds right," said Ray. "How do you know?"

"Your scrap rate on those days was about 10% higher than on other days. Every mistake you make is in this book, Ray."

Ray looked ill. He was breathing fast.

"Ray, you smell like a goddamn distillery. How late were you out drinking last night?"

The young man was silent.

"How late, Ray? You haven't got any Fifth Amendment rights here."

"I had a few beers and went to bed about 10:30. I got about 5 hours' sleep."

"A few beers, my ass! I bet you were boozing until an hour before you got to work. You aren't orienting these spools correctly because you're sick and drunk."

"Mr. Stark, I do not have any drinking problem."

"Well, you have a big Dan Stark problem, starting now. Shut down the blade processor and take a week off without pay. Think about your situation. You want to come back here next Saturday at 4 a.m. acting like a competent journeyman machinist, which is what you are paid very well to do, fine. If not, you can play broom jockey."

"Wait here," said Stark to David. "I've got to get someone sober to run this machine."

As Stark walked out, Ray said under his breath, "That son of a bitch!"

"Is he hard to work with?" asked David.

Ray gave David a dismissive glance and said, "Yeah, he's a real mother to work for. Who the hell are you? I never saw you before."

"My name is David Link. I am acting as a temporary consultant."

"Well, Dave," said Ray with some resonance, "this is none of your goddamn business. It's between me and The Man." He walked out moments later after shutting down the machine.

When Dan came back with a new operator, he took David aside and said, "You talked about the Hawthorne Effect. What you just saw was the Stark Effect."

"I don't think Ray likes you very much," said David.

"Ray lives only for the day he can shaft me," said Dan, happily. "But if he didn't hate me so much, he would have absolutely no reason to go on."

Later, they toured the design, forging, milling, punching, polishing, assembly and packing areas. As they walked, Stark chatted with a few workers in each department. He promised to arrange a company loan for a 25-year-old computer-aided design specialist who was about to buy a house. When they moved away, Dan whispered to David, "There is absolutely no way I can lose this guy. He's a brilliant, driven inventor. If he asked me, I'd buy him the house."

He paused next to a giant machine where metal rods were being chopped into two-inch sections inside a glassed-in chamber as a half dozen jets of oil cooled the chopper. Stark said, "Machine parts are born in oil. We have to account to the Massachusetts environmental protection authorities for every drop used. The Asians and Latin Americans can just dig a hole, dump it in and make it go away."

The machine operator came up, and Dan said: "Edgar, you spending any nights at home these days? Your wife tells me she hasn't seen you in a week." He spoke as if David were not present.

Edgar, a strapping man of about 33 with slicked-back hair, mumbled something about "other commitments" while looking at a young woman washing oil from her hands in a big circular industrial hygiene sink.

I 3

"Edgar, just remember those kids of yours are going to start understanding what's going on soon. Do you want that?" He moved on without waiting for a reply.

In the assembly room, he came up behind the forewoman without her noticing. He tapped on her shoulder. She turned, pulling a headset from her ears. She was about 40, very thin, with brown hair done up in a bun. She was chewing gum. "Hi, Dan," she said with a look of faintly discernible annoyance.

He detected her mood and said, "Hope I'm not bothering you, Wanda."

"Of course not," she said, brightening quickly. "Why should I be bothered?"

"Because I think I broke something up between you and your Walkman."

"Oh, no, it's no interruption."

The other women in the department, except for one, stopped their work to listen.

"Wanda, you are the head of this department. You are paid damn well to know everything that's going on here, to talk to people, to watch people. How can you possibly do that when you're cut off from the outside world by these damned earphones? I've told you before not to use them. Play a radio softly if you need music."

"The other girls don't want to listen to what I like. Dan, I mean really, it's a Saturday morning."

Stark's face darkened. "Wanda, do you think our customers give a flying dropkick that it's Saturday morning? A micrometer made on Saturday at 7 a.m. is supposed to work just like one made on Wednesday at 2 p.m.—perfectly out to one ten-thousandth of an inch. We don't make Saturday morning mikes."

Wanda looked away.

"I've got a good deal for you, Wanda. You keep your earphones and move over to where Juanita is sitting." Juanita, until now the only member of the department still working instead of watching the spectacle, lifted the jeweler's loupe from her eye and raised her head.

"Juanita, you have a new desk. You're trading with Wanda here. Come to my office Monday for a talk."

He and David left as the two exchanged desks amid excited murmurs. The assembly department had just witnessed a public execution.

The tour lasted 2½ hours. At the end, Dan said, "OK, Dave, your head should be reeling by now. Let's take an aerial tour."

A chauffeur met them in a moderately large Mercedes at the main gate at 9 a.m.

Inside the car, Stark cracked a window and lit a cigar as they pulled away.

David, trying to take in all he had seen, could think of nothing to say. Finally, he asked, "Where did you go to college, Dan?" David was genuinely curious to know what sort of institution could have produced the overbearing and outrageous Dan Stark.

"The South Norwalk Institute of Sports Broadcasting and Print Journalism," said Stark.

"What does that mean?" snapped David. This cur grew too bold. Stark was toying with him.

"I mean it isn't important," said Stark, calmly. "Not here. What do you think of the plant?"

"I think it's medieval."

"It's high-tech," rejoined Stark.

"OK, not medieval but early Industrial Revolution. From a labor relations standpoint, you are an anachronism. Your people have no privacy, no autonomy, no voice in decisions that affect their daily lives. You haven't organized your plant to maximize job satisfaction and productivity. If you had a union, you could never have gotten away with what I saw this morning."

"If I had a union, it would price me right out of Massachusetts. Then the union would berate me when I wanted to move to Arkansas or South Korea," said Dan. He then sat back in his seat and said, "Tell me your ideas."

David talked steadily for a half hour, describing Japanese quality circles and German work councils and their impact on job satisfaction, productivity and workers' sense of responsibility. Stark listened in silence. When David finished, Stark said, "I am not sure you are talking about Adamston, Massachusetts."

The driver turned off I-91 in Northampton and they arrived at the airport two minutes later.

"Dave, put on this flight suit," said Stark as they prepared in a hangar for the flight. "The helicopter isn't available this morning, so we'll take the little Cessna 206. We'll sit on the floor because there's only one seat and that's for the pilot. But the ride shouldn't last more than 45 minutes. You'll get a good look out the windows. It's a very clear day. The suit will keep your clothes from getting dirty."

David zipped himself into the coveralls.

The pilot, a blonde woman in her late 20s, started the engine when she saw Dan and David emerge from the hangar. Dan was carrying a large bag, which he said they could use as a makeshift chairback.

"Elsa, this is Dave," said Dan, as the two climbed into the rear of the small plane. The craft was too small to stand up in.

"Hi, Dave," said Elsa perfunctorily. She was concentrating on the plane.

"Take us up to three grand," said Dan. Elsa taxied the plane slowly past cornfields, then turned into an adjacent runway and gunned the small craft into the air. For the next 15 minutes, Dan pointed out the sights to Dave—the Connecticut and Mentors Rivers, Adamston Precision, Wachusett Mountain, and the area's main highways, rail lines and airports.

"Dip down over the Quabbin Reservoir," Dan told Elsa. He explained to Dave that "on a clear day like this, when there's been little rainfall for weeks, you can see down through the water to the remains of the old towns along the Swift River that was dammed in the 1930s to create the Quabbin. The reservoir supplies Boston with drinking water."

As they flew low, David caught glimpses of building foundations. The small ones likely were for houses. Bigger ones could have been for schools. Or churches. For a moment, he had an absurd image of a catfish playing the organ to a congregation of perch, bass and trout as minnows cavorted in the aisles. He was getting queasy. The plane was smaller than any craft he had flown in before, and altitude changes weren't helping. He started to taste the previous night's blackened red peppers.

"Elsa, Dave is looking a little green. Take it up to 8,500 grand so we can cool off a bit and get some fresh air."

"OK, but please move fast, Dan. I'm going to have just enough gas."

"Gas?" asked David. "How much gas does it take to get back to Northampton?"

"She's not going back to Northampton. She's flying to Teterboro, New Jersey," said Dan, with a wide smile.

David felt his teeth clench hard. Stark was playing with him again. Then David was shouting involuntarily.

"What in the goddamn hell are you talking about, Stark? Are you trying to jerk me around?"

His control had broken. He'd blown it. The semester in industry was over before it had begun.

But Stark kept grinning. "You're not a purebred, peace-loving, enlightened man of learning, are you, Dave? That gives me some small faint hope for you."

Dan continued, talking over the engine. "I am about to acquire a specialty textile plant in South Carolina. Among other things, it makes giant parachutes that carry two people. Some sports parachuting centers are starting to use them to teach new jumpers. The instructor and learner go down buckled together in what's called a tandem jump. I thought you might possibly be up to the challenge. We'd land right at the Northampton airport."

David swallowed. "This could be harmful to my health," he said.

"Yes, terminal in fact," replied Stark. "But I have made 51 tandem jumps and 103 solo jumps and have never suffered anything worse than a sprained ankle."

"I do not have to do this," said David.

"That's absolutely right," said Stark. "You can fly on to Teterboro now. I'll radio my driver from the plane and he'll be in Teterboro in four hours to pick you up. You can be back home by dinner. But I'm going to jump. Right, Elsa?"

"Right," replied Elsa.

David felt his heart racing. There were several ways out of this. He could demand to land at Northampton, rejecting the either/or choice that Stark presented. Let the co-conspirator Elsa gas up again in Northampton if she was short on fuel. Or he could fly to Teterboro, in effect saying that Stark's opinion didn't matter. Or he could jump.

The first two solutions, it became obvious after a few moments' reflection, were too "Cambridge," too ambiguous, too subtle—for Stark, anyway. There was only one totally honorable way out of this situation, and that was down.

"Let's jump," said David.

Stark looked at him appraisingly, then spoke. "Let me put the harness on you. Also, here's a rubber helmet and goggles. Put them on."

For the next five minutes, David tried not to think about what was happening. The harness was strapped over his shoulders, across his chest and back and under his thighs. Stark then donned his own harness and fastened it to the back of David's. David saw Dan was wearing a big "wristwatch" altimeter. It said 7,500 feet. Elsa was spiralling the little plane upward. A corkscrew path to oblivion, David thought.

"OK, Dave," said Stark. "We're fastened together with four buckles. Each buckle can hold 10,000 pounds. The chute probably could carry a young elephant. We're going to free-fall for about 33 seconds. That will take us down about a mile. Just above 3 grand, I'll open the chute."

David wondered whether his M-School life insurance would cover him. Most likely. What would Tatiana do? Maybe she'd be better off with someone else, someone ready to have children immediately. Maybe it was best in the long run. Tatiana the Merry Widow at 24. It was clear to him now that he had wanted children. They were the ordinary man's immortality. Maybe he would tell her that in the unlikely event he survived.

"Dave, are you listening?"

David listened, hard. "As soon as we leave the plane, you arch your body, chest stuck out, arms out at a 45 degree angle, legs apart a bit. You will be lying on the air. We will reach a maximum speed in free fall of 120 miles an hour.

"You don't have to tell me you're scared. All your survival instincts are telling you not to do this. But we are using one of man's tools—the parachute. Remember Carlyle: 'Winds and fire his unwearying steeds.' The winds will be our steed today."

Dan's wristwatch hit 8,500 feet. Dan reached over to one side of the plane and pulled at a handle along the floor. "I'm opening the door," he said.

The door slid up from the floor and across a track on the ceiling of the plane, clicking into place and creating a four foot square exit. David glanced out the big hole and felt the fear he remembered from looking straight down from the observation platform of a skyscraper. Only this fear was squared or cubed to terror. His crotch felt sick, vulnerable—some sensation from the race's ancient history.

Dan wasn't going to give him much time to think about it.

"Go!" said Stark. "Scoot to the door. You'll stay in the door 10 seconds with your feet dangling out, then I'll push off. Don't try to hang on to the doorway."

Below, David saw nothing but the I-91 and connecting roads. What if they landed in that 70-mile-an-hour traffic? It wouldn't really matter. David figured he'd die of a heart attack long before he hit the ground. He'd never feel a thing.

Suddenly, there was a push, and they were out of the plane, in the huge open skies. Nothing to hang onto. David was kicking, flailing, trying to swim without water. The wind was rushing past his face. His life was over.

A persistent noise above him became a voice. Saying what? He concentrated.

"Arch, dammit, arch," he heard faintly.

David, remembering now, spread his arms, put out his chest, stopped kicking.

After a few moments, Dan reached his own arms out in front and gave David a twin thumbs-up sign. Maybe David wasn't going to die immediately. He had some more seconds to live. The wind tore at his face, but he maintained his arch. Objects on the ground slowly got bigger. After an eternity, Dan shouted, "Chute opening."

David felt an upward jerk on his body for several seconds, as if a superfast descending elevator had stopped suddenly. Were they rising?

"Don't worry, It's called 'opening shock,'" said Stark. "It's over now."

The pressure ceased. The wind died, and they began floating down slowly in perfect silence, with their bodies now at right angles to the earth. There was nearly 3,000 feet to go, but somehow they seemed close to the ground.

"There goes Elsa," said Dan pointing into the far distance above them.

David looked up, past the edge of the giant yellow and red canopy above him, and saw a black dot, apparently headed for Teterboro.

"This is the part where you're supposed to feel like Superman," said Dan.

David didn't respond. He felt dizzy. His panoramic view of the earth gave little joy. He wanted nothing more than solid ground directly beneath his feet. Below, he now could see the white landing circle in a big green field 300 yards from the hangar. The circle widened as they descended.

They landed far more gently than David had imagined, but he stumbled, throwing them both to the ground in what seemed like slow motion. They rose together awkwardly. Dan unbuckled the rig, stretched, then began repacking the parachute, as David gratefully removed his goggles, helmet, harness and jump suit.

Dan said, "You made it. You did OK, except you kicked a lot when we exited. I'd give you a C+. You'll do better next time. Possibly."

"Maybe next time you'll hit the circle," rejoined David. "We missed it by a good 10 yards, for Christ's sake."

Dan grinned tightly.

"Why did you do this?" asked David.

"You really want to know?" asked Stark.

David nodded.

"I wanted you to go to the edge, get your blood running. I wanted to let you know what it is to be scared out of your mind—scared for your life. You guys in Cambridge, the only thing you're afraid of is not getting tenure. I run scared every day thinking the competition is going to drive me out of business. If API were to go down, I'd have betrayed my traditions and the people of Adamston." His voice rose. "And I'd have been beaten. I will not be beaten." The man was almost shouting.

Then, more softly, he added: "And I wanted to see if you would take a calculated risk."

David smiled with pride, despite himself.

Stark said quickly, "Yes, you took the risk, but you did it under pressure. I don't know how you'd do alone."

"I take risks, Dan," said David. "I took one coming to Adamston. Hopefully, it's going to work out."

Then they got into the Mercedes and rode without speaking for most of the journey back.

As they approached David's house, Stark finally said:

"Link, you are a product of the M-School. First you were a graduate student, now a teacher. The school has taught you about the rational deployment of human resources for maximum productivity. They taught you money, bread. But there's more to it.

"Did the School teach you to know each of your people, in all their strengths and weaknesses, and not just what workers in general tend to do under Controlled Conditions X, Y and Z?

"Did the statisticians and management-theory jockeys tell you about sloth, hate, pride, craftsmanship, envy and the ferocity of the human animal?

"Can you develop so much information about your workers' performance that they think of you as their conscience?

"Have you learned how to lay on guilt and grant absolution like a priest?

"Did the School show you how to terrorize screwups so badly that all they want is to redeem themselves in order to feel secure in your love and protection?

"Did you learn that Man needs circuses as well as bread—circuses to make him forget for a while that he lives under a sentence of death?"

The car stopped. David got out, and the two men talked through an open window.

"Those are rhetorical questions," said David, "so I am not going to answer them now. Just don't assume your way is the only way. I can help you. I can help your workers work better."

"OK, I am willing to learn, if you have anything to teach me, which I doubt," said Dan, now smiling. "Give me a written precis of your ideas for these worker-management whosits Monday morning. I don't want any sophomoric crap. I'm not going to play touchy-feely with Wanda and Ray and start tolerating sloppy work just so everyone can feel good about himself all the time.

"If your ideas are realistic, you can experiment with them cautiously. But you'll have responsibility for the results. That's something new for you. Some of you people don't really care whether your proposals work in the real world as long as they sound good to your colleagues. Let's talk at 6:15 a.m. Monday."

"6:15 a.m.?" That was the time David planned for his daily run. And what was this impudent bullshit about his not caring?

"That's my normal starting time," said Dan. "Didn't anyone tell you? If I start that early, I can usually be home in time for dinner with the family. That's a very important ritual at our house. Yes, let's do it Monday early. I'll have more time for you then than I will for five months. We're in a heavy period."

Stark had said that before. Was it a standard line?

"Thanks for the tour, Dan," David said.

"Don't be late," said Stark. The door window began closing as the car pulled away.

"I'll see you at 8 a.m. Monday," David said loudly, so that Stark definitely would hear.

The car stopped ten feet away. The rear window reversed direction and started opening. Then, after a moment, the vehicle moved forward and disappeared around a corner.

* * *

Inside their house, Tatiana was standing on a stool putting up new lace curtains.

"Hey," she said flatly, without turning away from the window. "Home is the hunter. These are what I bought with the Bingo money."

"They're great," said David.

"So how did it go?" she said, adjusting the curtains along the rod.

"I'm trying to sort out the detail, but the bottom line is that I'm in the ring with one mean son of a bitch."

"Yeah, I heard at Bingo that he was tough," Tatiana said to a curtain. "You know, David, I might like it around here. More than a semester, I mean."

She kept tugging at the curtains. "The river's polluted," she said, "but the Adamston Argus says Worcester County will get federal funding for a cleanup. And there's a nine-square mile nature preserve just north of here on the Mentors. And the schools are pretty good. They're always going to need good teachers, and I'm going to be the best, as you know."

"Creme de la creme," said David.

"The house prices are a dream," she said, looking back over her shoulder. "And the place is small enough to be understood; I already know where the sewage treatment plant is and who the five biggest local taxpayers are. I never knew that kind of stuff in Cambridge. And the pace is right. People have some time for each other. And we're not really that far from Boston."

"Yeah, it's possible the place could grow on you," said David. "There is work to be done at API, and it may take me more than a semester. But I'm a scholar, not a businessman. I'll go back eventually."

"But . . ."

"Back to teaching, I mean. Maybe, just maybe, not in Cambridge. There are other places. Anyway, its early days."

He felt adrenalin flow as he remembered the day's events. He had defied death in Northampton and had held Stark to a draw. "This Stark, I must emphasize, is a real bastard," said

David. "If he thinks he can push me around the way he tried to today, say the things he said, he has not reckoned with the Irish blood passed to me by my dear departed mother, Caitlin Caughey Link." He smiled at his words, which would have sounded impossibly embarrassing in Cambridge but somehow seemed to fit out here.

Something he couldn't place bothered him. What exactly had Stark said about circuses and why? David willed himself to dismiss the thought.

He ran his hand through his hair. A few strands came out. He brushed them off impatiently against his jacket.

"I have a thought," he said. "We'll buy a bottle of the best champagne available in Adamston for under $25 and put two glasses in the freezer to chill. At 7:30 tonight, after I have written out some proposals for Stark, we will raise our frosted glasses."

"'Beaded bubbles winking at the brim,'" she said.

"We will drink and talk of the future and of the ordinary man's immortality. And we will grill great chunks of red meat for dinner."

"Yes, definitely, yes," said Tatiana, turning around on the stool now to get a good look at him.

Jay A. Blumenthal

Amphibian at Midday

I

My horned claws rip at the pretender's dust jacket
until my skin crawls with disgust. This got published?
And by Plantagenet Press, with three hosannas from Donald Hall,
who, like my father, returned my manuscript unread?
My eyes fasten onto Miles Gumfy's long list of credentials.
Nine other collections! A MacArthur, two Guggenheims, a
Spandolini.
Recycled essays hyped for spring. M. Phil, Oxford;
Ph.D. Princeton; with a freshly minted MBA
from Sterling grafted on like a scholar's appendix.
Poet-in-residence at Brahman, editor of *Landfall*
(shouldn't it be *Landfill?*), and at 33 (he looks much older)
already touted as "the heir to the fertile tradition
of Ashbery and Blight." Pestiferous since my larval days,
I blaspheme the succession, or the need for it, then scavenge
through the text, all 276 pages, back to front,
front to back—it makes no difference—stopping to snout
at grade-A mulch (e.g., "the unrepentant hawk, wounded
by thought,/prayed at the altar of the mind"),
then fling bird and book among the remaindered dead.
Owls glower behind magazines, and I retreat,
a believer in my heresy: that, since breakfast alone,
I've thrown away far better poems.

Outside, crossing the deep furrow of Broad Street,
I'm struck by the world's grotesquery. Who would
have thought that vasectomies would catch on
or that Christine, my first wife, would leave me
to star in porno movies like *Queen du Passion*

and *X-Rated Suburb?* Or that the "lit" market would suddenly
heat up and turn Miles Gumfy into a hot commodity?
Caught in a stampede toward Broadway, I surrender
to its dumb instinct until nearly trampled at the foot
of Trinity Church. Springing to my feet, I recall my first
awkward steps on land and the long academic climb that led,
not to redemption, but to the pinnacle of romance:
a breathless honeymoon in the Alps. For two weeks
I was asphyxiated by scenery, while Christine,
still my professor, lectured me on my maladaption,
to wit, my refusal to mimic the chameleon,
forgetting that it has to change colors, not loyalties.
When I revived, my research trailed off into the empyrean
(while her chair in pragmatism remained sturdy),
and I descended—was pushed is more like it—into business,
my father's province. A lifetime of evasion gave way to panic.
Instead of some leafy grove, I found myself in a cesspit
of evolution where the air reeked of his sobriety
and the non-advancement of the spirit. The thick doors
of Global Security & Trust shut behind me. Fearing
each gasp in New York might be my last, I vowed,
once I made partner, to set sail for retirement, there
to immerse myself in the classics grad school had drained
of all meaning. In time I learned to breathe on Wall Street,
mainly by trading my gills for gilders, Krugerrands,
and the all-mighty yen, which meant my dream to return to the sea
never left port. With no partnership in sight, no university
position on the horizon, I clutched at shallow ambition,
hoping it contained the oxygen I needed.

II.

A steady stream of traffic exhausts the October air,
but the Sandpiper, a bar on Greenwich, helps to absorb
my anger. I dive into a schooner of Lowenbrau, empty it, pay,
then breeze down Rector, inhaling enough of its urgency
to resuscitate the perennial amphibian question: How could
Wallace Stevens, the granddaddy of the species, exist
in two worlds but write about only one? His pages are barren.
I can learn nothing of his jonquil's indemnity
or goldenrod's forfeiture of sun. About current yield

his bougainvilleas are silent. His flowers stem from pure mind,
and it was in this garden he sought asylum. Here, at night,
on weekends, during his vacations from the materialism
of wife and insurance, he cultivated his supreme fiction:
namely, that poems can be grown in such private soil.
To this day his work violates pure amphibian logic:
that the two realms must share the same premises—
if not in a marriage of the exotic and the mundane,
at least in a respectful cohabitation that we, his heirs,
can live with. But Stevens is more lizard than salamander
or frog, and once this truth takes root, the Emperor's kingdom,
for all its majesty, will wither like a morning-glory.
Until then we must pray for the fall of his dry reign.
Up ahead, my building shades into gloom, and I slow down
to bask in my regicide. I study the clear sky as if
it were unclouded memory, thinking no longer of Miles Gumfy
and his pedestrian lyrics, nor of this year's crop of bad poets,
nor of the invertebrate gods, beginning with my boss,
who demand my undying rectitude, but of this morning's
coffee break at the office when, with no one looking,
I fished through my waste basket for my scuttled poems.
Sure, they had sunk from insufficient craft,
but a certain buoyancy had lifted them from the slime
of imagination. During the stolen moments before clients again
weighed upon me, time floated without its usual gravity.
Swimming in the deep amnion of invention, my pores reveled
in their resurrection. My fear of discovery seemed groundless;
it felt as if my gills were growing back. For once
I was in my element, at a depth only I could fathom.

III.

Satisfied the heavens hold nothing for me today
and pleased, as always, I can navigate the streets unnoticed,
I scale the backstairs to my fishbowl of an office:
nine flights, my steps painstaking as I employ the darkness
to retract my claws and smooth out my skin—
just as my father taught me. His lessons about disguising
toad breath and webbed argument and hiding huge hindlegs
in a three-piece business suit kept my Global career
on a solid footing, and had enabled me to climb years before,

but as I reached the highest levels of international finance
I saw how the high priests soared only at the world's expense.

Among the vulturous, self-aggrandizement was viewed
as its own reward. Breathing in their presence came easily,
but lacking wings and a stomach for predation, I was demoted
to Corporate Limbo, the entry level for dull profit.
Darwin had exacted full payment for my investment in land,
and as a special bonus, had made my salvation, the ocean,
a forbidden woman whose ecstasy I could ill afford.
Yet my odyssey could not end without her deadly embrace,
for I believed, like Ulysses, that some noble deed might
yet be done before the long day waned into old age.

By now the spring is gone from my legs. I am bloated,
having fed on monarchs. Slipping past the receptionist,
I am indistinguishable from the other brokers, most of whom
work through lunch, their hunger calculated to take them far.
My secret is safe among the faithful, even though my mask
wears thin when I check the message board. A note, pinned
for all to see, announces that my new wife will be home late.
That was how my first marriage unravelled: memos, last-minute
calls that frayed my suspicion and tore at my underbelly.

When Christine left, I was stranded in my own body,
pleading with her to return. I claimed my spinelessness
was that of a mythic figure, an Achilles made weak by flannel
and herringbone, but she cared nothing for my classical posture.
When my letters came back unopened, her indifference ripped
through my insides, laying waste to huge tracts of intestine.
Without her response, my amphibianhood hung in the balance.
I took Seconal to kill thought, and when I awoke,
alcohol to erode consciousness, and when that wore off,
both at once to hasten my liquidation. By all accounts
I should have died. The will to live had deserted me,
but when I went under for the fourth time, animal fear
filled my lungs and sent me screaming toward the surface.
Caught in a nightmare, I was fished out, medicated,
tested, x-rayed, counseled, retested, explored, gutted,
deboned, filleted, and signed up for physical therapy.
My exercise in self-destruction ended in dorsal stretches
and tail bends, neither of which I've done for months.

Despite all the sermons about my "miraculous rebirth,"
my official conversion didn't occur until two years later
when my father, a professional amphibian, advised me
on how to divest emotional overhead from net worth.
Jewish stoicism, he called it, the first principle being
that survival was the true religion. From that it followed
that feelings were to be written off as liabilities,
then tucked beneath a corner of the balance sheet.
Surprisingly, his cool approach to bookkeeping was potent
enough to congeal rage; thus Gumfy's success could consume
my lunch hour and prey upon my soul, but once back
at the office, I could swallow hard and play the saint.

This stage precludes theatrics, so I withdraw to my desk.
My PC flashes news of all major currencies, in denominations
that elevate my blood. But the leap of faith required
to trade humor for energy does not materialize.
Anchored in pre-Christian doubt, I cannot evolve.
Instead of trawling my screen for conviction, I am lured
toward my window, where the Hudson lies stretched out below.
Untouched by poetry, it is the most businesslike of rivers,
and for a few moments I am calmed by its emptiness as it moves,
slowly and without purpose, toward the anonymity of the open sea.

The Virus

Craig Brown

IT WAS A fine April morning in
Peoria, Illinois, the 25th in fact, when Harley Longacre took his
station as Head Teller at the Third National Bank and Trust and
contemplated the immense pleasure he was about to derive from
a full day of bullying the Lesser Tellers who reported to him. It
was an activity he enjoyed with a fervor that others reserve for
sex. For nearly ten of the last twenty-three years Harley had been
Head Teller, and the fact he had fourteen years to go until he
reached age 65 gave him no reason to believe he wouldn't be the
Omnipotent Ruler of All Tellers until he retired. As Harley
looked down the still empty teller line he mentally reviewed the
rules that would allow him to "bring pee" (his words) on each
careless soul who committed an infraction. "Thank you, Lord,
for allowing me to have this job," he intoned, as he settled in to
await the arrival of his charges. Harley entered his password on
his computer terminal to bring it to life and was greeted with the
brief message: "Eat my shorts." Harley Longacre blinked on the
very fine morning of April 25 and then experienced an intestinal
fit that sent him scuttling to the men's restroom.

If that had been the only computer foul-up at Third
National Bank and Trust that morning I would not have been on
an airplane headed in the direction of Peoria on the very fine
morning of April 26. I am something of a wizard at finding and
eradicating computer problems, and while Peoria is not in the
99th percentile of places I would choose to visit, the rates I
charge are so outrageous I couldn't turn this assignment down.
Moreover, the nature of the problems at Third National
intrigued me.

If the insult issued at Harley Longacre's terminal had
been the only thing that had gone wrong that day, management
would have dismissed the issue with a snigger and again
considered if they should offer Harley a huge incentive to retire
early. As it was, that was only the first of many incidents. Each

person who signed on to the system received a message, ranging from "Take a bath, Dagwood," to a rather inventive innuendo directed toward Cheryl Fengler, who made no secret of the fact she wanted to know who or what was sending these messages. "I just can't imagine who would want to do a thing like that," Cheryl repeated twice to her co-workers, all the while smiling.

The insults to the personnel didn't send management over the edge, because each seemed to be a one time thing. As each terminal was turned on, it issued its message and then resumed normal operation. The devastating blow came from the customer terminals. These were a number of very user-friendly PCs on the network, placed at strategic locations for use by customers of Third National. They could be used to look up balances, transfer money between accounts, perform what-if situations on investments and loans and even help reconcile a customer's checkbook (although statistics showed they were rarely used for that, presumably because the customers who couldn't balance their checkbooks couldn't deal with computers, either).

The "Friendly Fannies," as the customer PCs were nicknamed, took a decidedly unfriendly turn. The first one to be accessed that day told Mr. Jack Peterson his money would be a lot safer anywhere else. Mr. Peterson didn't mention this to anyone but did take the Friendly Fannie's advice and withdrew his entire checking account balance. A system audit run later in the day showed that at least three more customers accessed the Friendly Fannies before noon, and, in all likelihood, received similarly disturbing information.

The stopper came when Mrs. Maude Ferguson sat down at a Friendly Fannie to see if her Social Security check had been deposited yet. It wouldn't arrive for another week, but her ritual was an established one. A pre-programmed sequence, triggered by the entry of her account number and password, would list the most recent deposits to her checking account. It would then affix an appropriate and personalized comment, such as "Your Social Security check has not been deposited yet, Mrs. Ferguson. Please try again tomorrow. Thank you for banking at the Third." On that one magical day of the month the comment would relay the happy news that the check was in the bank. On this magical day, however, Friendly Fannie did not list any deposits at all, and flashed this message instead: "Maudie, you look like two pigs fighting in a burlap bag!"

Unlike Harley Longacre, Maude Ferguson did not go to the restroom. She marched directly into the office of Henry Russell, President and CEO of Third National Bank and Trust and delivered a concise and colorful opinion of Friendly Fannie, Third National, Henry Russell and several other unrelated phenomena she was unhappy about. Henry (who was explaining one of the finer points of banking to Cheryl Fengler), was taken off guard. "I'm sure there's been some kind of mistake, Mrs. Ferguson," he said soothingly.

"Stuff a sock in it, Hank!" she replied as she moved her ample person out of Henry's office with an economy of motion he wouldn't have thought possible of someone her size. "I'm closing my accounts!" Maude yelled at no one in particular just prior to slamming the office door with enough force to make Cheryl Fengler take a small hop.

Within a couple of hours Henry had not only determined what had put the bee under Maude Ferguson's bonnet but had also reconstructed the events of the morning. Unfortunately he didn't have the Friendly Fannies shut down before they had insulted at least four more customers, not the least of whom was Stu Haworth, the attorney from Haworth, Haworth and Simpkins, who was told he could perform an unlikely acrobatic act involving a pastry in motion. Stu seemed to take it good-naturedly but warned Henry nonetheless, "Somebody's gonna sue your pants off if you don't shut those machines down." Henry called me after this.

"Shannon, I've got a computer virus and it's going to ruin me. I've got customers saying words like 'close' and 'account' in the same sentence and I don't like it!" He recapped the morning and told me he wanted me on the plane to Peoria yesterday. Henry and I had met several times at computer conferences, the kind that CEOs of medium size banks attend every now and then believing that they will somehow gain an understanding of current technology through osmosis. Henry's attitude toward me had always been that curious mixture of contempt and awe reserved for consultants.

"I need you here now, Shannon," he said. I suggested that he have someone turn off all the Friendly Fannies, that he alert all the bank personnel to report anything unusual from their terminals and PCs and told him that I would arrive on the earliest flight into Peoria on the morning of the 26th. It's something like the consultant's equivalent of take two aspirin and call me in the morning. Henry agreed reluctantly. He also agreed to my fee and expenses and was ready to hang up when he remembered to say, "You know that Terry Baker installed this system, don't you?"

I hadn't known that, but it didn't mean anything particular to me. Terry Baker was a hot-shot consultant who had made a living installing financial packages in small to mid-size banks throughout the country until December of the prior year, at which time he had purchased a Ferrari, a condo in Boca Raton, and a ketch that slept four.

"I didn't know Terry installed your system," I told Henry. "You don't think he had anything to do with the glitches, do you?"

"It sure seems strange to me that the guy got out of the business as abruptly as he did. Something funny going on."

It wasn't strange to me at all. Terry had worked his butt off for years and had squirreled away a small fortune. "I'll look into it, Henry," I said, "but it doesn't sound like something Terry Baker would do. The last time I talked with him he said he wouldn't even go into a bank anymore. Conducts all his banking through ATMs or over the phone. By the way, have you had any of these strange messages printing on your ATM receipts?"

That was the wrong thing to say to an already panicked Henry Russell. It hadn't occurred to him that Third National's proprietary money machine network might be routinely telling its customers to take their business elsewhere. Or worse.

"I've got to go. Be here tomorrow and be ready to walk on water!" Henry slammed the phone down. I didn't even have time to tell him I prefer changing water into wine so I dialed my travel agent instead. As unlikely as it seemed I was going to be in Peoria shortly after the bank opened its doors on the 26th. All I had to do was leave my own home at the reasonable hour of 3:00 AM, take a flight to the busiest airport in the free world and drive about ninety minutes from Chicago to Peoria, mostly in devastating rush-hour traffic. What a deal.

The next morning at the bank, I spent the first three hours closeted with Henry Russell. The man is an administrator above all and he had marshaled all the facts which he now paraded in front of me in chronological order. He did interrupt himself several times to tell me the "virus" hadn't invaded the money machines. His relief was obvious. He also told me he had not only disconnected all the Friendly Fannies but had them removed to a storage room on the third floor, as if they could somehow plug themselves back in and start insulting the customers again. The current state of affairs was that random bogus messages were still appearing, but only on the terminals and PCs of bank personnel. So far, everyone was coping with that as well as could be expected, with the exception of Harley Longacre. The insults on Harley's terminal had taken a different flavor, and usually ended with the message "Don't have a cow, man!" Harley was not amused.

When Henry had finished his presentation he perched himself on the edge of his desk and asked, "Do you think you can handle the situation, Jim?" Either my physical presence or the size of my fee had a calming effect on him and he had decided he could use my first name. Since it was approaching noon I suggested we have lunch.

"After that," I continued, "you can set me up in a vacant office with a programmer's terminal and let me do my stuff."

"Aren't you going to want to interview anyone?" Henry asked tentatively.

"The only interview I'll need to conduct is with your computer," I replied. Henry looked at me skeptically, so I explained, "When Terry Baker set up a system he always put in a little subsystem he designed that tracks all the entries made from anywhere and by anybody. Unless your operations staff has done some radical surgery on the system I suspect that will still be intact and that I'll be able to search the logs from now backwards until Day One. It really shouldn't take me long to find out who's at the bottom of all this mischief."

"Mischief?!" Henry cried. "This is more than mischief, it's a computer virus and it's spreading!"

Henry was one of those executives who always wanted to be on the leading edge, and since computer viruses were grabbing a lot of headlines recently he was going to be upset if he didn't have one. I gave in.

"OK, Henry, a virus. I'll still need a room to myself with a programmer's terminal. Are you ready for lunch?"

It is always a consultant's dream when on the road that his client will take him for lunch to a country club or to one of those fabulous members only clubs on the 29th floor of some posh building where there are at least two waiters per diner and a buffet table that is about to break from the weight of the lobsters and other delicacies piled on top of it. We ate, of course, in the employee dining room in the basement. Cold sandwiches, and hot coffee in the midst of a gaggle of employees re-hashing the morning's events.

I overheard one of them say, "Well you should have seen what Cheryl's terminal said to her today. Her face turned red as a beet."

"So what did it say?" asked the narrator's companion.

"You don't expect *me* to repeat it, do you?"

"Well, all mine ever said to me was, 'Have a great day, Blondie.' Pretty boring if you ask me."

I took in the background noise while Henry devoured two ham and Swiss on ryes and started quizzing me.

"How long do you think it'll take to track down the virus? Have you seen a virus like this one anywhere else? Do you think we're going to need someone else to help you?"

He could have asked the only question that was really on his mind, which was, "How much is it going to cost me to get out of this mess?" I contemplated my tuna sandwich as if it were going to yield some sort of answer and said, "If Terry's audit subsystem is still intact I should know what's going on by some time Friday." That answer translates to "Three days worth of fees plus expenses."

"Of course," I added, "I'll work into the evening if you can have some food brought in and a supply of hot coffee." The something for nothing gambit. In reality I work best without interruptions of any kind and the evening would suit me perfectly.

We finished our meals and Henry took me to an unused corner office on the fourth floor, which was occupied by the bank's trust Department and by one small law firm, which was not Haworth, Haworth and Simpkins. It already had nearly everything I needed: a desk, a comfortable chair, a bookcase with a full collection of system manuals and a terminal workstation behind the desk with one of the older PCs on it. "This used to belong to Perry West," Henry explained. "Senior VP. We gave him an early retirement last year, but we let him come in once or twice a week so he feels as if he's doing something useful. Give him a 'consultant's fee.' It keeps him happy."

"Is the PC connected?" I asked.

"Yes," Henry said. "Perry likes to watch the institution's cash position during the day. I'll have our security officer change the code on the terminal so you have full access to the network."

"I'll need an administrative clearance," I said, "the same as your security officer's."

"No problem," Henry replied, "at the fees you're charging you sure don't need to embezzle from us."

I must have pulled a face because he quickly added, "Sorry. Bad joke." He took a book from the shelf, thumbed through it a moment and said, "The Security Administrator is Arlene Tomlinson. She's our Cashier. Doesn't know beans about security but she liked the title so we gave it to her. Her password is 'Arlene.'"

"Are all your passwords that secure?" I asked, as my heart skipped a couple of beats.

Henry missed the sarcasm altogether. "Actually," he said, "most people just use their spouse's name for a password. It's easier for them to remember."

"How many copies of that security manual are lying around?" I asked, knowing the answer wasn't going to cheer me. I had virtually promised this man I was going to solve his "virus" problem in three days and was now discovering their security was Swiss cheese. A determined third-grade kid with a PC and a modem could penetrate their system in a matter of minutes. Henry took too long to answer the question as if calculating the number of copies of the security manual was yielding a very large sum.

"Oh, I'd guess there are twenty or thirty copies of this. We only give them to officers of the bank, though."

"That's a comfort," I offered.

"And to members of the board," he added.

"Can't forget the board members," I chimed, suppressing the urge to ask if Arlene had had the passwords published in the local newspaper. My mood was getting progressively worse when Harley Longacre entered the room. I'd never met Harley Longacre but I could have picked him out of a crowd. What he lacked in height he made up for in rotundity.

Harley cleared his throat, unnecessarily, since he already had our full attention and said, "I'm afraid there's a little problem, Mr. Russell." He paused, waiting for permission to continue.

"What is it, Harley?" Henry snapped irritably.

"Well, it seems that someone is moving some money around. You know, teller funds."

"You mean money is being taken out of the system?" I asked.

"Well, not exactly taking it out of the system," Harley continued. "Someone must have done a series of debits and credits during the lunch hour, and everybody has everybody else's cash drawer, if you know what I mean."

"Not exactly," Henry said, "what do you mean by not exactly?"

"Well, Janie's closing position when she went to lunch was debited off, then Ann's was credited with the same amount. Then Ann's old amount was debited off and credited to Sue. Then Sue's . . . ."

"You mean someone's been moving money around?" Henry asked. I loved that. Give the man a tiny clue and he makes quantum leaps of deduction.

"Is there any indication who made these transactions?" I asked.

"That's the strange thing," Harley said. "I can't actually find any transactions, per se. One of the tellers must have done it, but they couldn't have because I WAS WATCHING THEM MYSELF!"

"Shannon," Henry Russell said as he fixed me with a truly icy stare, "I want to see some water-walking and damned soon! Now I'm a man who believes in managing a situation. I'm going to get out of here and let you do your job. If you need anything—anything at all—call me. I'll stop in later this afternoon to see how you're doing." He turned to Harley and said, "Longacre, you and I are going to journal that money right back where it came from and then you are going to watch the teller line. Do you understand?"

Harley smiled grimly as if the task was a new one. Henry turned on his heels and left the room with Harley following him so closely there was going to be a collision if Henry came to a sudden stop.

I sat down in the chair in front of the terminal. I turned the PC on and entered the password "Arlene." The message that greeted me would normally have brought a chuckle: "Roses are red, orchids are black. I like you best when you lie on your back."

"Jim, old pal," I thought to myself, "you have here what the old-timers call an Opportunity." Then I settled in to do what I do best. The first couple of hours consisted of much technical mumbo-jumbo like loading the flat file from the audit subsystem (thankfully intact) into a relational database and constructing a meaningful set of queries to examine it. I also located a file on the mainframe which had all the passwords and terminal locations. This I downloaded into a spreadsheet. During this time Henry popped in to check on my progress at least three times. Each time he asked the same question: "How much progress have you made?" The last time I answered, "Right now I am about fifteen minutes behind where I would have been if you hadn't interrupted me."

The flippancy of my statement didn't affect Henry adversely. He left me alone for most of the rest of the afternoon, but stopped back in at about 6:00 to tell me where I could get a good meal nearby and to give me instructions on getting back into the building, just in case I wanted to work all night—as if there was an alternative for me. His timing was perfect. I had just finished the last bit of preparation before I began the huge search that would tell me what had gone awry with the system. A break now would give me a chance to clear my mind and prepare for the next task.

From the choice of restaurants Henry gave me I chose the one that sounded the least trendy, one that advertised Steaks and Chops. When I arrived there a short time later I was glad to see my instincts had served me well. The waitresses all wore white blouses and black skirts. That is a sure-fire indicator to me that I'm going to have a decent meal, quietly served and with a minimum of interruption. I asked for a booth and got one. After the waitress had taken my drink and food order I took out a small yellow pad and began to summarize the current status.

Fact One: Third National's security had been compromised, allowing someone to gain unauthorized access to the online system.

Fact Two: Whoever infiltrated the system was, in all likelihood a Third National employee, or at least someone who was intimately familiar with Third National personnel. I drew this conclusion from the fact that most of the messages appearing on terminals were personalized. It seemed obvious that whoever had caused the messages to appear had known exactly who would receive what message and, more interesting, what had to be said to get under the recipient's skin.

Fact Three: The infiltrator appeared to have gained a good working knowledge of the system, from the teleprocessing monitor on down. His achievements were on a skill level with a seasoned programmer. Too bad Third National didn't have any programmers.

Fact Four: The infiltrator apparently didn't have larceny in mind. So far. Some money had been moved around and some feathers had been ruffled, but so far there was nothing going on that would attract an audit. I had run a few quick preliminary audit programs of my own. None of the attractive targets like dormant accounts had been touched. So far, so good.

Fact Five: Judging from the level of security I had already seen at Third National I would probably be able to limit my list of suspects to fewer than a thousand people.

Fact Six: Finding out what went wrong was going to be only slightly easier than playing a blindfold chess match against Karpov and Kasparov while simultaneously composing an opera and finishing third in an iron man contest. Something like that.

My drink arrived and I thanked the waitress as if she had just saved my life. I decided to try to get my mind off the infiltration problem while I drank, but couldn't help wondering what tack I was going to take. Not only about the Third National problem but also what line of work I would pursue after this one. Shark wrestling in Pompano Beach was beginning to sound pretty good. "*Kyrie eleison,*" I said, as the waitress brought my food.

When I got back to the bank the night guard let me in. Henry's description of me must have been a good one. ("He'll look worried," I imagined Henry saying.) He buzzed the elevator to the fourth floor. I entered the office and turned the PC on, to be greeted by, "Having some problems, Dick Tracy?" Whoever this fox was he was penetrating the network right under my nose. Ignoring the insult, I accessed the most recent audit subsystem file. There were no accesses from the time I had left until now. That meant the system had been diddled earlier to have the message waiting for me.

What it also meant is that whoever had done the deed had waited until my services had been contracted. That meant I could narrow my search of accesses to those between 6:30 PM today and about 2:00 PM yesterday. Round that off to noon. My first query yielded too many accesses to be meaningful. Third National is a busy bank with several branch offices. For the second query I eliminated all dollar transactions. This gave me a much smaller number of transactions to examine, but it was still an impressive list. Next I got rid of all inquiries. In theory, one couldn't alter this system with a balance check. This yielded a manageable list of transactions I could start examining in detail. Next I sorted this list into order by password and user ID. I had been going through this list slowly and methodically, reading the particulars of each entry, so it took about fifteen minutes before I hit pay dirt. The password was "Shazam"and the user ID was "MARVEL" (presumably as in "Captain Marvel"). My spirits soared. Now all I had to do was toggle over to my spreadsheet and find out that the user name was . . .

Searching, searching, searching . . .

The user name was Steve Canyon? Yes. Canyon, Stephenson B., Colonel, USAF, retired. Retired? Yes, indeed, the Steve Canyon comic strip was retired with the demise of its brilliant creator, Milton Caniff.

My fox had a sense of humor and a penchant for comic strip characters. I toggled back to the query page and read the entry more carefully. The terminal or PC from which the entry had been made had an ID indicating it had been done on a dial-up line. That is to say, someone used their modem to dial a rotary line tied to the mainframe computer by another modem. Such lines are in common use for a dozen different reasons, such as remote analysis of problems, offsite programming and the like. They are usually secure in that the caller has to know the sign-on sequence and, in most instances, has to know a pretty obscure password. In this case, and much to my dismay, the caller only had to know the first name of the cashier of the bank.

I spent the rest of the evening gathering all the information I could about "Captain Marvel aka Steve Canyon." It wasn't too revealing. The access calls were all made during working hours, in broad daylight as it were. There was no way of telling if the calls were made locally or long distance. I might be able to confirm that with the phone company tomorrow. And other than the fact that most of the accesses were fairly brief in duration, which means the fox really knew what he (she) was doing, there weren't a lot of clues.

I punched up the command to sign off. For the first time, the PC flashed a goodbye message to me. "Giving up already, Dick Tracy?" I took ten more minutes to ascertain that no one else signed onto the system since I had returned from supper (no one had), turned off the PC and left. Sometimes a good night's sleep is the best way to get at a thorny problem. I had a feeling that such was not going to be the case tonight.

When I returned to the fourth floor office in the
morning my gloomy mood was not lightened by the fact that *my*
desk (we consultants sometimes get possessive) was occupied by
a stranger. "Uh oh," I thought, "the auditors have descended."
The stranger stood up and extended his hand.

"Hello. I'm Perry West. You must be Jim Shannon. How
was your flight in here? Let me get these things out of your way.
I'll just sit in the corner over there. You won't even know I'm
here. Beautiful morning isn't it? Might rain later, though. Are you
making any headway on the virus? Have you ever had any
experience with one like that? There. Now you can use my desk.
I'm going to the cafeteria. Can I get you a cup of coffee? Maybe
some tea? No, you don't look like the tea type. I just . . ."

"Whoa, Mr. West," I interjected. "If you slow down I'll
try to answer at least one of your five questions. Or was it six?"

He flashed a grin at me and said "My wife tells me I
should slow down. I try to but I guess I have too much energy. I
know I'm driving her crazy at home. That's why I try to get down
here a couple of times a week since I retired early. Gets me out
of her hair, you know. Sure I can't get you a cup of coffee?"

Perry was half way out of the room when I answered
that question positively and I wasn't sure if he heard me or even
cared. He was totally self-contained. The PC on my—that is
Perry's—desk was already signed on to the system with the Cash
Position inquiry called up. I presumed it reflected yesterday's
figures since the bank still wasn't open for business.

My only sure-fire strategy for the day was contacting the
phone company to see if the suspect calls originated from this
area code. To tell the truth I wasn't even sure they could get that
information for me. There are phone companies and there are
phone companies. I decided to wait another half hour before
calling them. I punched up the list of accesses. If I went through
that enough times I might see a different pattern, one that would
give me a clue. I needed a clue badly because I sure didn't have
one now. I was into the second page when Perry returned with
two huge cups of coffee.

"I didn't know how you like your coffee. Can you take it
industrial strength?" This time he actually paused to wait for an
answer.

"If you mean black, that's fine," I replied. That started
him up again and I decided I was going to have to tune Perry
West out like an unwanted TV station. I studied him while he

was talking. He was impeccably dressed. He had what a favorite aunt of mine called an "open face," by which she meant there were no secrets and you could trust this person at once. He was shorter than average but his posture was proud. I guessed at a military background. Since he was carrying on both sides of a conversation with me, asking and answering his own questions, I remained quiet and tried to concentrate on the screen ahead of me. There had to be a clue in here somewhere.

I have an excellent ability to concentrate, shutting out all distractions. After about fifteen minutes, however, I realized that I was being distracted by total silence. Perry had quit talking. I looked across at him sheepishly, realizing there was a good chance he had asked me a question to which he wanted an answer.

"I'm sorry," I said, "did you just ask me something?"

"Yes," he replied, "but I can see you're pretty busy."

"No, really," I said, "I have a habit of concentrating too hard sometimes. What was it you asked?" I try not to offend any customer personnel, even part-time, so-called consultants.

"I asked if you ever read the Captain Marvel comics, is all. They were a favorite of mine."

"I've heard of Captain Marvel," I said, "but that was a little before my time." To which I added the thought, "Sometimes, Jim, old buddy, you're only half fast."

I looked steadily at Perry. His open face revealed the start of a grin that might soon break into a full-fledged smile.

"Are you trying to tell me," I asked slowly, "that you are responsible for the pandemonium that's been going here for the past three days?"

Perry simply nodded. I could tell by his look that he was not only ready to acknowledge that, but was going to give me a blow-by-blow description of how he had breached the system.

"Do you mind telling me why?" I asked tentatively.

"They put me out to pasture, Jim. You don't mind if I call you Jim, do you?"

I nodded dumbly, while he continued.

"You probably know the script better than I do. I was the original programmer here. Back when we had the 1401. Ever work with a 1401?"

He didn't pause for an answer.

"I've been through every generation of computer they've installed. Worked my way up the ladder. Data processing manager, VP, Senior VP, all of it. Then they decided they needed an Information System. Brought in a bunch of high-priced fellows . . ." He paused a moment. "Don't mean to offend you, but the group they brought in was pretty slick. Knew all the latest buzzwords and catch phrases. They recommended a turnkey system, said it would practically run itself. And they were right. It almost does. They told the board they could get rid of their DP staff. Thing of the past. They were almost right about that, too. So they let the staff dwindle by attrition, moved some to other positions in the bank, offered some of us an incentive to retire early." He stopped and stared at the floor for a moment. "Guess you won't have to worry about early retirement, will you, Jim? Self-employed and all of that, you'll probably die with your boots on, right?"

I was still flabbergasted that Perry was telling me this much, but had to ask, "Why did you infiltrate the system? What did you hope to gain?"

"That's easy. You've seen what a shambles the so-called security is in. I decided to take a little chance. Show them they needed a real security officer and not someone who just holds the title.

"Take the dial-up lines, for instance. That's all backwards. The user should call in with a request. Then the computer calls them back at a pre-determined phone number and disconnects if it detects a call-forward.

"Management seems to think the whole data processing operation can be run by computers, no people involved. I decided to show them they're wrong."

"But Perry," I said, "you've created havoc with the system. You don't expect them to welcome that, do you? You've already caused at least two customers to close their accounts."

"One," he corrected. "Jack Peterson. It isn't a big deal. He's closed his account fifteen times in the last eleven years. He'll be back."

"What about the insults? What about Harley Longacre?" I asked. "He looked to me like he *was* going to have a cow."

"Don't worry about old Harley. Someone has to rattle his cage every now and then to keep him on his toes. He'll survive."

"But yesterday, there was some money moved around. Phantom debits and credits," I protested. "You can't just go moving money around."

"Didn't they tell you everything was back to normal by the end of the day? I didn't actually move any money. I just redirected some inquiries.

"Jim, I didn't do any real harm to anyone or anything. All I did was fire a shot across the bow. Now you don't know Hank Russell like I do. Give me half an hour alone with him and I believe I will have a position as the new Security Officer for Third National."

The look on Perry's face was one of supreme confidence. Somehow I had a suspicion he was right. I could imagine that he was good at smoothing ruffled feathers and righting all wrongs. Shazam!

"By the way," Perry went on, "I intend to give you all the credit for finding me out. You'll get your full fee. Don't worry about it."

I was beginning to love this man.

"Just one more thing," I asked, "you really teed off Maudie Ferguson. What are you going to do about that? From what I've heard the bank would hate to see her close her accounts."

"Well, Maudie's my sister. The scene she put on in Henry's office was a fraud, and she enjoyed every minute of it."

"She wasn't offended at all?" I asked incredulously.

"Oh, a little bit."

The morning of April 27th suddenly began looking very fine.

James A. Autry

Lights Flashing At O'Hare

Taxiing in on United at O'Hare
you see fire engines and an ambulance,
lights flashing,
and you think of snowy mornings
in a trailer somewhere in France,
near a runway of accelerating sounds,
loud but comforting in their consistency.
Then nothing,
and before you remember that silence
is not what you want to hear,
that fear born of something much older than
    airplanes
rises like a siren in your brain,
who who who who who?

In your briefcase is a calendar
filled for months to come,
time stretching like a chore
as far as you can turn the pages,
another week another year
to be played out in meetings and memos and trips.
Then, looking back toward the flashing lights,
ready by the runway,
you realize that out there somewhere
some poor son of a bitch
just wants the next five minutes
to be over.

Listening And Learning

There was a time I listened
to the men at the store,
thinking I could learn about farming
as they came dusty from the fields
in bib overalls and long-sleeved shirts,
their hands and faces dark red
save a white band where their straw hats sat.
They kicked their boots on the ground,
red clay dust rising to their knees,
and shook their heads as they came in the door.
Always shook their heads and met the eyes
of other farmers who shook their heads
and stood at the co-cola boxes
with a Coke or a Dr. Pepper or RC.
I listened about the weather
and the government
and the prices,
all of it turned against them.

Now, I watch businessmen
stretch and squeeze time on planes
and in offices,
measuring their days by meetings and phone calls,
then gather in clubs
and bars and restaurants
and shake their heads and talk and talk,
about inflation and disinflation,
about the government and the deficit
and the margins
and the share fights.

After a while, it sounds the same,
farmers and businessmen,
and what I hear
is how hard it is
for them to say how much they love it.

Romantic Revelations

My friend has an infallible rule
for spotting a romance in the office,
a rule true and proven over the years,
accurate in direct proportion
to how hard the lovers try to hide.
My friend calls it the Law of Romantic Revelation,
and it goes like this:
> *If you think they're doing it,*
> *they're doing it.*

Sounds silly but it's damn near perfect
if you have any power of observation at all.
If for instance a very solid citizen,
say a forty-five-year-old guy,
stops getting a haircut every other week,
and as the hair begins to hide his ears and collar,
you notice the gray ones are gone,
or if he shows up in an Italian blazer,
unvented,
with notched lapels,
watch out.
Next thing you know he's collecting wine
or original prints.
Then one day you're in a meeting
on personnel policy
and find he has become a feminist
since the last meeting,
or you notice in the corner of his office
a new Land's End canvas bag
for his running shoes and designer sweats
and one of those Fit at Fifty
posters on the wall.
You have but to keep your eyes open
and the object of his affections
will come into focus
and the Law of Romantic Revelation
will unveil its infallibility once again.

Recessions

Why do we keep on keeping on,
in the midst of such pressure,
when business is no good for no reason,
when everything done right turns out wrong,
when the Fed does something
and interest rates do something
and somebody's notion of consumer confidence does
       something
and the dogs won't eat the dog food?

What keeps us working late at night
and going back every morning,
living on coffee and waiting for things to bottom out,
crunching numbers as if some answer
lay buried in a computer
and not out among the people who
suddenly and for no reason
are leaving their money in their pockets
and the products on the shelves?

Why don't we just say screw it
instead of trying again,
instead of meandering into somebody's office
with half an idea,
hoping he'll have the other half,
hoping what sometimes happens will happen,
that thing, that click, that moment
when two or three of us
gathered together or hanging out
get hit by something we've never tried
but know we can make work the first time?

Could that be it,
that we do all the dull stuff
just for those times
when a revelation rises among us
like something borning,
a new life, another hope,
like something not visible catching the sun,
like a prayer answered?

Corporate Culture Shock

Ross Chichester

WHEN SIR JOHN Marks, managing director of the large Australian corporation that bought our little company, first visited us, he said he liked our "corporate culture." I wasn't sure what he meant, but I assumed it implied those ways of doing things that set one company apart from other companies.

What could I say? I said, "Thank you."

I wondered if Sir John had been attracted to us because he thought we were "exotic." If so, he was bound to be disappointed later on when he discovered how hard-working and ordinary we were. At least, I reflected, we had a good balance sheet and turned a good yearly profit. That should assure a stable relationship.

Our new parent, ACI, had 40,000 employees. Our company, Stonelight Tile, had 60. ACI's headquarter's were in Melbourne and Sydney, in tall buildings of glass and steel. Stonelight's were in a wooden lean-to, attached to a rusted quonset hut, in the Latino barrio of San Jose, California. ACI people spoke a strange English, sprinkled with "cheer-o's," "mates," and "birds." Our lingo was not much better, as the first language of 98 percent of us was Spanish, and about half of our talk was in a Chicano slang.

For some months after the new owners took over, our lives were unchanged. The kiln men sang as they unloaded the newly-fired tiles, particularly if the load was good. The delicious aroma of homemade Mexican food wafted from the kiln gas ports where breakfast, lunch, and snacks were always heating. We forgot about the Australians.

One hot spring day we were told to prepare for a visit and address by the president of ACI America, Inc., who had opened offices in Newport Beach, California. They had bought another California company, a roof-truss fabricator. We had, suddenly, a "sister." Officers of the two companies were to be introduced and the employees of both were to be made aware they were now part of a larger corporate family. We were told to choose an interpreter fluent in both Spanish and English, so that none of the president's words would be misunderstood.

I chose affable, intelligent Pat Ramirez, a second-generation Mexican-American, who was at home everywhere.

It turned out that Australian was as foreign to Pat as would have been Inuit or Samoan. I couldn't understand our new leader, either, but I had the advantage of having seen the words, "roof truss," on paper before the meeting.

The Newport Beach delegation arrived in a limo from the airport: giant pandas in black suits and white shirts. We greeted them dressed in jeans and covered with red clay dust from head to foot. Intent faces formed a semi-circle, dark eyes focused on the important visitors.

The "Chingon" (a word meaning "Big F- - - - -") spoke, turning to introduce the manager of our sister company, the roof-truss man. He said we were all now one family, sharing the same values and goals. At least, I think that's what he said, but his mumbled pronunciation was difficult to understand.

Pat gave a pretty continuous translation, but when the name of our sister company occurred, I always heard the Spanish word, "basura," which means "trash."

At last, the corporate president paused. "Any questions?"

Brown faces looked at him. There were low Spanish murmurs, and finally Pat, with a deep sigh, asked what was on everyone's mind. "We all want to know," he said, "what is roof trash?"

The Australian looked at me uncertainly. I was pretty sure I'd better not correct his pronunciation. I tried to explain to the group. "Trusses are what holds up roofs."

All those dark eyes regarded me with disbelief. The chingon had clearly (well, as clearly as he said anything) said, "roof trash." The English speakers had heard "roof trash," and their fellow worker, Pat, had said "roof trash" in Spanish.

"Basura para los techos," José Luis asked me. "¿Que es?"

I could only do what José Luis does when he's nonplussed: I grimaced and shrugged. Then I couldn't help it. I broke up. The meeting was dismissed with handshakes all around.

That evening over a beer Pat told me the rest of the workers thought the Australians were either crazy, or were playing everyone for fools.

"We'll have to be on our guard," he said. "Clearly, they don't know what they're talking about."

I finished my beer wondering what the future held for our little company and its new owners and I remembered for some reason a language difference that had nearly landed me in jail when I first came to Stonelight, fresh from the lilac areas of the University.

One morning, I had walked to the rear of the quonset where Florentino worked the tile press. He sang as he swung the heavy weight above him to bring a die down on the wet clay. I thought in my innocent, stereotypical way, How great not to have any worries like these guys!

"You're always happy, aren't you, Flori?" I said.

He looked at me, head on one side, pain showing in the creases of his forehead. "No," he said, "I think today I go to jail."

"But you're singing!"

"Takes my mind off my problems."

"Then I think I'd better learn that song. What is it?"

"*Preso Numero Nueve.* Cell Number Nine."

The rest of the factory crowded in on me, such as a nearby forklift that wouldn't start.

"What did you do," I asked, "that makes you think you'll go to jail?"

He answered simply, "I hit a chicken."

Of course I laughed. "They can't come and arrest you at work for hitting a chicken." Pomona Avenue, in front of our factory, was always full of confused chickens. "They can't lock you up for that!"

That afternoon, as I shared warmed-up enchiladas from somebody's lunch, two uniformed cops showed up and took the unprotesting Florentino away.

I leapt up and followed them to the door.

"You can't come in here and do that," I said. "Even if he did run over a chicken, think of his wife and kids. Think of the taxpayers. Think what locking him up will cost the government! You're crazy!"

I felt Richard Garcia behind me tugging at my shirt and I turned to see him shaking his head in warning. I clearly remember Juan standing beside him, shaking his head, and softly murmuring "tapado."

The two policemen grinned and escorted Flori to the police car.

The more I thought about it, the angrier I became. It wasn't just that we were left without our best pressman; it was the un-American aspect of the whole thing. How could we ever expect uneducated, poor people to have respect for our laws when they're trying to do a job and then get locked up for such trifling reasons?

I asked Richard, who seemed to be knowledgeable about such things, what would happen now.

"He'll have to go before the judge and plead guilty or not guilty. Probably tomorrow morning, because they picked him up today."

"I'm going to go talk to the judge," I said.

Richard regarded me with grave doubt. He said, "Well, you can if you want. It's a free country."

The next morning early I was in the courtroom when the prisoners were brought in for arraignment. Flori smiled over at me.

"I'm going to talk to the judge," I said loudly. "Don't worry. I'll get you out!"

Flori only raised his eyebrows and continued to smile.

I was shown to an office by a polite uniformed officer. There, behind an open door, a white-haired man sat reading at a desk.

"Your honor," the officer said, "this gentleman wants to speak to you."

The judge nodded. "Come in."

He didn't ask any questions, but just sat there looking at me; so I launched into my mentally-rehearsed lecture. Briefly, it involved justice, common sense, the Rights of Man, patriotism, the Constitution, the Pursuit of Happiness, and the oppression of the poor.

When I had finished, the judge frowned. He said, "Name?"

I replied, "Florentino whatever-it-was."

The judge said, "I mean *your* name."

I told him, and then he chewed me out for all he was worth.

"You come to me in my chambers before an arraignment and tell me how I must act. You insult my fairness, judgment, and knowledge of the law! I ought to have you locked up! Now get out of here before I do!"

I stood speechless, the officer still behind me. I thought I felt a nudge in my back and finally managed an apology.

"I'm sorry. It just seems like such a lot of trouble over hitting a chicken," I said.

The judge took a paper from the pile on his desk. "Your hard-working employee has been arrested for hit and run. He crashed broadside into a new Buick, causing more than a thousand dollars worth of damage, and then backed up and left the scene of the accident. Or so the witnesses say."

I brushed past the officer and hurried back to the courtroom. Florentino was seated at the end of the row where I could reach him.

"Flori," I said, "you told me you hit a chicken!" My voice was loud, and a uniformed guard moved in my direction.

"I know," Florentino said matter of factly. "That's what I did. I hit a 'chicken', a parked car."

When I got back to the plant I asked Richard, "What do you call a guy who is stupid?"

Richard said, "Tonto, but I don't think you're really tonto. You're just tapado." He pronounced it "top-pow."

"What is that, 'top-pow'?" I asked.

"Plugged up, constipated. In other words, innocent," he said.

I stayed on with ACI as Stonelight's manager for about five years after they had bought us. They were nice people, pleasant and generous, but our cultures never did come together. That corporation was taken over by another big corporation, and that one, I understand, by still another. New top management came and went nearly every year.

They became impossible to ignore. We had to talk to our employees through a union, which we'd never had before, but which, to the Aussies seemed a natural way of doing business. Our profit-sharing plan, in place for more than twenty years, was abolished. Tin Oxide, which makes the most beautiful white glaze, was eliminated as a raw material because it was "too expensive," though we charged more than enough for white tiles to compensate. Of course, when we left it out, we were told not to lower our price.

One day, one of the corporate executives said to me, "You know, when the telephone rings and the receptionist is busy, just let it ring. Don't answer it yourself. People are suspicious when the manager answers the company telephone."

I thought of the thousands of phone calls that had come in before there had been a "receptionist." I recalled contractor's wives calling in their husband's tile orders. I remembered noted architects and movie stars like Barbra Streisand and Kim Novak describing the kind of tiles they wanted. I remembered picking up the telephone and learning from the "Moshi, moshi," that Japan was on the line with a big order for a restaurant chain.

I looked at the bright young man sitting across from me and I thought "tapado." The world changes, businesses change, cultures either evolve or dry up. I thought I saw which way Stonelight's was headed.

I said, "Okay. My contract is up. I think it's time for me to say 'cheer-o'. What about the first of the month?"

He said, "Right. I understand." I knew he didn't and couldn't.

John Dickson

Oxygen Tent

Old office manager Nelson
lay there like a fly wrapped in amber—
eyes of a man who had drowned in his tub.
He could see us,
I'm sure he could hear us,
buried alive in his transparent coffin.

Half the office force came to smirk
at this petty tyrant who suffered angina
in Caroline Dawson's apartment.
And no one even aware that he knew her—
O'Rourke whom he fired
just before his pension was due,
Jimmy Martin, who hated his guts,
and all those others he had tortured
or lashed with his bullwhip eyes.

Such a lively gathering of people he hated.
Not a flower on the table or window sill,
just laughing and drinking and telling jokes—
a fiesta of those who came to see
how tough he was now with his heart sick.
Little Angie from Sales Records
actually wanted to blow him up
with her lit cigarette on his plastic tent.

But soon the joking died away.
The terror we saw beneath the sheet
brought an end to the stupid laughing.
His was the silent scream of lobsters
trapped in their nets.

We watched the crest of his swollen fear
slip down from its flood stage,
down to a weaving, winding flow
to a faint hope of rebirth
complete with manger bathed in light
and meek lamb and pensive cow—
all of this floating in his eyes
with bottled messages to us
recounting what little good he'd done
as though they were moments of saving grace.

Monday morning when they asked
if we had a chance to visit Nelson
we answered,
"Yeah . . . we saw him."

The Retirement of Louie Berman

On this, his final day,
he awakens to the gold-sky morning
and boards his Garden of Agony train.
The merest tremble invades his hands.
Capillary veins lace his nose and cheeks.

O who will figure the warehouse report
now that Louie is leaving?
Who will balance the customer's ledger?

The girls from Cost Accounting touch his arm.
The blur of their faces
has the sparkle of precious stones.
The men from Sales Records shake his hand.
Their smiles are warm with years of friendship.

They remove his clothes and shave his skin
and wrap him gently in mango leaves.
He is roasted twelve hours over heated rocks.
His rich juices
are allowed to gather in an earthen jar
and he is sliced into equal portions
with ceremonial precision.
The partaking of his flesh,
the sipping of his warm gravy
are deeply symbolic acts.
He is giving them all his friendship and wisdom.
From now on he will always be part of them.

He could have chosen to lock himself
in the cloister of his age
with his severance pay and his company pension
snipping roses and playing cards,
lost in his memories of jumbled years
while his marrow dries
and a haze of frost gathers between his legs.
But once in his life, at least,
every man must behave in the grand manner.

Gavin Ewart

The Caged Copywriter

"Office life, investment, interest rates, corporate politics, annual
reports,—these are not subjects which would seem especially congenial to
poetry"
                    —Dana Gioia, *The Hudson Review*

I sat alone in so many small rooms
behind glass partitions,
or open plan with others,
and wrestled all day with the headlines,
with the hundreds of words of copy,
biro and two-finger-tapping
on the beaten-up old typewriter . . . .

I sat in on so many meetings
where they told us the Unique Sales Proposition
and listed the Sales Points:
it's blue, it's chemically neutral, it's waterproof.
And the boys from Research narrowed down the copy
to the angelic head of a pin.

Requisitions, work demanded, campaigns with posters—
all filtered through a Copy Chief or Creative Director,
typists making nonsense of the carefullest copy
(the clever writers wooed them into clean Top Copies).

After the liquid lunches the authoritarians were mellow . . . .

And this went on for days and weeks and years,
tedium tempered by occasional entertainment,
the good expensive food wilted in the face of the clients
(the talk was of cars, they never read a book,
just once somebody mentioned Dornford Yates with approval),

you couldn't get drunk because of The Image.
It was, virtually, a Tantalus Situation.

The clients bullied the agencies, the Account Executives
bullied the Creative Departments—
they had Brigade of Guards ties and friends in the City.
Money may be "a kind of poetry." It certainly talks.
From the Fifties to the Seventies I heard it talking.

We were pedestrians on the plains of the working week,
the expendable infantry below the peaks of Success.
Who wants to read about a routine?
No love affairs, no murders, no adventures.
Just the summer lightning of a sparkling campaign.
Just a lot of figures, a lot of sums of money.

In a big store, does a shoe
ever write a poem about the Carpet Department?

Virtual Romance

Paulina Borsook

I WAS AT a conference with the usual
assortment of tech-weenies, dweebs, programmer geeks,
wireheads, and brainy-type science guys. There were lots of
academics and Grand Old Men of computing and foreigners
that could be spotted immediately because they were too
well-dressed. There were a few Internet wizards that could be
identified by their combination of hair and aging: some had
sloppy Pigpen hair on receding hairlines, some had grey-haired
ponytails.

Anyway, I was in line at the dinner buffet, for once
having decided to forego room service. The allure of being one
of the few women in a male-dominated setting, the promise of
easy pickings, had long since worn off but here, at least, there
weren't any industry touts to be run away from, no flacks, no
managers of marketing communication who would score points
with their bosses if they lassoed me into having dinner with
them. Why not try to be sociable for a change, momentarily
forget my raving misanthropy, and cultivate industry contacts as
my boss kept hinting that he was paying my salary for me to do.

As I was standing holding a plate, and knife and fork
rolled up in a napkin, I glanced up at this guy who had just
butted into line. What's that, I thought? He was tall, he had a
good haircut, he wore his suit well, he was consciously groomed
the way only European men can be, his wing tips were shined.
His name tag said "Dirk Van Hooeven, Salomon Brothers."
What was he doing here?

Dirk introduced himself to me and the two or three
other men around me. We all sat together; Dirk piled lots of
sweets on his dessert plate, which seemed out of character with
his general correctness as bond analyst. Dirk suggested that we
all go to a nearby jazz club. I hate jazz, but I was too curious
about him to let on; besides, this crowd of innocent nerds would
be puzzled by my explanation of why I hate jazz, how I had tried

to like it by listening to it a lot, that I'd even had a jazz bass-player boyfriend, that I knew it was a lapse in taste like liking George Winston or not liking Robert Rauschenberg. The poor darlings would be scared and confused by such talk, and if Dirk liked jazz, as a lot of Europeans do in their infatuation with all things exotically American, I didn't want to scare him off.

So we went off to the jazz club, a product manager from DEC, a QA engineer from Wang, an MIS director from an army base near Sacramento that I'd never heard of, Dirk the Wall Street quant, and me. Everyone was scrupulously polite. The married ones brought out pictures of their kids. The music wasn't intrusive at all. I noticed Dirk's nails were very short, very pink, perfectly manicured.

He offered to walk me back to my hotel. Oh goody, I thought. He escorted me to my elevator and said goodnight. Dammit. When I got back to my room I watched the 1 AM showing of *Top Gun* on the in-room pay-per-view TV channel. That was the great thing about business travel: I lived better on the road than I did at home, got my fix on popular culture in my favorite way—randomly, passively—, and never had to pay for any of it.

The next morning while checking in to get copies of the conference proceedings, I saw an information packet with the initials "DVH" lying on the table. I took out one of my business cards and scribbled "hi, I couldn't resist leaving you a note when I saw your stuff here," and stuck it beneath the rubber band that had been stretched around the packet.

I sat down on a folding chair along the edge of the conference room. This morning's panel discussion had promised to be the most heated because it had sprung from a Birds-of-a-Feather session the night before. While Dirk and I had been exchanging pleasantries at the Holiday Inn's Cherries lounge, TCP/IP gurus had been plotting the migration to OSI standards. Because the technical session was ad-hoc, there might be shouting.

I always enjoyed the religious wars in the scientific community, though I almost never understood what they were about without taking aside a native informant and having him explain what the two warring factions believed in. The partisans of connectionless transport squaring off against the partisans of connection-oriented: it didn't matter that what they said made no sense, because the invective was great. "Brain-dead," "trivial," "obvious." Such language.

I turned on the new mini-cassette tape recorder that a vendor had given my boss. It was no longer the fashion to give out such expensive freebies, but this was from a startup in Florida that was kind of out of it anyway, judging by the parity-product nature of their initial offering, which might turn out to be vaporware anyway. It figured that they didn't know what they were doing, because all those guys down there were spinoffs from aerospace or Harris or any of those other companies that had specialized in military junk, and they just didn't understand how things were different now. Silicon Valley spent its marketing money differently.

My boss had enough electronic toys as it was—in fact, we had a five-dollar bet going on how soon I was going to buy a VCR, easy money for one of us because he was a classic early adapter, I was the classic Luddite—so he offered it to me, half as a joke, if I'd get their matrix switch into the book. I didn't mind; while I didn't much care about the new information technologies, much less want to think about how I should spend my money on them, I didn't mind being given a piece of them for free.

Dirk sat down beside me. He asked me what I was working on. I said I didn't know yet, that I wouldn't know until I got back to my office what was worth writing about. He asked me what magazines I thought he should read. He industriously wrote down all the titles I listed, but I knew he would never look at them. He might as well have been asking me about my hobbies, my pets, what I did with my spare time. His point was to keep me talking about things I could seem to be expert in. Then I noticed my tape recorder had stopped running.

I asked him if he could figure out what was wrong with it. I had long since given up being worried about appearing to be a woman who is useless with machines: I was, and there was real power in self-acceptance.

Dirk picked it up from where it had been lying on the seat between us. The way he flipped the hand-sized device on its back, the knowledge in his finger tips as he poked and prodded at the buttons, the knowing what to do with what he had been presented with, broadcast erotic competence. He was the dream of sensorimotor intelligence married to expensive after-shave.

Dirk told me the problem was that the machine was in voice-activated mode, and because we were sitting so far away from the speakers, and our whisperings had been so quiet, the tape-recorder was stopping and starting. I proposed that we leave the session anyway, because neither of us was paying any attention to it.

He agreed, and we decided to take a walk along Cannery Row. I took secret glee in having this gleaming whippersnapper with his peculiar animal radiance tagging along beside me in view of the blue Pacific. It was my personal revenge on the cosmos. For all the times I had been obliged to listen to spiels on V.22 *bis* and packet-switching and why this year was going to be the year of the LAN. For having been forced to dine with all the company drones who might well have been Disney Audioanimatronics dolls, except that they had crusty skin. For all strange-looking, well-intentioned, maladroit men I had been forced to occupy common space-time coordinates with for professional reasons. Whereas with Dirk, the most banal of his comments on the weather held charm.

Dirk said he was going to be in San Francisco the next day talking to the operations manager in Salomon Brothers' office in the Bank of America building. He asked me if I wanted to have lunch.

* * *

I had just bought a laptop computer, which I was fooling around with, trying to use it in addition to the IBM PC my company had provided for me. I was on the phone to New York to a systems-analyst friend of mine, having him talk me through a DOS installation-problem, when call-waiting beeped. I put my friend who grovels at computers on hold and took the call. The receptionist said Mr. Van Hooeven was there to see me, and she complimented me on figuring out how to use the new phone system so soon. I told her that it was OK to buzz him in. I hung up on my friend, and by then Dirk was standing outside my office.

He looked down at the laptop. He was too polite to ask if I were having problems, and I intuited there were limits to the attractiveness of my female learned-helplessness. I was sure Dirk knew women investment bankers, whizzes with spreadsheets if not rocket scientists themselves, so he probably would not look kindly on incompetence. I didn't mind being Exotic Other: I just didn't want to look stupid.

He said that he had sold computers the summer between his sophomore and junior year of college, and had gotten pretty good at tech support on both Macs and PCs. He asked me if he could play with my Toshiba. I said sure, and it was a treat, thrilling almost, watching the knowing way he flipped the laptop's screen to adjust for the way the light struck the LCD display, the deft couple of keystrokes he used to generate a screen-dump to activate my printer. He had never seen a portable printer like mine before.

We went to Ciao for lunch, a yupscale place around the corner, because it was yet-another-expense-account-place I hadn't tried near my office. I was methodically working my way through all of them within a ten-block radius, and so far had no favorites. He ordered pasta with three cheeses. He insisted on picking up the tab, though he could have just as easily been listed on my T+E as an "industry consultant" or "user" as I was going to be listed on his as "media contact." I pointed out that since he didn't know the Bay Area and was going to be there for the weekend, I could play tour guide.

☆ ☆ ☆

When I called his room from the house phone at Campton Place, I told him that he should bring along a bathing suit, because I was going to take him to the Platonic Ideal of a Marin County hot-tub place. That is, if he wanted to go. He agreed that might be a good idea and said he would be right down. But he didn't invite me up.

As soon as we got into my car, he started twiddling with the controls on the radio. I was stunned by how large his hands were, how thick and blunt his fingers. I had to stop myself from staring or saying anything about them. He asked me if I were thinking about getting a cellular phone; I said no, because I wasn't a stockbroker or selling real estate.

By the time we had driven through the redwoods in Samuel P. Taylor state park, and he had seen the West Marin cows grazing on clover, he was reminiscing about when he lived in England. There had been cows there, but none on hills so steep. He didn't remember the cows of his native Holland very well; he had been six when his family had left. There had been poppies in England, too, but none so saturated in color as the California golden poppy.

I took him to McClure's beach, which is about as far west on the continent as you can go at Point Reyes National Seashore. The San Andreas fault runs out to sea there, and you pretty much feel you can't go much farther, that things are about as extreme as you could want them to get. I had him climb up with me on my favorite set of rocks, where we stared out to Taiwan; when we started climbing back down, he commented that at grammar school in England he had been taught that a man should always precede a woman up a staircase, because otherwise he might be able to look up her skirt. He was such a gentleman that he wouldn't have mentioned it until we were no longer replicating those potentially scandalous postures.

On the way back to the car, he stopped to pick up an undistinguished sea-rounded rock. He said he was going to take it back to keep on his desk in New York because he was the sentimental type. I said nothing, because I could not deal with the statement. I couldn't have made his declaration of strong liking, of letting me know that he was recording our scrabbling on top of cliffs as This Was A Romantic Moment To Be Remembered, for I was a scaredy-cat. The silence as I drove was companionable, even more unsettling than the sexual tension.

Floating World, the hot-tub place in Sausalito, was just around the corner from Whole Earth headquarters and a couple of yachting supply places. It was also about half a mile away from where I'd had my first technical writing job at a small Microdata and Honeywell software shop that wrote Pick-based vertical accounting packages for construction firms.

When you walked in the front door of Floating World, you immediately got a Twilight Zone feeling of Moonie mind control; there was watery New Age music playing, the staff all wore pastels and were horribly relaxed, there were expensive and exotic brands of skin-care products for sale at the counter, and the interior overall evoked a resort in Bermuda.

Dirk and I went off to the men's and women's bathrooms to change into our bathing suits. I wanted him too much not to be worried about seeing him half-naked; no clothes at all would have been even scarier. He was waiting patiently for me by the door of our suite. I was grateful that he was wearing standard department-store baggies: some perfectly nice men show alarming lapses in taste when it comes to bathing suits. After I closed the door behind us, I showed him which knobs governed the volume of the piped-in music, which buttons determined the degree and kind of bubbliness of the water jets, which switch turned on the light in the sauna. The suite had a clerestory window which did not that night frame the moon; I pointed out the wind chimes hung in front of a small air vent, which would be jangled gently by a gust of air five minutes before our time was up.

I told him what I normally do is turn off all lights except the ones that illuminated the bottom of the redwood tub. I explained as we got into the water how Floating World used an oxygen-filtration system pioneered by NASA for the astronauts instead of conventional swimming-pool chlorination—much healthier. I thought this would interest him because he had been a chemistry major at Dartmouth. I pointed out the Japanese-influenced joinery in the woodworking, very typical of Northern California wood-butcher style. I hoped he found my pedantry entertaining. I wanted to make sure I seemed no more than friendly and helpful. We were careful not to let our knees touch underwater.

For dinner, he said we ought to go back to Campton Place, because they were famous for their food. He asked me if I minded room service; that way we wouldn't have to change out of our jeans for the dining room downstairs. I said sure.

In his room, we used the excuse of being flushed and wet-headed from Floating World to change into matching and ugly white terry-cloth robes provided by the hotel.

He noticed that the red message-light on his phone was blinking, so he called down to the desk before he placed our food orders. He also called his answering machine in Brooklyn Heights, using a hand-held beeper to punch in the touch-tones of his remote code. He told me who the messages were from (his college roommate, a co-worker) as he listened, a good sign, I thought.

We had green-lipped New Zealand mussels, which made Dirk nervous. In spite of being Dutch, he turned out not to be a fan of bivalves. We drank far more than we ate.

I was sitting in an armchair next to the bed as he stood with the cable program guide in his hand, pulled from the top shelf of the armoire that held the TV and the in-room bar and stocked refrigerator. When I said there was nothing in particular that I felt like watching, he walked over to me and sat on the edge of the bed. I asked him what we were doing here. He leaned over, lifted the hair off the back of my neck, and kissed me there.

When he stopped, I kissed him full on the mouth, cupping his face with both of my hands. I knocked him back onto the bed. When we came up for air, I asked him how old he was. He said he was twenty-three. Dirk was only two years older than my oldest nephew. I shrieked, laughed, and crawled under the covers, pulling the sheet over my head.

Dirk looked worried. How old are you, he said. I said I was thirty-three. He said that in August he would be twenty-four, the way a kindergartner says he will be five and a half next month, every little increment of age counting. I said yes, but in September I would be thirty-four.

I became a little hesitant, and he moved too quickly and roughly at first. But when I whispered easy, easy, we became miraculously in-sync. I had never run into his mix of strength and sweetness before. He was so powerful, but anything I tried made him tremble.

There was a purity to him, a psychosexual gentility, that humbled me. In his immaculateness, no matter how intense things got, he had no smell, except for the faint remains of his cologne.

How could anything that huge and passionate be so minutely sensitive: beautiful living contradiction. You don't expect fine instruments to be as responsive in the high notes as well as in the low ones, piano and forte, but he was, he was. I had never known that masculine strength could be so inspirational. As he lifted and moved me down from where I had been driven up against the headboard of the bed, the tenderness in his massive, Nautilused-out upper torso was almost unbearable.

We were in that divine state of telepathy that I had even forgotten existed, and he blew me away. He was oxen-hearted, and exquisite. It was sacramental, alright.

We stayed up all night. He was impressed that I carried rubbers with me. Not sleeping didn't matter that much because he had to be in the office by 5:30 AM that morning anyway in time for the market's opening back east. Salomon Brothers kept a black middle-aged woman, a former employee of a once-famous Pacific Heights hostess, as a cook for the morning staff, so Dirk knew he could stay awake once he got there, primed by coffee and sugar and the good grease of a traditional breakfast.

Dirk said he would call me at lunch, and that we would spend the next night together before he had to fly back to New York.

He dressed in a suit; I had only my jeans to get back into. We agreed that we should walk out at different times, to not advertise to the desk crew What We Had Been Up To. I walked out about five minutes after Dirk did, attempting to look impassive and cool, scowling even. The night-clerk behind the desk smiled at me with the same smile a stewardess had given me when I and my ex-husband had ducked out of the bathroom on our honeymoon redeye flight to Jamaica. Service personnel pretty rapidly get familiarized with the little wings that appear an inch and a half above the ankles after mad love-making.

I dashed home, changed into standard business attire, and came back to work. I was loathe to go out for lunch, waiting for Dirk's call. I was too nervous to eat anything anyway, so I stayed in. He didn't call. I took out the tapes I'd made at the conference. Sure enough, there was one where Dirk and I could be heard to be talking and giggling, with someone droning on in the background about network management. It was a tape of him fixing my tape recorder, and I was stunned by how flirtatious we both were, even then. We might as well have been fucking on the floor of the Doubletree Inn lobby. Hearing him was painful, so I did not finish the tape out.

By four o'clock when Dirk finally called, I was in despair. He had been called into meeting after meeting; instead of staying the night in San Francisco, he had had to take an evening flight to O'Hare to do fire-fighting having to do with some kludgy graphics workstations in the Chicago office.

I got squeaky. I found myself slipping into the worst sort of clinginess, asking Dirk when I was going to see him again. I realized I didn't have his office phone number, his home address or phone number. He spelled them all out, said he could be out in San Francisco for a weekend in a month, and that he would call me when he got back to New York.

Two days later, there was a pink telephone message slip from Mr. Van Hooeven of Salomon Brothers waiting for me when I walked in to work. My chin was still chapped from having kissed him so much. I called him back immediately.

After telling each other how much we missed each other, and how tired we both were, Dirk asked me what my facsimile number was, because he wanted to send me something that described how he felt when he got back to New York after two days of getting no sleep and getting hard-ons from thinking about me as he sat in on meetings where the competitive advantages of different kinds of twisted-pair cabling were being discussed.

I put Dirk on hold. I had to ask my secretary for the facsimile number. No one had ever asked me for that before. We kept on talking, and soon there was a knock on my door. The fax had arrived, a "Far Side" cartoon of a fellow in free-flight, who had a grand piano and an anchor at the ends of his parachute lines instead of the hoped-for parachute.

It amused me that Dirk had so officially filled out the facsimile cover sheet (TO: J. Mergner, FROM: D. Van Hooeven), down to a chargeback number in the upper left-hand corner. As if there were anything official or business-like about what he had transmitted.

Dirk and I agreed to call each other daily. I said I had been writing him a letter; he wanted to know what I said in it. I said that would be cheating, and besides, I was much too shy to read out loud what I had written. He said he didn't want to wait for me to mail it, and asked if I could fax it to him. I said I had never sent a fax before, and besides, there were things in my letter I wouldn't want anyone else to read. Dirk tried to coax me on, assuring me he would stand right by the machine to pick up the letter as soon as it arrived so no one else could see it.

I caved in. I had my secretary transfer his call to the phone on her desk, so Dirk could coach me through the steps I needed to take. He patiently talked me through the numbers I had to punch in, the buttons I had to push. I giggled throughout, feeling scared and excited and on an adventure and doubting the whole thing would work. Then I heard the answer-tone of the receiving facsimile machine, and saw my facsimile machine print out "SALOMON BROS—WATERSIDE PLAZA—212-555-6097" on its display.

The whole exercise made me giddy. I was able to talk on the phone with Dirk simultaneous with him guiding me through this set of moves that would get my letter to him in realtime. I marvelled at how he just knew what to do without ever having seen my facsimile machine. The power of his knowingness gave me the shivers.

I asked Dirk if it had come through OK. He assured me it had, and I could hear his snorts of amused pleasure through the phone as he read what I had written.

I had my secretary transfer his call back to my office, where I could close the door.

So our pattern began. We called each other several times a day, courtesy of our employers. We left messages on each other's answering machines, sometimes calling midday when neither of us could possibly have been at home just to hear the sound of each other's voice. He used the Salomon Brothers mailroom to Federal Express me a favorite kind of cookie he had heard me mention I could only get in New York. I started hoarding the pink message slips where the space that said "M" was filled in by D. Van Hooeven, "company" by Salomon Brothers and where the two boxes "called" and "please call back" were checked. I prized the one where in the space for "number," my secretary had written "u-no." It was a signal to me, and to my office, and to the world, that we were an item.

Every time he called, as soon as I heard his voice I would flush and stammer. I would close the door to my office and hunch over the phone. Every time after we finished talking, I would look as though I had just had sex, because my eyes were shiny and my hair was mussed from my nervously running my fingers through it as we talked. I would walk around afterwards with a secret smile for about half an hour. Very soon we had spent more time on the phone than we ever had in person. And none of this would have been possible if our companies hadn't negotiated corporate bloc-discounts with interexchange carriers, letting us run amuck with AT&T and MCI. We were treating long-distance as if it were a basic human right like heat or potable water: life was grand in the wake of the breakup of the monopoly of the Bell System.

I could date when I officially fell in love with him to a particular phone call. We had been arguing about GOSIP timetables. Dirk maintained that the OSI standard was going to become mandatory for all government procurements; I said that my sources indicated that grassroots protocol stacks could still be bought and used, as long as the OSI products were in there in the RFP too. I went out to lunch; there was a message from Dirk marked URGENT when I got back. He had called one of the vendors that he had a privileged non-disclosure relationship with in order to corroborate his position in our argument. Dirk gave me the phone number of his contact, the head of the company's development team, so I could hear first-hand from someone else the reasons for Dirk's contrary position. I didn't want to get myself into some sort of pre-announcement embargo, which my company policies forbade, but I promised Dirk I would call. Dirk said he was concerned that I would admit an error into my story. I thanked him, and hung up. Not only did he think I was the best lover he had ever had, he did not want me to look bad in print.

After about a week of this, of my living on ice water and take-out fruit salad and wandering around the Embarcadero with my hands in my pockets, autistically and repetitively whistling the dippy top-forty love song from *Top Gun*, Dirk escalated our relationship.

Since I was writing letters on my computer anyway, Dirk suggested that I upload my letter to him at work, so he could read it right away. I was skeptical about systems like that: I hate machines, they hate me, and there was always some damned thing that would come up, or wouldn't work as it was supposed to, or made no sense. But he was sure he could make the setup function; he had all this experience giving people help over the phone with their computers.

Dirk had told me he needed to know what my data-line phone number was, so I had to drag the office manager into the PBX closet and have her help me paw through yards of spaghetti cabling, checking ports against the wiring chart.

I called Dirk back with the number. Before he configured his computer to receive a file transfer from mine, he walked me through the command sequence so that my computer would be slaved to his as soon as he dialed in. Keeping me on the telephone, Dirk initiated the connection. As I was talking to him, I saw

    hi. can you read this?

appearing across my display, the characters coming into light as he was typing them back in New York. I squealed, told him that I could. He brought out my getting-to-be-the-girl, o take me James. Or Dirk, in this case. He then asked me the filename I had given to the letter. I told him "Dirk7," and watched as the letter streamed across the screen, paragraphing lost in one continuous flow of ASCII. His sureness was reminiscent of when he had stuck his hand in exactly the right place between my shoulder blades. It was unsettling and strange and exciting to watch him enter and work my computer that way.

After I had acquiesced in the file upload, he proposed that we start sending each other electronic mail. I freaked out. I was beginning to feel corrupted.

No, no, no, I said. That's what those weird people do who get into computer dating and marry people they've never met and have no social skills and have those weird pear-shaped flabby DP bodies from too many hours sitting and staring at computer terminals.

Dirk disagreed. He had met one of his college girlfriends through electronic mail. He used to run the Arpanet node at the

Dartmouth computer center and got into a CHAT with a woman who was a Berkeley graduate student one night. Their conversation turned into a nightly flirtation after Dirk found a picture of her in an old Dartmouth yearbook: she had gone there as an undergraduate, which had been one of their initial points of tangency. They met after speed-rapping and making goo-goo eyes at each other online for several months. Dirk said it had been weird to make her actual, physical, and not virtual, acquaintance. But it wasn't as weird as I might have thought, and that he and she carried on a nice summer romance after they met, and besides, he and I had already met and knew we liked each other.

I protested. BBSes are weird, I said, people who hang out on them are weird.

Dirk said that there were all kinds of people on the Internet and that there were conferences on everything from politics to cooking to the Grateful Dead—in fact, Dirk's immediate vice-president was a Deadhead, and had been grateful when Dirk downloaded the most current postings on the Dead SIG.

I said I liked writing real letters. That virtual communities were to real communities as catsup is to a vegetable.

Dirk kept on. He said that this way, our letters could get to each other right away. That we could be reading and writing to each other from work when it would look like we were doing other things. That the three-hour time difference between us wouldn't matter as much, because he could write me in the morning before I came into work, and I could write him after he had gone to sleep.

I said I had never had any ambitions to be a hacker and I had never wanted to be a ham radio operator either.

He persisted. He said that if I started sending him electronic mail, we wouldn't be playing as much telephone tag. And when we were both on the road, it would be even easier to stay in touch, because anywhere either of us stayed, we would be able to log on through the phone jacks in our hotel rooms. Assuming they had RJ11 connectors.

I relented, because being an ageing hippy made me want to try anything once. Besides, I didn't want to keep acting so un-with-it. Also, if it was just another way of sending and receiving love letters, only faster, then I was all for it. I didn't want to appear more hung-up than any of his past girlfriends.

I told Dirk I'd figure out a way to get to him electronically.

I asked my boss if he would pay for me to subscribe to an electronic mail service. He was reluctant, but I said it would better my contacts around the country, help with research. He said OK, but to keep the monthly expenditure under $25, the amount where the bean counters automatically started asking questions and demanding receipts.

After I asked around, it seemed like the only way I would be able to hook up to Dirk was through the Well. The Well stood for Whole Earth 'Lectronic Link, and was connected to Whole Earth magazine. The people who ran it were also ageing hippies—escapees from intentional communities, they were civil libertarians and communications junkies. If I could stomach this email stuff at all, it would be through them.

Once I decided to commit the crime of going electronic, I was impatient with how long the administrative tasks took. If I were going to participate in *folie a deux*, I wanted to get on with it, get it over with.

While I waited, I was reduced to going to the men's fragrance counter at Macy's where I sprayed Xeryus on my forearm. I had spotted Dirk's canister of it on the ledge of the sherbet-colored fake marble sink at Campton Place; but on me the stuff only smelt insipid and metallic. I tried other means to make Dirk real. On my office bulletin board, I tacked up articles on Salomon Brothers, or Holland, and even a soft feature from *The Wall Street Journal* on a church in Cornwall called St. Dirk's-in-the-Field. These were the best I could do.

It took the Well a couple of days to enter my name, address, and Mastercard number in their records. Then I had to wait until their manual arrived in the mail. The manual was like most manuals in that you already had to know how things worked in order to use it, you couldn't find anything in the table of contents or index, and it relied on a knowledge of Unix and data communications that I just didn't have. What was a parity bit, and how was I supposed to find out how many I was supposed to have? Did I want to be full-duplex? Have the echo on? And what the hell did "mark" mean here? It was as tedious as when I used to try to read articles on building your own grey-water recycling system for the home in my brother's issues of *Popular Mechanics*. Why would anyone *voluntarily* do this to themselves.

I had to come up with a login/user ID. It had to be something that I didn't think anyone else on the Well would have, and that I could remember easily. I chose "potto," a favorite woodland creature. And for my password, "redux," somehow having to do with the self-referential, worm-ourobouros, infinitely recursive quality of it all. I knew better than to choose something like the name of my cat, or my birthday, or anything that someone could easily link to me. Basic network-security hygiene dictated obscurity of password.

I kept on trying to log on until the day when I got the sequence

```
This is the Well.

Dynix (R) V3.0.14   (well)
Type your user name or "newuser" to register
login: potto
Password:
last login: Tue Apr 7 1987 14:35:37 on ttyxa
Copyright 1984 Sequent Computer Systems, Inc.
Picospan T3.3 designed by Marcus Watts
licensed by Unicon Inc.

You have reached the WELL (Whole Earth
Lectronic Link). Material posted on the
WELL is the sole property of its author.
Reproduction in any medium without the
express permission of the individual
author is strictly prohibited.

**************************************************
     Welcome to the Entry Conference   !
**************************************************

The following commands can all be given at
the "OK (? for help):" prompt. All
commands on the WELL are followed by a
carriage return:

Type: welltour .. to read the WELL's
                  introductory Guided
                  Tour.
Type: manual   .. for instruction on
                  how to read The WELL's
                  online User Manual
                  (intermediate level).
```

```
Type: support    .. for instructions on
                    getting online help.
Type: b          .. to browse the list of
                    topics  in this
                    conference.
Type: tips       .. to see a list of
                    lively discussions on
                    The WELL.

*LONG DISTANCE CALLERS*
Type: access     .. for information on
                    long-distance connect
                    alternatives.

4 newresponse topics and 22 brandnew topics.
First topic 1, last 72
```

The password didn't show up on the screen as I typed. I immediately called Dirk, even though he told me he was going to be at a meeting where secret strategic plans for FDDI and IRIS workstations and more he wouldn't tell me about were going to be discussed.

While waiting for him to call me back, I called what the Well called voice support to ask them what my Internet email address was. I had no idea. The person who took my call had no idea either, but said she would find someone who knew and would call me back. Out of edginess, I logged back onto the Well again, just to prowl around. There were things called conferences, where people who didn't know each other would yammer on about designated topics. There were conferences on different kinds of computers (natch), but also on true confessions where people got publicly and mentally undressed, on singles and parenting and the media and health. The idea of carrying on conversations with people I had never met, and probably wouldn't like if I ever did meet them, was repellent. Here these people were, making like they were each other's best friends, flirting with each other and often making silly, sci-fi-inflected jokes like Cal Tech undergraduates make to each other. It seemed like the worst of the 60s rap groups, only carried on by people who were addicted to keyboarding.

Dirk got back to me before the Well did, and gave me an address of his for me to try in electronic mail syntax:

```
!mail salomon@tuck.dart.edu
```

So I typed that in, and got a prompt for "subject." Being shy, I typed in

```
first try
```

Not knowing what to put in the message itself, I wrote

```
let's see if this works
```

We hung up. The Well then called me back, and tried to come up with an addressing syntax that would route email through the Lawrence Livermore Laboratory node onto the Internet. They were uncertain that it would work. I sent two messages, the first using the syntax that had originated with Dirk and the second using what the Well had cobbled together for me.

My first message never got to him. It bounced back hours later; something was wrong with the addressing:

```
9 Apr 87 15:18:58 PST
Date: Thu, 9 Apr 87 15:18:58 PST
From: Mail Delivery Subsystem
<111-1cc!MAILER-DAEMON>
Subject: Returned mail: Host unknown
Message-ID: <8704212318.AA1521@11-1cc.ARPA>
To: well!potto
Status: RO

——Transcript of session follows——
550 tuck.dart.edu.tcp...550 Host unknown
550 salomon@tuck.dart.edu... Host unknown

——Unsent message follows——
Received: Thu, 9 Apr 87 15:18:58 PST by
111-1cc.ARPA
(5.51)
id AA15209; Thu, 9 Apr 87 15:18:58 PST
Received: by well.UUCP (4.12/4.7)
id AA29107; Thu, 9 Apr 14:46:43 pst
Date: Thur, 9 Apr 87 14:46:43 pst
From: well!potto (Justine Mergner)
Message-ID: <8704212256.AA29107@well.UUCP
To: salomon@tuck.dart.edu
Subject: first try

let's see if this works
```

Somehow it was humiliating to see my message back in my face. I never liked seeing my mailed letters at friends' houses either; my letters always reminded me of used Kleenex. Here, my ignorance was being indicted, too. This was Fate intervening between two lovers as surely as war or moving to another high school would have done. And though I knew DAEMON was a name for a Unix utility, it looked too much like demon, and I felt I had been condemned to Hell. For trying this unnatural medium against my will. For worse, failing at it. You made me play by your rules and I didn't even win.

I called Dirk back when the mail bounced. He asked me to read the message back to him. He decided that I needed to better identify his host gateway, and that he would try sending me a test message of his own to see if at least, he could get to me. He came up with a new address to try, adding a host number to the host name:

```
!mail salomon@tuck-10.dart.edu
```

We talked some more, about what he was going to do that night and what I was going to do that night and how both of our jobs were going. He had just seen the movie *Something Wild* and said it reminded him of us. He made a few affectionate double entendres in that patented chesty rumble of his that always made me feel like the RCA dog listening to His Master's Voice. They were particularly ticklish because I knew he did not have his own office; how could he say stuff like that with someone within earshot? Or possibly within earshot? He was a risk-taker, that was for sure.

When I got to work the next morning, there was a message waiting for me on the Well; he had gotten the second message using the Well's addressing scheme.

```
From 111-1cc!tuck-10.arpa!salomon Fri Apr
10 6:21:08 1987
Date: 10 Apr 87 08:43:00 EDT
From: "DIRK VAN HOOEVEN"
<11-1cc!tuck-10.arpa!salomon>
Subject: your mail...only took 12 minutes
Reply-To: "DIRK VAN HOOEVEN"
<11-1cc!tuck-10.arpa!salomon>

I really don't know what the panic was all
about. From when you sent it to your
```

```
mailer on the Well (15:26 to when it was
forwarded 15:37 to when it was received by
me 18:38, it only took 12 minutes... not
bad, huh?

your message came through L. Livermore
Labs and I think the Well is on Usenet.

Dirk
—
```

I called Dirk immediately and told him that the system at last
seemed to be working, because the second message had gotten
through. He had also gotten my third message, which had
addressed him by a numbered host. I was getting initiated into a
new level of vice.

I felt like a French girl who by falling in love with a
handsome and sweet German soldier, had become a
collaborationist. Dirk was on the side of greenmail and
arbitrageurs and program-trading, employed by the running dogs
of Yankee capitalism, an accessory to the ruin of traditional
American industries and neighborhoods. He was a technocrat, a
digitizer, an ambassador of the future that preferred, nay,
expected the engineered and the simulated and their MTV. This
naive, post-literate Reaganite was actively participating in the
downfall of the West, because he was contributing to the
creation of ever-more-tricky financial instruments instead of
working on a cure for cancer with his training as a scientist. He
would have had no idea what the personal being political meant,
or how I would have argued for the unmediated and the
authentic. I was fraternizing with the enemy and I didn't care.
My embrace of this emissary of everything that was politically
incorrect was total.

Dirk and I still talked as much as ever, whether at work
or using our business credit cards when we were anyplace else.
But email entered the cycle, in that often after hanging up from
talking with him, I would compulsively dash off a note on
something left unsaid. He would receive it an hour or two or
three later, and call me back with a response. Or immediately
dash off one of his own. I would log on after lunch, in the
middle of working on something else, or almost hourly, just to
see if there were something there from him. We were linking up
in every virtual way we could. The prompt line at the bottom of
my communications software said

while it was making the call across the Bay to Sausalito. I'll say.

As soon as I saw the

```
You have mail.
```

message, I would let the message scroll down my screen. Then I would turn my printer on, reprint the message onto paper, turn the printer off, store the message in my Well mailbox, and log off. If it was a short message, I would read it as it appeared, but if it was longer than the twenty-five lines that comprised a screenful of data, I wouldn't even try and would let the printer handle it. All that great mush would be going by too fast for me to read it. I never could figure out how to stop and then restart the scrolling of the message.

I would then rip the message off my printer, and one time out of two, laugh out loud. I was sure my officemates thought I was insane, for I would be sitting in my office, clearly with no one else there, I was audibly not on the phone, but I was laughing, nonetheless. The printouts I kept in a file folder labeled with Dirk's name, hanging in the top drawer of my file cabinets.

I wasn't with this man nor was I sharing his bed, as I was dying to. But I could share the phatic act of sending him email: the fact that I would have sent him something, I kind of figured, was the point, and that he and I would consider that our link was virtually instantaneous. That it took twenty minutes, or three hours, or however long it would take to make the hops through network gateways from Sausalito to Manhattan, was immaterial. I guessed to Dirk that the communication itself created intimacy.

I thought that was perverse, but it seemed no more major a concession than wearing a perfume or garments to bed you knew a guy liked. It seemed an acceptable deformation of character for such a hunk. There was no pain, and a minimal amount of hardware. And I got to participate in the communications revolution of our time.

I was also shocked at how bald his email was. He was willing to write and transmit messages that were extremely personal, yet I had always been told that you shouldn't ever put into electronic mail anything that you wouldn't want read by others. Privacy cannot be guaranteed over a network. But Dirk did it anyway, and joked about how maybe some of the Internet types that he knew well and that I had met at our sainted conference of memory in Monterey might be reading our mail at points along the way because it was so hot. We might be giving thrills to late-night network operators in Omaha, Minneapolis, and Philadelphia as our mail went charging back and forth between the Coasts at 56 kilobits per second.

> You have proposed an entire weekend of
> sexual activities, taking recesses only to
> eat and bathe. Now you can imagine how
> enticing and appealing that sounds...I'm
> at the office, and just as I am saying to
> you that I would be VERY happy with that
> scenario, my VP asked me into his office.
> Now you must realize that talking about
> this made the front of my pants look like
> Mt. Fuji, not exactly a way to go into
> conference with your manager.
>
> Ever caring, Dirk

So I went along, tentative, anxious, goofily grinning. I felt that Dirk was challenging me to break taboos. In terms of heterosexual behavior, I thought I had done all that as a teenager, found doing so for its own sake boring, and had gone back to being conventional. I hadn't thought it would have been possible for there to be any new taboos I had not yet considered as worthy of being broken.

Dirk would tell me his sexual fantasies. He liked playing guessing games, and having me give him hints daily about things I thought we ought to try when we next got together:

> As for your hint of the day, smaller than
> a breadbox, huh?
>
> 1. sensory deprivation (I'd be interested
> in this even if it's not what you're
> hinting at :-)
> 2. it could be some kind of oil for
> massage, but that's a guess, and since you
> said it's smaller than a breadbox, I can't
> imagine that oil would qualify.
>
> How about if you include price ranges for
> these "objects"?
>
> I'll be looking forward to the next hint!
> Speak with you soon...
>
> EOM - 19 lines

I had to be told that ":-)" was the online glyph for a smiley face. It signified a joke.

The fantasy I found most puzzling was one he had of making love blindfolded. I had never done this, nor wanted to, but if that's what he wanted, I could be a sport. But something happened with the message I sent in reply to his talk of silk scarves. I had to call the Well tech support to help me figure out what had happened, to retrieve the misfired mail. The woman helping me out with the errant email had to actually go into the text of files, searching for mine in order to figure out what happened. Certain of my words would have jumped out at anyone. My Well helper was too polite to say anything, but I felt as if I were standing on top of my desk, naked, so anyone passing by could remark on my figure flaws.

I had never been involved with a workaholic before; to me it was part of his appeal:

> My worry is that should I get too caught
> up, or personally attached (as in I can't
> stop thinking about you), I might louse up
> the work opportunities that arise. Now I
> know that seems very nerd-like, but
> nevertheless it really matters to me that
> I succeed here. When I have more staff
> working for me so I can exert a little
> Human Resources Management (read: whip and
> slavedrive), the situation could change.

Dirk had to fly to London and Frankfurt to check up on the installations there. He borrowed some kind of a Trash-80 clone from work. He sent me a message just before he took off for the airport. What a great guy:

> I'm logging on from my workslate, and i
> can read your two messaegs at 300 baud. I
> can't really write a very long response on
> tis little keyboard, but I wanted you to
> know I had read it. I managed to get the
> morning flight on Sunday, so I'll be off
> bright and early, and off to the
> Marlborough Arms Sunday night and flying
> to Frankfurt on Monday night, and staying
> at some little hotle sorry hotel called
> the Hilton neat our office there. In case
> you haven't noticed, I dont have a working

```
backspace, since I can't figure out how to
make this ting create a true DEL character.
<kiss>
Ciao
Dirk
```
———

I tried to imagine if the notebook-sized computer had an internal modem, or if Dirk had gone to the effort for me of using an acoustic coupler.

He called me from his London hotel room and drove me wild by putting on a fruity British public-school accent. We both wished I was there with him. We arranged that I should call him in Frankfurt, because the German PTT slapped on a massive surcharge on outgoing FX calls: why give the hopelessly old-fashioned Deutsche Bundepost any more money than we had to. We talked about when he was going to be coming out to San Francisco for a clothing-optional weekend. As soon as he got back from Europe, we decided. All he had to do was cash in some of his frequent-flyer miles using overnight mail, have the tickets Fedexed to him at Salomon Brothers, and I'd see him on Friday. I was going to take that afternoon off.

He showed up at my office straight from the airport with his garment bag. I blushed when I saw him again for the first time in six weeks; seeing the object that had inspired all that hot-and-botheredness made me bashful, because of course I didn't know him: he was a stranger, though one I was really delighted to see.

We drove to my house and with barely suppressed impatience, fell into bed. It was ecstatic, celestial, angelic, transcendental. When we were done, Dirk said he couldn't do this with me anymore. I said what? Cradling my shoulders in the crook of his arm, with his other hand he took out from his wallet that he had laid on the bedside table his American Airlines AAdvantage card. It listed the toll-free reservations numbers for major cities in the United States. Including San Francisco.

I asked him what he was doing. He said he was looking for the next flight out. I said I wasn't going to argue with him, but I thought he was crazy for walking away from what we had. He said that the sooner we disengaged, the sooner we could each find someone at home, him in New York, me in San Francisco.

He made a reservation for a flight out the next morning. We stayed in bed, got up to make dinner when the sun was going down. He complimented me on how I looked in my bathrobe, calling it a gown in the British fashion.

I would not beg him to stay; with my pride I could not throw my arms around his knees in a fit of female weakness. I have a kind of tramp-dignity: if you were offering me lunch because you took pity on my hunger, homelessness, and joblessness, I would still insist on raking the leaves in your backyard first. And I never wanted to talk anyone into anything.

As I was stuffing the remains of the food I could not eat down the garbage disposal, Dirk came up from behind and hugged me. He pulled me away from what he saw was a dangerous task, the best little boy in the world and former Medevac volunteer horrified by what he saw as a dismemberment in the making. I swung around and slightly out of his embrace and thrust my splayed fingers out in front of me, dancing them in his face. Three decades! Ten fingers! All there! I said. He pulled me to him and said, you drive me crazy. It put me in mind of the scene in *Annie Hall*, where Woody Allen and Diane Keaton were photographing lobsters on the kitchen floor. Once Dirk grabbed me, he carried me off to bed up the stairs Rhett Butler-style. More incandescence.

I watched him sleep, because I could not. With Dirk, I had lost my immunity. Every moment with him had been a found one, all sixty hours of them. When he woke up that morning and came downstairs, he found me in a rocking chair. He asked me what I was thinking. I said I was thinking about how much he pleased me. He looked stunned at my reply.

When I dropped him off at the airport the next morning, he said he thought we should cool things for awhile. I drove back to my office, leaving him a message on his answering machine, just to hear his voice one last time. I logged on and sent him a note I hoped was neither too anguished nor too drippy.

When I got back to work on Monday, I kept logging on hourly to see if there was anything from him. There wasn't, but the habit had grown too strong to break. With no positive reinforcement after a week or so, it dropped down to once a day. After a week or two of that, it dropped further down to once a week. One time I logged onto the Well with the intention of capturing to disk all the messages he and I had sent each other, cleaning out my Well mailbox. While I couldn't stand the idea of all that heavy breathing and pent-up yearning just sitting there in binary in my mbox, I found I couldn't stand even more removing the record of what we had been to each other.

It was about then that I got my first Well bill: it was less than $40 for hours of virtual lovemaking. After a month had gone by, I regained enough composure to have a friend return the scarves to Saks and credit them to her account. She then gave me back the cash. I couldn't go through the transaction myself.

I had to go to Seattle to attend an IEEE conference and interview the Marconi Award-winning muckymuck from Bell Labs who had invented adaptive equalization. I brought my laptop with me because I decided I had to write to Dirk as we had planned, from a hotel room. But I mailed the letter to him at work in the ordinary way, with stamps. There was no answer.

All that summer, as I had that spring from the time Dirk had said we would have to part, I walked around with a virtual spear in my chest. I logged onto the Well once a month, but there was never anything there.

The fall came and there were massive layoffs at Salomon Brothers followed immediately by the October stock-market crash. I decided I would contact Dirk to see if he was OK. Also, we had spoken of meeting at the fall Comdex back in the spring, and if he were going to be there, I wanted to be prepared. To avoid him or drag him back into bed. I did not want to be caught by surprise.

About a week after I sent him the message through the Well, I got this back:

```
Hi. I haven't been reading my mail for a
while, so I just got your note.

I won't be coming out to Vegas,
unfortunately. My new boss went to Comdex
a few years ago, and thought it was the
biggest excuse for a party he'd ever seen.
I will be making a Silicon Valley trip,
but on a date to be determined. I'll let
you know here.

Dirk
```

But he never did.

About a year later, when I logged onto the Well because some other friends had joined, I decided enough time had elapsed that I could bear to look again at what Dirk had sent me, but I couldn't find any of it. By then I had learned to compose offline and save myself money; even without Dirk's expertise I had learned how to use Crosstalk Xmodem with Xywrite. I sent an email message to the Well system administrator asking him what he thought had happened. After several messages back and forth, we both decided that Dirk had been lost in one of the Well's many disk crashes. The sysop couldn't help me.

Not Quite
Out-of-Business

Surrounded by white sheets,
fly-specked with numbers,
he stares at monstrous phone
that just swiped graduate school
from his daughter.

Thinks about pushing ex-client
in front of fast-moving Yellow cab.
Wonders why he didn't become a poet,
what to tell wife in Darien,
whether mistress on Bleecker Street
should get same story.

Hungers for martini, winning ticket at Lotto.
Then he spins Rolo-dex, reaches for phone
and launches another cold, cold sales call.

NW Flight 1482
Seat 6A

Running last quarter numbers
across his Zenith laptop,
wishing he could get back
to Tom Clancy,
fantasizing about
burying face in
stewardess' blonde muff,
wondering if Nintendo
jammed in his carry-on
was what Ronnie wanted,
counting times he cheated on
Cynthia this year
(only four),
not seeing wing of
speeding 727 peeling
through fuselage of
his silver cocoon,
strangling in
smoke at Detroit Metro
two weeks before his
Christmas bonus.

Robert J. McKenty

The Anointed One

"Wang Laboratories Inc. said Frederick A. Wang... was named to the post of president, succeeding his father, An Wang. The appointment... appears to ensure that Frederick Wang will eventually head the company."
—*Dow Jones News Service*, November 19, 1986

Thanks to the chrism
Of nepotism,
Wang knows that *their* head
Will be an *heir* head.

Heir Head Steps Down

"Frederick A. Wang, president of beleaguered Wang Laboratories, Inc., resigned yesterday.... Last week... Wang reported a $424 million loss for fiscal 1989...."
—*The New York Times*, August 9, 1989

The reign of a son or a daughter
May come to an end with a thud,
For though blood may be thicker than water,
Red ink's even thicker than blood.

"other"

Lawrence Coates

SHE IS, NOW, ideal.

Ideal and typical. Are the terms really so different? About her, everything is known. The questionnaires with which I worked she could fill out easily, never have to use the box marked "other."

Age 26 - 39

The sacrifice I made would not have been made by every man. But it has paid me well, personally and in terms of my career. The other satisfaction is bonus: the unselfish joy I find in the happiness of others.

I was the Chief of Soliciting Advertising for a San Francisco magazine. Soliciting advertising consists of making many phone calls to many businesses and convincing them that your magazine is the perfect medium through which to discuss the virtues of their product. This is an undertaking in which rejection is a constant and tenacity is a must. To be a good telephone solicitor, one must have a visceral belief in the importance of the work.

I had no illusions about why I was given my job. It was not because of special skills which I alone hold, nor for my resume, nor for my advanced degree in business administration. I was given the job because, to my superior, I had the appearance of a homosexual.

Sex: M ☐   F ☐

We used women to make the phone calls. Like the lieutenant and quartermaster of a small platoon of soldiers, I armed the women with marketing surveys, supplied them with details about who reads our magazine, their age, sex, race, average yearly income, informed them of target groups to which certain types of ads would be directed.

I gave them lists of businesses, names, phone numbers and I sent them out to the phones to battle with indifferent secretaries and tape recorded messages, to get behind the lines to the man making the decisions, and once that was achieved, to combat apathy and complacency, to make him realize the urgent necessity he has to place an ad in *our* magazine rather than any other.

That is where the questionnaires were applicable; we had a profile of the readership of our magazine, gained through years of analyzing questionnaires. The perfect reader would use all the products advertised in our magazine: all the products advertised in our magazine would appeal to the perfect reader. The man who decides to place an advertisement in our magazine knows with whom he is communicating; his products helped create that person, and, conversely, that person helped shape his products.

What is your average monthly

Victories were few in the battles for new advertisers, and there was never a final victory, only the ongoing struggle. For that reason we kept the telephone solicitors' salaries relatively low. We liked women who looked just a bit hungry. It was important that they feel a slight need, a slight dissatisfaction with their lives. Then, on a subliminal, inarticulate level, they understood the mainspring that drives all advertising, and were more effective in their work. As soon as a bit of languor creeps into their manner, the moony indifference that accompanies too many canelones in white sauce with Chardonnay, they grow indignant over the low salary. Corrupted by satisfaction they are no longer suitable for the job. They leave, of their own accord, *they think.* To be replaced by another slightly undernourished woman. I have never had to fire anyone. The case with Fanny was a bit different; not really a firing, more like a change of venue.

How many times a week do you normally

In my superior's very limited mind, the correct person for my job was a homosexual. Women are needed to do the soliciting because the person who makes the decision is a man. But to supervise women, who better than the homosexual? There can never be flirtations, the little sexual intimations that might cause a supervisor to turn a blind eye to a subordinate's deficiencies. Also, there is the presumed frustration of the homosexual who sees before him what he wants to be and cannot be; he will therefore, to use my superior's phrase, "stay on their ass."

I was not, in fact, a homosexual; I was celibate. Advertising deals with sex; by doing without sex, leaving myself frustrated, I was more devoted to advertising. I was "married to my work," and I continued that way until the case with Fanny.

I hired Fanny because she met my criteria. She was a big boned woman, Swedish stock I guessed, who'd never had a chance to put on weight. She looked like she needed money, as though her whole body needed money. Within her was a healthy, plump woman striving to break out. Her cheeks longed to become fat and rosy, her buttocks and breast to turn round and full, but "necessity's sharp pinch" had frustrated her. She would therefore understand that soliciting advertising was important, because our magazine was like her body, and in her work she would nourish both.

Where did you purchase our

She got on well in the job at first. She had a deep husky voice and spoke well, and was bright enough to memorize the standard lines I had provided. She was hungry, and she was successful in bringing new advertising within the covers of our magazine. I thought she was on the way to becoming a fine solicitor.

After some time, however, I noticed an estrangement between her and the other eight women in the office. She would not, it seemed, "talk about her things." At coffee breaks and during lunch hour there was usually a constant chatter about men, and eye shadow, and dinner dates and movies, and clothes. They always talked as though I wasn't there, because they too thought I was homosexual.

This kind of chatter I always found useful; those who couldn't see the big picture needed another kind of incentive. If they didn't know that their job was vital to the magazine's health, they could look at it as a means to obtain those always-talked-of things. The state of perpetual longing, of dissatisfaction, was just the spur needed to make them work. I was always gratified to note that they usually talked of things that had appeared in our magazine, even though I knew that if they ever obtained them they would be of no more use to me.

Fanny did not join in the chatter. She took her coffee back to her desk and sat alone. At times she leafed through a book. Not our magazine.

How many and of what age?

Helen was the woman with the most seniority in the office; I looked at her as a kind of top sergeant. She was married, but fortunately her husband was unemployed and there were two small children at home. I also think perhaps that her husband was impotent. Helen told me that none of the other women knew a thing about Fanny, that she was aloof and standoffish. They didn't know where she bought her clothes or what perfume she wore, how often she went out or whether she had a boy friend and what he did for a living and how much he earned. They wanted to know, essentially, the same facts about Fanny that we know about our readership.

Helen wanted me to do something about Fanny. Disingenuously, I asked her why she thought it necessary to know these things. Helen looked at me with a mixture of pity and disgust.

"You wouldn't understand because you're a . . . man."

Fanny was, at the time, bringing in more new advertising than the other women. It often happens that the newest and hungriest solicitor is the most successful, but Fanny was extraordinary even by those standards. To exploit the estrangement, I put up a bulletin board at the entrance to the office with each woman's name and began to record graphically the numbers of new accounts. Every Monday I started with a clean board and by Friday I had colored blocks of paper stretching from left to right beside the names.

Naturally the colored blocks beside Fanny's name stretched the farthest. This did not help her popularity with the other women in the office but it did lead to a substantial increment in the growth of advertising. The other women wanted to show that this new girl, who acted differently, was no better than them.

The increment in advertising was, of course, well received by my superior; he congratulated me for "staying on those women's asses."

In spite of the other women's efforts, Fanny's line of paper continued to be the longest every Friday. I was not above adding a few unearned blocks to Fanny's name, to increase the discontent of the other women. This was justified of course by the concurrent increase in advertising. But, one week, I found that I had to add blocks to Fanny's name just to keep her ahead of Helen. Tracy and Shirley were also on the verge of overtaking her. Was this because my strategy had functioned perfectly? Or was it because, yes, Fanny's cheeks were a bit fuller, a bit rounder.

I suspected the normal explanation: a man. She had found a man to buy her shrimp scampi and chianti and long loaves of Italian bread. My ploy of adding blocks to her name would not work indefinitely; the other women would see that she was putting on weight, and notice how her work level dropped. Somewhat sadly I began to record the new accounts with fidelity and Fanny's name inevitably dropped from first place. I felt that the era of rapid increments was over; things would return to normal, and the usual *denouement*, with Fanny growing disgusted with the low pay and leaving, would occur sooner or later.

Is your status that of

She grew plumper and the lines behind her name grew shorter in an inverse function. But she did not quit, nor did she begin to tell "her things" to the other women in the office. She continued aloof until Helen said to me:

"Fanny isn't doing her job."

I was already aware that Fanny's production had dropped to barely acceptable levels, but what did she mean exactly by "isn't doing her job?" Helen explained, patiently as to a child, that Fanny had stopped wearing earrings. She had stopped wearing perfume of any kind. She no longer wore make up. Her permanent had lost its curl weeks ago and she never spoke about going to the hairdresser. It was rumored that she only had one pair of shoes. I asked, again disingenuously, why it was important when all our work was done over the phone. Helen looked at me with an identical mixture of pity and disgust.

"She's dressed the same way three days in a row."

Was it true? This was, perhaps, much more dangerous than I'd thought.

The following day I took note and it was true: she was dressed the same way as the previous day. In an office of beige and grey and blue serge, her manner of dressing was shockingly different. It clashed with the vestments of the other women, clashed with the office decor. It was of a style that some might call "provocative" or "alluring," but which I found frightening. It was different than anything I'd ever seen worn to work; simply didn't *go* with our working environment. And the paramount consideration . . . it was the sort of thing that we do not normally advertise in our magazine.

If a single woman dresses the same way two days in a row, it is usually the cause for snickering. Her co-workers assume that she spent the night "over," somewhere other than her home. "Getting any lately?" But three days in a row was completely unheard of.

The next day, Friday, she was again dressed identically. That made three days by the official count and five days by Helen's count. Mercifully the weekend came and so the crisis was postponed until Monday. The situation called for careful thought and tactics.

Where did you first

Her action was very bad for morale in the office. The other women would begin to ask why they had to spend time arranging themselves to come to work when one of their number got away without doing so. It would lead to discontent in the office, but not a productive discontent. Potentially a very counter-productive discontent.

I knew that through the effort made to look smart and ready the women gained the moral force necessary to do their jobs. Because they used the products advertised in our pages, they wanted other people to buy the products also. They were all dissatisfied, because they wanted to become the perfect reader. But they longed for others to want the same things, to prove them fashionable, to justify them.

For that reason, they had to believe in the importance of advertising the products they used. If they didn't take part, they would become ineffective as soliciting women. This is what Helen meant by "not doing her job."

It was clearly very dangerous. Suppose, just suppose, another woman in the office wore the same thing two days in a row. The thing could spread like the plague through all the magazine's offices. With its origins in my troops. It would end my career.

But there was another level of thought, a more disinterested, altruistic level, which told me I had to stamp this out before it spread. If this fledgling movement spread, advertising itself would be endangered. And with it large sectors of the non-defense economy. I, as the holder of an advanced degree in business administration, could see this very clearly.

That was when I solved one part of the enigma. It was not a man who had changed Fanny, subverted her with hollandaise sauce and cherries jubilee. It was, I realized in a flash of illumination, that she had stopped buying clothes. She had stopped buying clothes and was, perniciously, buying food instead.

But why did she not want what other women want? How could she feel satisfied dressing identically every day? That remained an enigma.

It didn't matter, I decided. My course was clear.

On Monday morning my superior called me in on my way to the office. He said he was sorry he had to get on my ass a little bit, but that results had gone to shit lately. I told him there was a problem with our *esprit de corps*, that one woman was causing a problem but I thought I could resolve it. He told me he would back me up if I wanted to fire her ass, only be sure to have a good pretext, record verbal warnings in personnel file, etc.

To dismiss her would be the worst thing to do, but my superior would not be able to grasp the implications. To avoid creating a movement, we had to avoid creating a martyr. Even though the women office workers had no union, there was no shortage of agitators who could use Fanny as a figurehead for their own agenda. It would be easy with television and posters to make of her a charismatic heroine.

What was needed instead was a kind of public recanting. I told my superior that I didn't think it would be wise to fire her.

The next day I gave the plan of the day to the other women, then asked Fanny into my inner office. I sat behind my desk and told her to be seated. Across the desk, I said to her:

"Will you have lunch with me?"

She accepted. I am convinced that the desk, my implied rank of lieutenant, helped.

On the advice of a friend

We went to lunch together every day that week, at some very fine restaurants. I ordered for us both, always the dishes with creamy sauces of butter and egg yolk, always the pastas rich with olive oil. She continued to dress the same way, but on Friday she also wore a pair of earrings, and I knew I was making progress.

The following week we began to go on dinner dates, and over the souviaki I gave her the first gift: a bottle of perfume. She ran off to the powder room to try some on.

I gave her many gifts after that, I showered her with gifts. It was never difficult to decide what to give her; I merely looked in the pages of our magazine.

As I saw her begin to give in, as I saw her resistance fail bit by bit, it became a very powerful experience for me. It was a confirmation of my own deepest beliefs—the advertising we carried really was correct and justified, it had the power to move people, to change people. Not just the way they dressed or ate, but also the way they thought and felt, the way they loved. Our advertising *worked*—in every sense of the word.

Finally I gave her the gift we had both been expecting. It came in a long flat box, white and tied with ribbons. I gave it to her after a dinner of paella, rice yellow with saffron and glistening with Spanish oil. She untied the ribbon and peeked in the box, then closed it quickly. She began to cry and confusedly kiss my wristwatch. I called for champagne.

All this I had done for my career, for the magazine. Also, I had done it for all of us. I had succeeded in stamping out a potential brush fire and although the world would never know, business and advertising would never know, I knew, and I drew a deep satisfaction from the knowledge. My thanks I would receive in some fashion every time I saw the crowds in Union Square buying, happily buying, what they had seen in our magazine.

Married ☐

The wedding was a civil ceremony, but Fanny wore the white dress I had given her that night. The other women in the office pitched in and bought her a trousseau: lingerie, peignoirs, frilly things in light blues and pastel pinks. From page thirty-three of the June issue, I think.

She left the office, and I soon had the crew back into shape. But then I was promoted out of my job. My superior told me frankly that he didn't think a man getting a regular piece of ass was right for the job; it was taken by a younger man named

Edward, who seems to fit my superior's criterion. My new job in finance is on a faster track.

Fanny is at home now. She has grown pleasingly plump, and takes cooking classes at the community center. We don't ever talk about our unusual courtship, but she has her own credit card with a high monthly limit, and she also reads our magazine constantly. She is, now, ideal.

That night, with the champagne, she'd seen what would be her wedding dress. And although she was about to compromise forever and take her place in the scheme of things, when I asked her why she had done it, she whispered in my ear:

"It is how I see myself when I dream."

And I knew I had been right, that such things are best hidden away, that the battle had been a worthy one in the ongoing struggle.

G. E. Murray

Crossings: November 21-22

For Dana Gioia

Chicago—Paris, the business again,
and again all the high-order reasoning
of night flight takes hold as we shed coat,
trade smiles, stow gear, ease down, shake hands,
latch table, stretch out, rub feet, buckle up,
talk small, pop mint, press light, and bless self
while instructed in the rites of safety,
and all cabins cross-checked, prepared for departure,
and all of us brought to a full, upright
and locked position as we rumble down
the runway lifting off into roseate twilight
and jetstream, hung out, exhausted, gone. And soon,
we become part of the going rate—climbing
yet fixed, floating too predictably.
Thus, we assume elevation's space and, sooner
bumps from things in the night. And soon enough,
all the rich meats of Air France run bloody
and cool, duck bonne femme muddled
in peppercorn sauce, spoils of Madagascar,
another freshly boned truth to feed upon.
So we're up and outrunning vibration,
banking through a touch of turbulence,
head winds seemingly deep and fluent as tides.
So we too become matters for complex negotiation,
due diligence, higher net worth.
As we smooth to new cruising altitude,
I level off with an Armagnac and faint smile
from the long-legged woman across the aisle,
maybe headed the way of strangers and dangers,
an idea left unbuttoned as imagination.
Just now she leans over to whisper:

"When leaving the country these days, don't
forget to put a stop-loss on your portfolio . . . ."

It occurs to me at 40,000 feet we count
too much upon implausible returns. With any luck
unwinding empty in a suit, it's conceivable
I've had enough of the plentiful stuff
of which schemes are made—capital ventured,
offers tendered. Tonight, queuing up
alongside stars, I rifle my briefcase
for other game, for poems, and in the black
of this blue interception find you and yours,
blessings and lessons for flying cloud legends,
somehow collecting time while spending it.
This is straight time I'm doing, doing
a subtitled movie before lights out.
And the 747 surges, hums itself into a lullaby
for those hundreds now sleeping, slack-jawed,
blankets tucked, spittle on chins,
twitching from an occasional love instinct,
a few hands slaving under covers,
all through this soft doze in the muff of space.
Out of porthole, patroling the night watch
for death winds or a perfect prayer,
I write, "Love demands the slipstream night,
the flight in which you ride it, and it
rides you, until what happens, happens,"
into another notebook from another ocean crossing.

So I'm mid-Atlantic and forty years into a life
official as a passport, equally unquestioned;
me, gaining critical mass and balance,
if only in the spirit of a midcourse correction.
Nearing dateline, darkness soon to be day,
I remember John Kennedy shot dead
decades ago tomorrow or tonight, whichever;
Kennedy eternally dying on film,
America exploded in black and white,
America crying to "God Bless America,"
its face shattered by the shards of mirror,
the dreaming now naked, Kennedy forever
collapsing into myth, proposition, dilemma,
a distant bygone, as if spilled milk.

I'm still glazed, utterly. Memories await
exquisite remaking as institutional history. Ha,
big money still costs way too much. Ha,
we still believe the world so rich
one ought to cheat more than a bit. So go
such dim arguments of generations
set loose and lost upon each other. I think,
keep the deep shining and those sermonettes
irrelevant. Too many of us are still missing
in action, unable to finance a memorable warmth.
Inklings of a bad moon rising whenever
I'm part of the sky. Grindings of expectation
whenever I'm sitting pretty. How I marvel
at last at the unravelings I count
as liabilities of your average hopefulness.
So many slogans of revolution, half-turned loves
returned to me tonight, like projections,
still reminding of what to believe in in America:
our jazz, our wildness, all our unresolved
lumps still bubbling up through melting pots . . . .

Ah, foraging on the run, on the circuit,
in the necessitarian thick of cost
containment, competitive advantage, 3-D
spread sheets, and tiered-contribution analysis.
At times afraid of flying this high, this fast,
this hard, I reflect on deals struck
and done and see only myself staring out
the black oval, blinking back
at new-found stars, counting my ways
a part of such inconclusive, ongoing
presentlessness, immeasurably alone
with my own retellings, private traces,
elations, hesitations, realignments, and more.
How I love this window-shopping for soul,
for each piece of heaven's fancy,
for some better way to muscle history,
for taking possession of my own remains
and knowing what to make of them. I shift
positions and guess there's sloppy weather
ahead, as the plane twists beyond midnight,
inveigling, intransitive, intractable.
In no time we'll dip toward a distinct line

of dove-gray sky, horizon cut
into darker flannel, the clearing edge
of earth unending. In this dead stretch,
I greet myself halfway across the sky,
whether an initiative or erasure.
It might help to understand my reluctance
to be earthed or sucked forth by speed
that punctures every safe reserve of this
blinking-blanking world I've secured
as if a loan. Just take me away, nose up,
lavishly thankful for all I see that goes
blessedly unsaid. I know events
necessarily outrace strategies; assets
perform accordingly, as if miracles.
Rubbing hands in anticipation of who-knows-what,
some life of spill and hurry, I harbor
no hard feelings for the rimes of our times:
grim and trim; persuasion as evasion; fake songs
and wrong mistakes. Do we require rescue
or refuge, moment or episode, from a republic
of pleasure, some Switzerland of interpretation?
I have learned from a distance even fog
holds a cutting edge; that a mask can be worn
on the groin, how weather is nearly essential.
Someone coughs. It's Friday night
over Halifax and quite early tomorrow
down in the skinhead dawn of downtown Belfast.

Someone still thinks it's an age when loneliness
figures to be as repetitive as it is
decorative, when market forces are still
as purely coincidental as freedom's twitch.
I prefer all of this peculiar space
and its incurable view. Such is order
and strangeness. Such will be continuation.
I ride the good ride Air France provides,
coming alive to descent, discontinuing monologue
with the bulkhead, surrendering earphones,
unused. I'm cheerful this hazy morning aloft,
bearing down upon Europe; for now, seamless
in either skin or sky. There's Paris
in autumn morning haze, iced by rain
before first welcome. Sunrise blocked,

but nonetheless a light source dispassionate
as we swing into final approach
to the desires of Paris just waking
when it is almost winter and before-hours.
I think there's enough time left to avoid
repentance, to sell originality as insurance,
to establish interests in the name of fiasco,
to pain and wretch among our borrowings.
By noon I'll be in conference on Rue St. Honore;
by eight, asleep over dinner at Guy Savoy.
This is as stunning as the future becomes.

Pat and the American Dream

Betty Sherwood

THIS IS A story about Pat—actually five stories about five people named Pat, although they might all be one person—if they were interested in becoming a national symbol that is. Their names are Pat because Pat can be either a male or female and in the 1980s you just can't tell anymore. Things are no longer as clear cut as they once were. I will, however, use the masculine personal pronouns because I am old and I still tend to think of these Pats as "he." Pay close attention to each story because you will be required to take a short quiz at the end.

We will start with Pat Morgan because he would insist. Pat is 50 and has long ago given up referring to his hair as "thinning on top." It is now quite gone and looks very unlike anything that once supported hair; he compensated when it began to falter by growing a very thick mustache and taking up racquetball. He quit playing racquetball about five years ago because he was running into too many of his subordinates at the racquetball courts. He took up handball instead, and lately he has begun to make an effort at squash. He is also thinking seriously about jai alai because the other day he saw two of his underlings in the locker room after handball.

Now this Pat *is* male because he is an Executive Vice President of a multinational conglomerate headquartered in New York City. He has been an Executive Vice President for eight years now, and he wants very much to be President, so you see he just couldn't possibly be a female. If I rewrite this before I die, I may be able to give him a sex change operation. I don't know if I like that possibility or not.

Pat lives in a condominium in Manhattan—Upper East Side. He knows he should live on Long Island, but New York City is so very . . . appropriate for his self-image. He has close relationships with maitre d's at several of the top restaurants in the city. He worries that this might change if he moved out to the Island. His condo does have 12 rooms, though, and three rooms for a live-in servant, and three balconies, and a sauna, which slightly offsets the absence of a tennis court and pool. If he gets the Presidency, he will buy a second home on Long Island and send his wife out there.

Pat is in charge of sales for Africa and for Madagascar (which the company has decided is not a part of Africa for sales purposes). The particular thing that Pat is selling is drugs: antihistamines, antibiotics and anticoagulants. These don't do too well in Africa because: Africans don't get clogged up; another company got there first; Africans aren't real big on discernable blood clots. In spite of these problems, Pat has done a terrific promotional job in Africa, and he sees an even better chance in the future with a new antibiotic his company has discovered which is powerful enough to kill the herpes bug.

They are currently having some problems with the drug because it also kills the body's defenses against minor infections that usually accompany cuts and other sores. The FDA is trying to decide whether they should notice some missing test data before they give approval. They meet a lot with the President. However, this only affects U.S. Sales and Pat's closest rival for the Presidency is in charge of U.S. Sales. Pat wonders for a while whether he should bring to the attention of the FDA (anonymously) a memo he discovered, after a painstaking search, which relates to the missing data. He wonders whether this would be to his advantage or not. He decides if he becomes President, he will need U.S. Sales of the drug, so, in a cunning political move, he mentions the memo privately and casually to three other top executives who are extremely ambitious. One of them is the Executive Vice President of U.S. Sales.

In any case, the FDA doesn't affect Africa sales, so Pat decides to mount a major sales campaign. In an inspired marketing strategy, he promotes the antibiotic not only for specific illnesses, but for inclusion in cattle feed to prevent the horrors of serious disease.

Many of the African nations are very enthusiastic about the drug. Some of the infections found there have quite appalling effects on the population and certainly on the economy, and they are quite difficult to defeat, particularly in an epidemic situation. The nations' leaders also see a chance to increase their personal fortunes. Pat personally makes several trips to various African nations, promoting the drug with hospitals, physicians' organizations, and national health ministries—or whatever the bureaucracy is in a particular country. He is careful to confine his visits to the major cities. Several countries buy a great deal of Pat's drug.

During the following three years, Pat's company's revenues rose 8% due solely to increased sales in Africa (which rose 60%). International Health organizations estimated that during these three years, six million Africans died of minor cuts and cold sores. Another seven million died in five countries as a result of serious famine caused by wholesale deaths of cattle from minor infections.

* * *

Pat Stanley lives exactly two miles away from Pat Morgan. Pat Stanley is a 43-year-old partner in a very prominent investment brokerage firm. Pat loves the brokerage game. He quite often visits the floor, or as he prefers to call it, "the ring" because he loves to "duke it out" on "the mean streets." Pat talks this way. Really.

Pat spends all his free time training to be a prizefighter. He knows he is too old, but he doesn't really believe it. His trainer, who has worked with some of the best, is on retainer so that Pat can call him any time when he has a spare hour or two to work out. His trainer watches him work out and encourages him. Pat lives in an 8-room, rent-controlled apartment. One of his greatest accomplishments was finding that apartment, and it took two people working for a full year to get it for him. He brags about it to every new acquaintance, but he will never say who these two people are. Pat also owns a house in Connecticut which he bought for his 72-year-old mother, and he has put his three nephews through college. He likes to do these things since he has no family of his own, and it makes him feel good. Besides, he really doesn't have time to spend all his money on himself, and the fun is in making it—not in spending it.

Pat loves his work and works very hard at least 10 hours a day. Often longer. And he gets involved with some very complicated trading. Once when the market dropped 75 points in three hours, he had four phones going with eight runners on the other end. He was just sorry he didn't have time to get down on the floor himself. Pat's suite of offices was done by a professional decorator in dark wood, velvet, and leather to make clients feel wealthy and secure. People who feel wealthy and secure get expansive and are willing to risk more, which means Pat gets higher commissions. Pat calls his office "Ex-Lax."

Pat uses cocaine on weekends. He hates weekends. There aren't any deals, no excitement, no killings. And he can't box for 48 hours straight. So he takes coke and parties. He only sleeps for five hours a night. It isn't exciting to sleep either.

Pat has a partnership involving himself and five executives who work in five different major holding companies. When something happens at one of the companies, Pat gets the tip, buys or sells as much stock as possible in that company under the other four executives' names, and all six split the profits. One evening at 8 p.m., Pat got a tip that one of the companies among the 23 which were held by his partners' companies was going to be sold the next day. The deal was a very big one and had been cut in the deepest secrecy, and they just hadn't known about it earlier. Stocks of five different companies would be involved in the transaction. Pat was in the office at 5 a.m. the next day, and he began trading as soon as the bell sounded on the floor. When he came in, there was a big buy order from a pension account manager on his desk, but things were so hectic he didn't get around to executing it until 11:30. By that time, the DOW was up 38 points and the stock for the pension fund client was $125,000 more than it would have been when the market opened. Pat and his partners made $348,000 in four hours.

The night Pat executed this deal, he was flying so high he went to a singles' bar, and for a change he met someone very appropriate to his sense of self-importance—a really enthusiastic listener. Pat became more expansive with each drink. The person he picked up happened to be a dewy-eyed business school student who had worked as a runner that past summer "for the experience." The next morning the student did some research involving the stock reports, Dunn & Bradstreet, and "Who's Who in Business." Two days later, the letter which arrived at the SEC caused three investigators to be pulled off of other cases and assigned to look into Pat's dealings before the week ended.

Pat's heavy trading caused the five stocks to fluctuate by up to $25 per share. The seller company received a decreased cash portion in the deal since the stock portion had risen so precipitously. This caused profits of both the buyer and seller companies to fall for the year, which meant that the stockholders would've lost about $6.50 per share in dividends. To offset this loss, both companies raised the prices of their products 3%

across the board, and laid off 6% of their employees. Of the people they laid off, 16 never managed to find another job, eight of these went on welfare, and two children of ex-employees died, one in childbirth and one from measles complications, when the ex-employees' health insurance expired and the families couldn't afford proper medical care.

✻ ✻ ✻

Pat number three, Pat Mowbray, lives in Queens. He has a charming supportive wife and two children who are both a credit to him. He is a Manager in the Information Systems Department of a major uptown bank. He hates his job. He loves his work. He has three personal computers at home and is currently rebuilding a mini which he found in a secondhand computer clearance barn. He has developed an operating system that is similar to MVS, but simpler to use, and in some ways more powerful. Pat wants to sell his operating system, but he just can't get any mainframe manufacturer to listen to him or to try it.

Pat has worked at the bank for 15 years now. Fifteen years of getting up at 5:30 a.m. taking the 6:45 train and walking in the door at the exact same time and riding the elevators with the same people every day. Fifteen years. 3600 mornings, 3600 lunches from 11:45 to 12:30. Fifteen years of people bitching at him about the stupid computer breaking down. *He* didn't tell them to buy that thing. *He* can't fix it when it goes down. He is a system programmer not a computer repair man. Sometimes he thinks he'll go nuts with the sheer silliness of it all. If it wasn't for his operating system and his yearly vacations in Cancun, he doesn't think he could have stood it. Oh, of course, he loves his family. His marriage is . . . comfortable. His kids are good kids—no drugs, no alcohol, good grades, good future. But still . . . .

There is so much he wants from life. Sometimes, he daydreams about going to Cancun every six months instead of once a year. Or maybe even Hawaii. And a new house. A house with a special room for his computer equipment. For fifteen years he has waited and worked and wanted.

And then one day he saw how stupid he had been. He was reading about some politician who had gone to South America, Europe, Australia, etc. every six weeks or so with his secretary and the taxpayers' money (or PAC money) for "Studies." Pat changed that day. Oh, not that very minute. He just grimaced at the story, went to work and listened to people gripe about the computer. But sometime during the day, he decided that he was every bit as good as the politician, and by the end of the month he had everything set up.

He wrote a program and hid it in the operating system. The program took 1/10 of 1% off the interest of the biggest depositors' accounts at random, two accounts per month, and diverted the money to a bogus account he set up for a business. It then automatically transferred the money daily to another bank to another business account and from there to a money fund and a stock fund, both in the name of different businesses which he had set up in his name. He knew better than to go around cashing checks made out to himself drawn on the bank where he worked. Too many people got caught by tellers who remembered strange coincidences like that.

In addition, since the bank, once deregulated, had decided to earn a great deal of money on the customers' floats by delaying transfer time from the bank to the payee (but not from the payor to the bank) by one day, they could damn well share that with him. It was only right. After all, some of that money they were using was his. So he gradually cut into the interest on the float over a period of eight months until he was taking a full percent of that, too.

This caused the bank's profits, which had been climbing at a steady 2% per quarter, to suddenly level off. Actually, their profits were bouncing up and down like an aerobics class, but this was due to ill-advised and risky speculation as the bank, now free of the regulation fretter, tried to make a killing. However, these bad debts were always factored out by the analysts when evaluating operations, and what they saw was flat profitability, which baffled them completely.

They put six of their best new MBA's to work on it. After three months, when the MBA's couldn't figure out what was happening, they presented their report recommending that the bank raise the minimum deposit on checking and savings accounts, (thus increasing the money they could earn interest on), get rid of low profit areas with high overhead (such as pass book savings and cashier's checks) and downgrade a few of the jobs in the bank. They did this and their profitability rose again and they were happy.

Some of their customers weren't too happy, though. Most of the pensioners couldn't afford to tie up that much money in minimum deposits and thus were forced to go to a cash basis, which made them more vulnerable to robberies and mugging on the day the Social Security checks arrived. It also meant that many young people gave up trying to save some of their income because there just wasn't any place they could put their savings other than the sock drawer. Several of the clerks, whose jobs were downgraded, had to put off purchases and vacations this year and began having worse headaches and stomach pains, more frequently, from worrying about providing for their families and themselves.

Within a year, Pat had accumulated enough money to spend six months in Cancun and start his own business. His wife had a new refrigerator, his son had his own car, and they had signed the deed for a new house. Then something very strange happened. A very inept hacker got into the operating system one night. The next morning when Pat came into work he found the computer down, and the place crawling with computer technicians and engineers. It seems the hacker had blown a control in the operating system and thoroughly mixed everything up. A complete audit was ordered. The hacker was caught and thrown in jail.

Three weeks later the confused hacker was literally thrown out of jail and told to keep his mouth shut about what he had seen. He hadn't seen anything, of course, but he promised faithfully. The audit had uncovered Pat's program. Or rather, the hacker's messing around had caused it to just pop to the surface where the auditors stumbled over it. In addition, the program had stopped short of transferring the funds, so Pat's bogus account was full of money, and they found that too, and followed the transfer—and went to the next bank and followed that too. Right to the door of Pat's new house.

* * *

Pat Jones is a factory worker. He puts eight screws in eight holes on the backs of TV sets in a factory in the Bronx. He has been doing that for 12 years—ever since he was 16. If anyone were to ask him if he liked it, he'd just shrug and say it was OK. He doesn't think about whether he likes it or not. It just isn't something you think about. Neither does he think about whether he likes to go bowling on Tuesday night or play poker on Thursdays. He just does these things. And he works really hard at doing them well—or at least better than his fellow bowlers and poker players do. He talks about bowling, poker, work, women, baseball and football teams and games, cars, and how computers are taking over the world. Sometimes he talks about politicians. Occasionally he talks about what is happening in South America or Nuclear War, but not often.

Some evenings he watches TV. He stops in a bar near the plant every Friday night for two or three hours. Sometimes he gets drunk. Most of the time he just laughs a lot and does silly things with the other guys like making book on who can spit further or trying to set up a betting pool on some woman's chest measurement.

He listens to news on TV and reads sports magazines. He doesn't buy "girlie" magazines. It's too much to pay for a few pictures. Sometimes a friend gives him old copies. He hides these from his children.

Pat has four children. Three years ago he had five, but his second son was killed by a drunk driver outside the school along with three other kids. The driver was sentenced to two years in prison. Pat never talks about it to anyone. There simply isn't any way he could express the total bewilderment that he feels. He is supposed to be angry, but he can't seem to sort things out enough to be angry. Oh, he wants to kill the driver with his bare hands, but that isn't really anger. It is just a fact.

Pat only goes to church about six times a year, but he believes in God; he also believes in his country, some of the people that run it, American-made goods, and the Union. He also believes that the rich people and corporations don't pay any taxes because of all the loopholes, and this isn't going to change when the tax reform bill is passed, and he believes he is every bit as good as they are and has just as much right to keep his money as they do.

Every year for the past 11 years, he has deducted uniforms from his tax return although he isn't required to wear a uniform at work. All the guys do it. He also deducted tools, although the company provides them, and he has never reported any of the income he gets from doing building work on the weekends and on holidays and vacations. He figures that money is his, since he doesn't charge as much as a regular construction worker would get. Also, he needs the extra money. There is no way he could make it without that money. Not with four kids and a wife who insists they all have to have braces and go to college. That's really what he is busting his ass about anyhow. So his kids can have a better chance than he had; and all that extra moonlighting money goes into a bank account just for them and for their education. He figures the government owes him that much. Had he been able to afford advice from a tax expert, he would have found out about trusts and reporting the income under his children's names and setting up his moonlighting as a separate business complete with expenses for tools and supplies and an office. But, he doesn't know about these things, so when he got called in for an IRS audit, he figured they had finally caught him.

The audit was actually about the heavy medical expenses the year his son died (it took several months for his son to defeat all the hospital machines) and the notice just said to bring receipts for medical expenses. The IRS always audits for heavy medical expenses rather than taking the easier and cheaper way and asking if anyone had been sick or died that year. But Pat didn't know about this. And he couldn't understand a word on the official IRS audit notice, except for the date, the place, and the word "audit." Some lawyers and accountants can understand the IRS notices, particularly if they have been drinking heavily, but no one else can figure them out. So Pat went in and took all his records, and looked so guilty that the agent decided to do a complete audit. The audit, at a total cost to taxpayers of $18,000, uncovered back taxes of $23,000 (including interest and penalties) of which $19,233 was finally recovered. Had Pat set up a business for his moonlighting, the IRS would have had to refund $6,243 to Pat. However, no one at the IRS suggested this possibility, and besides, they could open up all 11 years, but Pat couldn't retroactively set up his business. Pat never did understand that if his son hadn't died, the IRS would never have questioned his tax return.

* * *

Pat Michaels is the youngest Pat. He is only 19 and he also lives in New York City even further uptown than Pat Morgan does. Too far uptown in fact. He has three brothers and two sisters. Another sister died before she even began to walk. The Michaels children have three different fathers. Or at least that's what Pat's mother says, so he guesses it must be true. He has never met his father, but the other two fathers come around occasionally. Usually to try to get some money out of his mother's welfare check or the tips she makes when she fills in for a friend at a neighborhood bar.

Pat decided when he was really young that his mother was a jerk. She was always letting those damn welfare people push her around. If she had any damn brains she'd be getting three welfare checks like Lottie downstairs. God, she was dumb. It was no wonder Sam and Arnie (the other fathers) were always punching her around. Pat had let her have it a couple times himself when her whining and begging got on his nerves too much. She was always after him to go to school or go talk to the minister or stay home nights. He had things to do. Big things. He was damned if he was going to end up like Sam or Arnie or Harry or Pete working day labor and then partying 'til the money was gone and living wherever they could find a landlord to carry them for a few months. No sir. Not him. Not Pat. He had big plans.

He was going to get him some sharp clothes, a real bad car, and at least three foxy ladies. And he was making it. He had worked hard and got a piece of the action pushing Crack and Pot and a few select pills at the branch campus downtown. He was headed for big things. It was just a matter of working hard and getting the right people to take an interest. Of course it got a little rough during breaks and vacations. So sometimes he had to fall back on his former line of work—taking money from old people who had just cashed their welfare or Social Security checks. That had kept him in clothes and pocket money before he was old enough to get in with the right businessmen. He had been good at that, too. Really worked hard at it. Studied all the places where old people went to cash their checks, and when they went. And he practiced shoving them down, grabbing the money and taking off at top speed, throwing purse or wallet away as he ran, until he was so fast, he could be out of the area before the old fart let out the second yell. He was practically a legend in the neighborhood.

Pat smiled to himself with pride. He had been the best. He hated to go back to it, even for just the slow periods, because now he was older and had a more lucrative and respectable position, and well . . . it was just beneath him. He sighed and shrugged. Well, nothing for it. He picked out a rabbity looking old lady as she went into the store, checked through the window to see that she was cashing the check and just waited until she came out. I wish I could say it was Pat Stanley's mother, but she lives in Connecticut, or that she was cashing it because a branch of Pat Mowbray's bank had increased minimum deposits so that the old lady had to close her account, but it wasn't. (They wouldn't have had a branch in this neighborhood in any case.) It was just an old lady with a very small Social Security check and food stamps to look forward to each month.

Pat followed the old lady for two blocks then gave her a shove and grabbed her purse and started to take off.

But something went wrong. She wouldn't let go. She just yelled and held on like a vise. Pat pulled and kicked at her, but she wouldn't let go. She couldn't. It was all the money she had. If he got this, she would die. She had no relatives or friends who could lend her any even if she could pay it back, which she couldn't, since even with a full check, she sometimes had to go a day or two without food. So she just held on desperately. And Pat pulled and kicked and punched at her. Goddamn, it was his money. He worked for it. Tailed her, picked her out, practiced all those hours. He worked for it. It was his money. And how would he look if anyone found out he wasn't as strong as an old lady. She *was* just an old lady for Christ's sakes. What the hell could she do with all that money? So he kept hitting and kicking her and finally she let go and he took off, but it had taken too long. A policeman in a patrol car had spotted him. And he didn't quite make two blocks, even as good as he was.

☆ ☆ ☆

Now the quiz. Please match each Pat with the end of his story.

1. Received $898,000 total in bonuses, followed by a promotion to President with a $250,000 salary benefit package increase. Was invited to speak at commencement exercises for one of the most prestigious colleges in the country.

2. After an expenditure of about $150,000 of the taxpayers' money on investigations, received a nasty letter from the SEC. The story was reported on the second page of the financial section and clients/commissions increased by about 18%.

3. Was laid off with a year's severance pay in lieu of notice. He also kept the money, since the employer couldn't recover without prosecuting, which they couldn't do without making the whole story public. Moved to Pennsylvania when offered a job by the computer company that manufactured the bank's computer. They also bought his operating system for $3 million.

4. Spent four years in prison for fraud, lost his house, and never was able to send his children to college. His daughter is a waitress, one son is a truck driver who hauls chemical waste to illegal dump sites, the other works in the same factory as his father did, and the last has completely disappeared.

5. Went to prison for four years for murder and was killed in a riot when opposing gang members disagreed over who had the drug concession in the prison.

6. Define Victimless Crime.
   Define White Collar Crime.
   Define Crime.

7. Go for a walk in the business area of your city during lunch hour. Can you identify any criminals?

Business Class

The flight attendants maneuver their way
down the darkened aisles, bending and smiling,
checking our condition. After three good
bourbons, I look around. I'm surrounded
by people in business suits who look
like me, the older ones reading,
the younger ones pointing out bonus rewards
in their sales catalogues. "Have a nice day,"
the recorded message at the airport urges
in all sincerity, and we've tried,
in all sincerity. We've tried to make money,
for ourselves, for our homes and families.
We're doing the best we can, living
out of briefcases filled with reports,
PERT charts and letters, tickets and Rolaids,
stock quotes, Maalox, cigarettes and gum.
On the seat beside me, a senior man
is already asleep, a finance report
resting on his stomach, his mouth half open.
Each year I tell myself that I'm leaving
in the next few years. A writer can't
live like this, can't think, and yet
if I had the perfect leisure to think,
with long, expansive mornings and a solid desk
overlooking the ocean, perhaps
I would think of nothing at all, or a little
less each year, more baffled and secure
than I already am. No, I have my heavy
bills to pay, like every other poet
on this plane. So tell me this is not
a life or a living. Tell me that it all
doesn't count.

Dignity

So at last I've finished
writing this sales
brochure on mid-sized
business computers,
right on dead-
line (from the chalk
line drawn around POW
camps in the Civil War,
if a prisoner crossed it
they shot to kill), the way
it's done in the business world,
so I treat myself
to a cab and go bombing
up Third Avenue to visit
Major Client, and just
for today, I'm beginning to feel
on top of things
for a change. The afternoon
is autumn glorious, brilliant
with the smell of leaves,
and I get chills
as the driver dodges, darts
through traffic like a bicycle
messenger. We even pass
poetry in the street,
police barricades set up,
city workers in orange jackets,
dragging out jackhammers, teaspoons
and whatever else
they need to repair the state
of the art (assuming
that's what this city needs).
And we pass other cabs
and even an ambulance late
for Bellevue, making
midtown in record time,
and I tip the driver

and float upstairs in a huge
elevator and sit down with
Client who reads the copy,
scratches his head, and
loves it.
                    So we shake hands
all around and, what the hell,
I take another cab, and
God, the city is looking
even better than before,
and I've got a check.
Yeah! Got a check
for twelve hundred dollars
and I'm going to the bank
and I'm making a deposit
for the rent and the groceries
and a few days of peace
to write all this down
and I'll look that teller
right in the eye and sign my name
with dignity.

Success Stories

I

I'm still addicted to the *New York Times*.
On Saturday nights, I walk down Flatbush Avenue
for the Sunday edition. Vertical Manhattan
glitters in the distance, all "threats and diamonds."

I reach for the Arts and Leisure section,
the Book Review next, irritated with myself
for wanting to know the latest
about all those famous
artists and intellectuals, the ones
with massive, dramatically carved heads
and powerful hair.

I sometimes see them on the street
avoiding eye contact or listening to a young
delighted companion. They look exhausted,
but in the papers they lean back
self-assured for the interview, attractively
potent and laughing with large, yellowed teeth.

I wonder what they're really like:
the fabulously affluent painter with his soft,
Virginia manners and ice cream suits,
the sculptor in his spartan loft, gesturing
wildly with a blowtorch as he makes his point,
or the East Village novelist brooding at the camera,
slightly impatient, pressed for time, thoughts
flashing from her lowered brow.

I imagine their light, sure fingers
playing on the singing cables of Manhattan.
They have it made, I tell myself.
They work for themselves. They can write
their own ticket.

II

"We're not the geniuses we thought we were,"
my wife says, and of course, she's right.
Self-pity only goes so far, so every morning
I go to work on the F train, briefcase packed
with desperate journals, Whitman and Rilke,
minor notes to myself, and lunch.

"Ninety-nine percent of poetry
is in the living," Dr. Williams said.
So where do the poets in America belong?
That is to say, what do they do
for a living?

I work in an ad agency, writing spec sheets
and sales brochures for computer systems.
Each night, I go home to Brooklyn,
hang up my coat, say hello to my wife.
I'm an old hand at the office now,
on the same account for seven years,

God help me . . . . Shouldn't life be going
faster than this? I meet with the sponsors
from Boston to discuss a new campaign.
I get things accomplished. I nail things down.

Others are promoted past me, but that's OK,
I tell myself. I'm left alone to think,
and I do. I shut my office door each morning,
remembering how I used to storm to work
along Park Avenue, hating my wife, my obligations,
my lack of time to write, and repeating Rembrandt's motto:
"Concedo Nulli!" Yield To No One! I thought

I was drowning. Now, I have a view of the Hudson,
if I lean over my desk and twist slightly to the right.
I watch the holiday ships as they leave for Bermuda,
backing slowly away from the pier, tiny arms waving.

III

I wanted to vanish into the woods and re-emerge
with something wonderful, a white light
cupped in my hands. I wanted to astonish.

Monday morning, 8:00 a.m. It's raining.
On the subway, we smell like big wet dogs
jammed together, hunched in our raincoats, umbrellas
dripping on our shoes. My little book says,
"Surrender your will. Only then can the rest
of your life begin." We slowly emerge
from the ground and pause at an elevated station.
The doors open. For a moment, I can feel
the cool, fresh air on my face. Miles
of low, gray buildings, overcast skies . . .
And seagulls! The cries of seagulls
circling somewhere in the fog overhead.
Then the doors squeeze shut, and we're
rumbling down into the earth again toward
Manhattan, wealth, and our steady jobs.

Project Black Knight

James Shepard

STARING OUT AT the
moon-shadows on that bright July night, my mind drifted off as
the Gulfstream IV began a gentle descent into Pittsburgh.

I found it ironic to be facilitating the take-over and
liquidation of a Fortune 500 company in my hometown. I had
always dreamed of returning a hero of one kind or another, but
there I was, representing a group of stockholders in a raid on
International Steel Industries. *I'll be in and out in twenty-four hours*, I
thought to myself, *taking a piece of American corporate history with me.*

With the exodus of the eighties and the decline of the
junk bond market, self-proclaimed shareholders' rights activists
were turning to an age-old weapon of corporate governance—the
Proxy Fight.

In 1931, A.P. Giannini, founder of both Bank of America
and Transamerica, met with shareholders in various cities
throughout the southwest garnering support—and
proxies—from Transamerica shareholders to win back the
Chairmanship of a bank that was losing deposits, loans and
marketshare. In recent years, some of the most established and
respected companies such as Gulf Oil, Texaco, USX and AT&T
have found themselves embroiled in Proxy Contests.

The proxy has become the new weapon of Wall Street
and proxy firms like mine are engaged to formulate a tactical
assault (or defense) and to go forth into battle, much like the
warriors of old, only having exchanged suits of armor for
Armani; a cellular phone in one hand and Sun Tzu's *The Art Of
War* in the other. We lobby for stockholder support and guide
proxies through the labyrinth that is the bank and brokerage
system.

Outright victory over an incumbent board of directors
of a billion-dollar company is a formidable task and the odds are
stacked high against you. The cost of attempting their ouster
runs into the millions. The stakes are high, but so are the rewards.

Bastille Partners, my client, had picked the right target. Affected by the declining domestic steel industry, International Steel Industries chose to diversify rather than streamline. They bought into an airline that crashed in a splash of red ink and invested in a fast growing restaurant conglomerate that acquired itself into oblivion. Nothing was left but a struggling steel company and the embarrassment of a monumental waste of money. Five consecutive years of losses, concurrent with increasing management salaries and bonuses had left the stockholders angry and frustrated. Their board of directors had raised a gun to its head and was begging the stockholders to pull the trigger.

Several would-be acquirers made overtures, but were spurned. Two years back, a French company launched a tender offer that failed when their banks got skittish and nixed the deal. ISI languished, red-faced, with no White Knight savior in sight. Then Bastille accumulated its state.

Bastille Partners nominated its own slate of directors and presented a plan to liquidate the company which, utilizing the net operating loss carryforwards, would deliver to the shareholders twice the market value of the stock.

Four months of law suits, Fight Letters, telephone calls to stockholders and media manipulation come down to the presentation of the proxies at the annual meeting. ISI had collected proxies voting for their director nominees and we had collected proxies voting for our nominees.

All the marbles are riding on that day. If someone screws up and the proxies don't make it to the meeting site, or if a few hundred thousand shares slip through the cracks, it could cost the fight—and a million dollar fee.

Every time I go through this, I think back with a shudder to the time in St. Louis, when we *lost* a limo carrying all of our five million votes. After sending four rented cars and eight frantic executives on a hell-bent search through the streets of the city, we found the limo parked in an alley behind the wrong building.

My thoughts turned back to the matters at hand as our wheels kissed the runway. *Everything should be set. The only wild card is Mary. If I can stay one step ahead of her, this'll be a slam-dunk.*

At about eleven p.m., Mark and Lori, members of my crew, and I disembarked from Bastille's Gulfstream. We loaded our baggage and three leather cases containing several thousand cards representing about eighteen million votes into a waiting limousine.

Heading into town, we emerged from the Fort Pitt Tunnels and were awed by the glorious Pittsburgh skyline. The night lights were mirrored by the Monongahela River as we crossed the Fort Pitt Bridge enroute to a rendezvous with our advance team.

We had leased a temporary office close to the hotel where the meeting was to be held in order to better handle the preparations. International Steel Industries was the home team in this engagement, so we had to take extra precautions to ensure secrecy.

At the office, we met up with advance team members Steven and Barbara, and locked the proxy cards away in a rented fire-proof safe for the night. Along with the proxies were boxes containing the envelopes that the proxies were received in; all date and time-stamped for presentation to the Official Judge of Elections.

On the ride to the hotel, Steven brought us up to speed on the status of preparations.

The War Room was set up and ready to go. We had gone in a month earlier under an assumed name and rented the Echelon Room which was right across the hall from the Grand Ballroom where the meeting would take place. Then we had the hotel install the electrical wires and telephone lines that we needed for our equipment. The equipment arrived today and everything was locked and under guard.

"We did have some foul play with the reservations," Steven told me. "Somebody moved my suite to the eleventh floor. All the others are just where we reserved them."

"What about Bastille's rooms?" I asked.

"All in place. In fact, they checked in an hour ago."

"Then the decoy worked."

"Like a charm."

We reserved all of our rooms, including fifteen for Bastille's principals, director nominees and the lawyers and investment bankers in their contingent, under bogus names—all except Steven's, that is. He was always head of our advance team and Dexter & Company, the opposing proxy firm, knew it. So we reserved, in his name, a suite close to the conference room floor with extra phone lines added for fax machines. Working for the dissident shareholder group and being in the company's hometown, we were very susceptible to sabotage. We anticipated the assumption by Dexter & Co. that Steven's suite would be used as our War Room, and their changing the reservations to a different suite, far away from the conference room floor, confirmed our suspicion that they would try to trip us up.

We checked in and then made our way to the War Room. The hallway on the conference room floor was long and wide and elegant. An electronic events board glared: *International Steel Industries - Annual Meeting 10 AM Grand Ballroom/Trojan Equine Assoc. 8 AM Echelon Room.* The only soul around was the security guard posted outside the Grand Ballroom. We smiled innocently and approached the Echelon Room. Barbara knocked once, paused, and then there was a knock on the inside.

"Mustang," Barbara whispered to the door.

The door opened and we were ushered in by Tom, the third member of our advance team.

"Welcome to the front line," Tom said with a grin.

I surveyed the War Room. Straight ahead were three portable personal computers wired to three portable printers. Along the right wall was a bank of six fax machines.

"Have the fax machines been tested?" I asked.

Barbara picked up a piece of fax paper. "Yes, they're operational and the lines are set to roll over, one to the other. We'll be able to receive transmissions from all points simultaneously." She held up the test message. It read: GOOD LUCK PROJECT BLACK KNIGHT.

To the left were three high-speed photocopy machines and several long banquet tables, on top of which were four cellular telephones, a stack of manila envelopes, reams of copier paper, staplers, tape, badges, an authorized admittance list and a detailed, color-coded, multi-floor plan for the hotel, outlining rooms, doorways, elevators, stairwells, emergency exits and pay phones. This was to ensure that no act of God or man kept us from delivering our proxies to the Judge of Elections.

I turned to Tom, who was on guard and would be sleeping in the War Room. "Any sign of Mary or the other Dexter people?"

"A little while ago, the guard from across the hall came over and let two people into the room right next door. It sounded like a man and a woman."

"What were they doing?"

"The man asked the woman where she wanted the fax machines and then after about a half an hour, they were gone."

"That sounds like them. No trouble from the guard?"

"No. I don't think he knows I'm in here."

"Good."

Just then, we heard several voices outside and I motioned to Tom who killed the lights. The voices seemed somewhat familiar, but we kept silent. Suddenly, someone tried the door handle.

"It's locked," a voice I recognized said.

"That's Ruben, " I said. "Open it up."

Tom turned the lights on and Barbara opened the door.

"Hey, what are you doing, hiding in here?"

"Yeah," I said. "Come on in."

Ruben, an attorney for Bastille, walked in, flanked by four investment bankers from Sherman—Wilkes & Co. After inspecting the War Room, they said that the principals wanted to see me upstairs.

"Sleep with an eye open," I told Tom. "Everybody get some rest. We rock 'n' roll at eight a.m."

I met briefly with the rest of the bankers and lawyers and nominees who had retired to one of the rooms for several rounds of victory toasts. We had been informed before we left New York that Goldberg, Weinman and Company, a major money management firm, had voted a block of about a half million shares in our favor. We had lobbied fervently for their support and anticipated getting it, but their investment committee didn't come down with a decision until late the day before and their treasurer wouldn't be in the office to sign the proxy until the morning of the meeting. We needed that block faxed to us by the time the polls closed to put us over the top. It was going to be a Maalox morning.

After settling into my room, I picked up the phone and dialed the hotel operator. "Mary Sanders' room, please."

After a moment, she said, "I'm sorry, we have no one registered under that name."

"Oh. Try Mary Snyder."

"Just a moment."

I kept forgetting that she'd gotten married since the last time I'd seen her.

"Here it is, sir. I'll ring it for you."

When Mary answered and I heard her voice, I wanted to hang up, but I knew that our meeting on this trip was inevitable.

"Hi, Mary." There was a slight pause and for an instant I thought that *she* might hang up.

"Hello," she said.

"I'm sorry it's so late. Did I wake you?"

"No . . . yes . . . How are you?"

"Good. How's Dexter & Company treating you?"

"Fine. Funny we should be meeting head to head like this, isn't it?"

"I wish it didn't have to happen."

"When I left for Dexter, we knew it was bound to."

"I know. Listen, I—"

"Any word on the Goldberg vote?"

"You haven't heard?"

"No. Have you?"

I didn't know what to say. Within hours she would find out, but I didn't want to be the one to tell her. She should have known by now, anyway. Was she bluffing? Did she know something I didn't?

"No, I haven't heard." I figured I'd play it out. "Can I see you?"

"When?"

"Now. Just for a while."

"Okay."

I hadn't seen her in several years and this was probably a bad idea, but it was something I had to do. A wave of trepidation flowed over me as I knocked on her door. I wondered if I had time to run away. She opened the door and said, "Hi. Come in." Her silk robe highlighted the contour of her body and her hair was longer than I remembered. It accentuated the lines of her face in a way that made my heart ache. I knew then that it *was* a very bad idea.

"How's married life?" I asked.

"Good," she said, too cheerily.

"Too bad," I half-jested.

"Hey, you left me, sweetheart. Remember?"

"I know, I know. So why don't you just kick me in the nuts and get it over with?"

She retrieved a bottle of champagne from the wet bar and with her back to me, muttered, "Because I still love you."

I approached her and gently kissed her neck. "I still love *you*," I whispered. She turned and we kissed. The taste of her lips made my mind swim. I wrapped my arms around her and held her tightly to me.

"If we get caught," she said, "by your people or my people, we're in big trouble."

Then I said probably the dumbest thing I'd said in a long time: "I don't care."

She dropped her robe and then began to undress me. We lay upon the bed. The world disappeared for those few hours and I hated to leave her *again*. Whatever its cause or reason, and whatever happened in the morning, she would go back to her husband and I would go home alone.

"We shouldn't have done this," she said quietly.

After I dressed, I looked deep into her eyes. "Are you happy?" I asked.

"Yes. Are you?"

"If you're happy, I'm happy," I lied, and turned for the door.

"Question."

I turned back. "What?"

"You got the Goldberg vote, didn't you."

"Yes."

"Good night," was all she said.

After I left, she picked up the phone and placed a call to New York.

At seven a.m., Lori and Steven awoke to their own alarms and began a chain of wake-up calls. We have brought our own alarms since three years ago in San Francisco when the Dexter people called the front desk in the middle of the night and canceled our wake-up calls. At about eight-fifteen, our team convened in the War Room for a final strategy session. Steven logged on the computers and dialed one into our New York office and one into the electronic mail system of Independent Tabulation Systems. ITS mails, collects and tabulates votes from clients of brokerage firms and banks that don't have the resources or desire to run their own Proxy Department. The third computer was dialed into the Proxy-Gram system, which, in the final days and hours, collects proxy votes from shareholders that call a pre-established toll-free 800 number. Within minutes, these electronically generated proxies would begin spilling out of the portable computer printers.

In the next room, Mary and Dexter's people would be pulling in their own votes.

Barbara, Tom and I slipped cellular phones into our pockets and headed out to the hallway. The conference room area was beginning to buzz with people. A reception area was being set up with programs, sign-in sheets, stockholder lists and admittance badges. We signed in and obtained our badges, each being record owners of one share of stock, then Barbara and

Tom started walking down the hallway and I turned to go back to the Echelon Room. As I did, Mary passed by. She smiled politely and entered Dexter's War Room. For some reason, I became uneasy.

Barbara and Tom rode the elevator to the basement-level garage and drove separate rented cars to the temporary office. The proxies and envelopes would fill one trunk, but at this point, "back-up" was the name of the game.

At the office, they retrieved the proxies from the fireproof safe, loaded them onto a dolly and then waited for the overnight delivery of proxies collected the day before at our firm's other offices across the country.

In the Echelon Room, Lori and I took the proxies that began rolling off the fax machines and printers from our offices that received them that morning from banks and funds in their territories, and handed them to Mark, who made photocopies of them all and stuffed them into manila envelopes. At ten a.m., when the stockholders' meeting was convened and the polls opened, they would be delivered to the Official Judge of Elections.

By nine a.m., our own security guards were posted with an admittance list. The lawyers and bankers began to arrive, but had been given instructions to stay clear of our operation. Our director nominees would, no doubt, choose to make their entrance at ten.

I pulled out my phone and dialed New York. The Goldberg proxy was still not signed. The treasurer hadn't arrived at his office, but was on his way. His 500,000 shares were ours, but time was ticking away and the window for delivery was closing.

Our adrenaline and anxiety was beginning to peak as it always does, but something else, unknown, was gnawing at me. Mary was on my mind. It may have just been her presence, but something wasn't right; she was too calm.

Next, I called Tom. The overnight delivery had arrived with about another 90,000 shares. They were on their way and their E.T.A. was 9:40. Too close.

In the midst of rush-hour gridlock in Lower Manhattan, the gray-haired treasurer of Goldberg, Weinman and Company sat in the back of his chauffeur-driven Mercedes at the corner of Broadway and Maiden Lane. As the light turned and an opening cleared, the driver began the left turn onto Maiden Lane. Suddenly, a chorus of blaring horns announced that something was going wrong. Before either man could react, a nondescript, four-door sedan peeled through the chaos and barreled across Broadway, slamming into the right-front side of the Mercedes, sliding it, on a bed of tire tracks and broken glass, into a sidewalk newsstand, sending magazines and newspapers flying.

The driver of the sedan, a dark man with a full, not too authentic looking beard, tried to open his door, but it was jammed shut by the twisted metal. He crawled over and climbed out of the passenger's side.

The treasurer and his driver were shaken, but unharmed. By the time they got out to survey the damage, the man with the beard had disappeared into the gathering crowd.

I was waiting with one of our security guards outside the hotel for Tom and Barbara when my phone chirped. It was New York. Goldberg's treasurer had been in an accident and wouldn't make it to the office for another hour. That would put our receipt of his signature at about 10:45. We'd be lucky if management didn't close the polls by then. We were pushing the outside of the envelope and without those shares, we crash and burn.

"Get to him!" I screamed. "Broadway's only four blocks from you. Have him sign it on the street!"

"I'm doin' it!" New York shot back. "I got two on foot and one in a cab. We're checking on places around the accident site to fax from."

Barbara and Tom drove up to the curb and screeched to a stop.

"Keep me informed, I gotta go," I said and then clicked the phone off.

A bellman wheeled a luggage cart over to the car and we unloaded the cases of proxies and boxes of envelopes. Barbara parked the cars while Tom and I, escorted by the bellman and the guard, rolled the proxies through the lobby and onto an elevator.

"We have a problem," I told Tom. "Somebody tried to eighty-six our Goldberg vote."

"How?" Tom asked, in shock.

"An unidentified man ran him off the road on his way to the office and then split."

"Was he hurt?"

"No. It's gonna be close."

We were on the elevator with the guard and the bellman, all of us watching the changing numbers overhead. Without looking at him, I said to Tom, "We're gonna have to stop the clock."

"Gotcha."

We wheeled the proxies toward the Echelon Room. The hallway was filled with stockholders, employees, retirees and the press. Heads turned and people stepped aside as we made our way through. The lady at the company's reception desk looked down at the proxies and then up at us. If looks could kill, we'd have been dead on the floor.

The stockholders' meeting was brought to order at ten o'clock sharp and the Chairman began his review of the year's results. Tom took a seat among the other shareholders as Mark, Lori, Barbara and I began a relay, passing cases, boxes and envelopes from the War Room to the Judge of Elections, seated in the back of the Ballroom. Mary and the other Dexter people did the same, though working for the company, she had the advantage of being able to deliver the bulk of her proxies well before the start of the meeting.

At 10:25, everything was delivered—except the Goldberg proxy. Without it, we were 150,000 shares down. I stepped out of the Ballroom, pulled out my phone and dialed New York again. Mary came out behind me.

"You look worried," she said. "What's the matter?"

I looked at her and that uneasy feeling came back.

She cocked an eyebrow and then asked, "Traffic problems?"

I felt the blood drain from my face. "How could you . . ." was all I could say.

"You taught me well," she said and then turned and walked away.

My man in New York came on the line. "Five minutes," he said excitedly. "He signed it and they're on their way to a fax machine."

I ran into the Echelon Room and got Mark, Lori and Steven into position on the machines. My heart was racing as Barbara and I went back into the Ballroom. She took a seat next to Tom while I stood near the doorway.

The board's representatives had given their reports and our nominees had made a brief, but passionate plea for support. New proxies had been passed out to stockholders who wished to change their votes and a short question and answer period was just concluding.

"Well, now," the Chairman's voice boomed over the P.A. system, "if there are no further questions, I believe we can close the—"

"Excuse me, Mr. Chairman!" Tom stood and bellowed. "One short question, please."

The Chairman, anxious to end the proceedings, motioned Tom to the microphone in the middle of the center aisle. Mary joined me at the doorway as Tom made his way over.

"What's goin' on?" she asked.

I just shrugged.

Tom stated his name and shareholdings as is customary. A few chuckles rippled through the audience when Tom announced his one share holding. "Mr. Chairman," he began, "in the most recent annual report to shareholders, on . . . ah . . . page seventeen, I think, anyway, ah, it says that by closing the company's plants in Tennessee and Virginia and, as the report puts it, 'otherwise downsizing the Mid-Atlantic Division,' the company will be able to create what the report refers to as 'critical mass' in the areas of distribution and— "

"Please, sir," the Chairman interrupted, his patience spent, "the point?"

Mary tapped me on the arm. "I'm serious. What's going on?"

"School's not out yet, sweetheart," I said. "Pay attention."

"Yes sir, my question is, sir," Tom rambled on, his face turning white, "what, in your estimation, will be the economic impact of these plant closings on the surrounding commun . . . commun . . . co— "

Tom's mouth fell open. Electronically amplified gurgling sounds resonated throughout the Ballroom. There were horrified gasps in the crowd and then Tom toppled over, crashing to the floor atop the microphone. Immediately, Barbara stood up and screamed, "Oh my God!" at the top of her lungs. The audience broke into panic. A man and a woman comforted Barbara. A group gathered around Tom.

A voice shouted, "Give him room!"

Another voice cried, "Give him air!"

Mary didn't leave my side.

Suddenly the door burst open and Steven reached in with a manila envelope clenched in his hand. I snatched it from him and swung around avoiding a reflexive swipe from Mary.

"Hey!" she yelled.

I ran across the back of the Ballroom toward the Judge's table as I heard Mary call out, "Johnny, stop him!"

A man I recognized from Mary's team stepped out in front of me. I looked into his eyes and in a voice as cold as ice, I said, "Touch me and I'll drop you." Our shoulders brushed as I passed by him and tossed the envelope onto the Judge's table.

The crowd calmed down as Tom recovered from his fainting spell and apologized for the disruption.

Outside the Ballroom, I looked around for Mary, but she was gone. I could hear the Chairman's voice, "Well, that concludes the business. The polls are now closed."

"More champagne, sir?" The attendant filled my flute again. Congratulatory high-fives, clinking Baccarat and laughter filled the Gulfstream's cabin as we climbed through the afternoon cloud-cover.

My thoughts turned to Mary as one of the investment bankers, with a phone pressed to his ear, yelled out, "Quiet down, quiet down! It just came over the wire, 'Today, International Steel Industries' Chairman conceded that the company's incumbent directors were defeated by a narrow margin at its annual stockholder's meeting, held this morning in Pittsburgh.'"

Robert Orndorff

Sometimes We Let the Mail Go Until Tomorrow

Done with work, ready to go home,
We pick up the stuff in our office that we want to take with us, but
We forgot to send an important electronic mail message, so
We set down the stuff, send the message, pick up the stuff and
       get to the front door of the building, but
We forgot the envelope that we need to take home, so
As much as we hate to walk back past people still in their offices
       once we've decided to leave
We walk back and set down the stuff and locate the envelope
       and pick up the stuff
Again.

Walking out the door,
We can't remember where we parked the car.
We walk up the slope in the back which is where
We parked in the morning. We walk left which is where
We parked after lunch. We walk towards the green corrugated
       dumpster enclosure which is where
We parked after a bank errand, which is where
The car is.

From Route 520 heading West,
We can take the Arboretum exit but that's slower unless we want
       to stop for dinner at the Surrogate Hostess or
       somewhere along Fifteenth. We can
Take the Montlake exit but we only usually do that when we have
       night classes at the University of Washington. We can
Take the Route 5 North exit since we have leftover pizza at
       home, since we don't have a night class tonight. We can
And we do.

In the neighborhood we look for a parking space
On Bellevue between the grocery store corner and Roy. If no luck,
From the corner we visually check further south on Bellevue. If
    no luck,
From the corner we visually check left up the hill on Roy. If no luck,
We drive to the right down the hill on Roy and try to park
        illegally. If the building manager
Sticks his head out the window and says he'll have us towed if we
        park there,
We do it all again, not wanting to park out of the light or
        anywhere we don't usually park.

Not wanting to set the stuff down on the ground but needing to
Lock the car door and check once more that it is locked.
        Needing to
Open the front door of our apartment building but getting the
        wrong key,
Apartment and building keys looking alike but not working
        interchangeably. Needing to
Open the mail box with the third smaller slippery mailbox key
        that once in the key hole tends to fall back and out to
        the floor even before the mailbox is unlocked. Needing to
Pick up the key. If mail, needing to
Find a hand for it but not set stuff down. Still needing to
Open apartment door with two large bags and envelope and mail
    in hand

Sometimes we let the mail go until tomorrow.

Dialog Between Manager and Employee

Not a big thing in and of itself
But part of a continuing pattern that makes one think of a trend.
You have a tendency to ignore these things or dismiss them as
    isolated incidents

So don't respond until you've given this some thought.
It's not easy for me to do this
(I'm grinning but then I grin at inappropriate times.)
But I must put you on probation.
(I suppose I'm grinning because your humiliation embarrasses me.)
Not something I want to do
But a procedure that I must follow.
God knows we don't like to fire people
(I'm looking out my window but not because there's anything
     outside I want to see.)
So it's hard to fire people, hard to fire people.
We must give evidence of effort.
In your case this means
We must tell you what your problems are, give you a fair chance
     to improve, and simultaneously make your employment
     probationary.
(So that eventually it's easier to fire you.)
Not something I want to do.
Nobody likes this, neither you nor me.
What does it mean to be probationary?
It means you have 5 months.
God knows these things are easy enough to do,
You certainly have the innate skills,
You're bright enough
Why in the world don't you do them?
I don't see any reason why you cannot improve, any reason.
(I twist strands of hair between thumb and fingers.)
I really think you can improve.
Don't think it's likely that we'll fire you or anything.
We'll revisit in 5 months and then decide whether you can
     continue to work in my group.
You do still want to continue to work in my group don't you?
You underestimate the importance of other people's perceptions
     of you, of the little things,
And, by the way, you have no instinct whatsoever for
     self-preservation, no instinct.

C. Allan May, Jr.

layoff

one day i was told by my company
i was no longer needed, my manager's voice,
in the telling, soft, measured, and gentle,
like tissues offered for tears.
the guilt of his remaining had tamed him,
brought him to that quiet place
all bearers of bad news know,
the safe white space of reprieve.

the four small walls of the conference room
boxed him in, held him both literally and symbolically
in the smallness of corporate life,
forced to do what he had no heart to do,
to be what no free heart should be;
so he focused on the bright side, the severance
benefits, the luck of escaping the uncertainty of it all.

but in the quiet, still air of that room
i felt his dread easing out, easing in, like his breath,
shallow and subdued. would i rave accusations at him,
would i throw back on him the despair he expected,
would i—god help him if i did—break down and weep?

> *there was no window in that room,*
> *but i felt nonetheless the sunlight,*
> *felt the walls opening like rows of black dominoes*
> *tipping over, tipping over, and the wind*
> *rushing in like wings. set free, i knew at last*
> *how captured i had been, chained, blindfolded,*
> *gagged by a thousand minor seductions,*
> *my dreams wrenched loose from their roots*
> *and left quivering in the naked air.*

I tried to reassure him, the survivor
(nos morituri salutamus),
and like a priest at confession, to absolve him
of any guilt he imagined. i spoke of changes,
of roads diverging, opportunities springing up like hyacinths
after a long winter. i smiled and was happy,
and not just for his benefit. i spoke truth to him,
saying "listen, i'm scared to death—
but i needed this, i was drowning in this little pond
with all these frightened, hungry fish,"
and i know he knew what i meant,
though he could not believe my relief.

> and listen, all you who have never
> been laid aside:
> it doesn't hurt like you thought it would,
> and the hand that pushes you out
> is a friendlier hand than you have believed
> and older, and wiser:
>> even the sun knows when to set,
>> and the rain falls when the conditions
>> are exactly, precisely correct.

Irreverent Thoughts About Organization Charts

James A. Autry

IN ALMOST THIRTY-FIVE years of organizational life, I've never figured out what useful purpose organization charts serve, and if I had my choice, we'd do away with them.

But they seem so firmly embedded into the consciousness of every American, from Boy Scouts to school boards to corporations, that I know organization charts will outlive me. All I can do is warn everyone who'll listen: Learn and remember the laws of organization charts:

1. They mainly are about egos, and they serve to inflate egos in a roughly ten-to-one inverse ratio with the egos they deflate.

2. An organization chart, posted in an obvious place, is a proven morale killer.

3. Organization charts are *always* inaccurate, even as some poor bored secretary is carefully lining out the new one and sending it off for photocopying. And if the chart is not inaccurate, the organization does not have enough change, thus is in big trouble.

4. Organization charts in a company neither define relationships as they actually exist nor direct the lines of communication. People do all this for themselves, and the realities of relationships and lines of communication never match the charts. When you find the rare company in which the charts do define relationships and do direct lines of communication, sell your stock at once. There's not an ounce of imagination in the whole place.

If the "organization" does not exist in the minds and hearts of the people, it does not exist. No chart can fix that. An organization's function is simple: to provide a framework, a format, a context in which people can effectively use resources to accomplish their goals.

Among their most important resources are their relationships with one another. Who's on top and who's on bottom, according to the chart, is among the least important information. Besides, we all know who the boss is, and our employees know who we are.

So why make a diagram out of the obvious?

All the Young Fausts

Mark Hall

Many of the high technology firms in Silicon Valley encourage their employees to dress up for Halloween. Mine is no different. At least a hundred-and-fifty of us, more than half of the company, donned masks, came in drag, wore elaborate make-up and costume, or tore our clothes and greased our hair in imitation of punk rockers. It was great fun, and the personnel manager felt she had succeeded in raising our morale.

Then why am I depressed?

I came as Mephistopheles. My wife spent a half-hour making up my face. I had a dark cape. My hair was black and slicked back. I looked, I must say, foreboding.

When I arrived at work everyone was thrilled that I had gone to such lengths. The first people who saw me, the women in the accounting department, made quite a fuss. They said I made a devastating Dracula. Or, was it Wolfman?

Now, I didn't mind being mis-cast. After all, my costume did not come from the dressing rooms of Hollywood, but from my own meager closets. I corrected them in a friendly way.

"I am Mephisto," I said.

Their faces went blank.

"Mephistopheles."

More blankness.

"Faust? Dr. Faustus? Christopher Marlowe? Goethe?"

They stared at me uncomprehendingly.

I explained the literary allusion of my costume and they were very interested, glad to know. When we parted, I excused their ignorance (in my élitist, sexist snobbery) by saying to myself, "Those were just the girls from accounting. Why should they know anything of English and German literary tradition?" Why indeed.

My depression lingers not because of that first encounter, but because my day was filled with blank faces. Not one—not a single employee—knew Mephistopheles from third base. Again, I didn't mind being praised for my likeness to Dracula (or Wolfman), but when corrected, everyone, without exception, said, "Who's Mephistopheles?"

These are not uneducated people. After a while I kept track of those who did not know: an MBA from Stanford, two MBAs from Santa Clara University, a Ph.D. from Case Western Reserve, a business major from Boston University, a BSEE from Kansas State, a Master's from Columbia, a BA from San Diego State, a BSCS from the University of North Carolina, a BA from the University of Wisconsin. The list goes on.

The one thing all of these people have in common, besides their ignorance of Mephisto, is their involvement in high technology. These people are, as they like to say, the "shakers and movers" of tomorrow's technology, tomorrow's economy, tomorrow's society. Having been involved with high technology for more than five years now, and noting the glamour, appeal, and the undue influence it has on society, I fear they may be right.

High technology, and the scientific achievement that drives it, seems to be enough for them. The knowing and understanding of literature and the arts is irrelevant to them. As one young computer science genius said to me after I had explained (for the umpteenth time) just who Mephistopheles was, "I didn't study any of that stuff. It was unimportant."

I suppose I could have rationalized that the Mephisto character was an obscure aberration in Western thought, but that's not so. He is critical to our tradition of defining good and evil, right and wrong, commitment and deception, justice and salvation. The idea of Mephistopheles fueled the imaginations of Marlowe, Goethe, Mozart, Shaw, and Mann, among others. When our young "shakers and movers" of tomorrow believe such work and ideas to be "unimportant," what does that tell us about our future?

Joseph Wiezenbaum, a computer scientist at MIT, wrote in his book *Computer Power and Human Reason* that science "has virtually delegitimatized all other ways of understanding." He added that contemporary literature and art, once the educated person's foundation for "intellectual nourishment and understanding," have become "perceived largely as entertainments." We have, in other words, become hoodwinked by science and technology.

Our new generation of technologists does not seem to bother with literary tradition and the intellectual dilemmas that provoke great art. To them, the world and those of us who dwell in it can be reduced to a knowable formula, computed and filed. There is no room for questions without answers, ideas that don't fit into the equation. What they know *is*. What they don't know *isn't*.

Perhaps through the tools of science and technology Mephistopheles has bargained for the souls of all our young Fausts. Perhaps he has finally won.

View From the Front Desk

I'm in before anyone. I'm a sterling employee.
I'm here when the first hiss of air whooshes
from the vents, sibilant as a librarian's shushes.
Then the phones ring, the bosses come, the raree

begins. I take it all in. Whatever messengers bring—
the mail, deli lunches, roses—I accept.
If all three come at once, I'm quite adept!
There's room in my lap for everything.

It's the lulls that throw me: minutes that drag
on and on and no bells ring. Workers from inside
rush past me, flushing with purpose and pride!
I drum my ragged nails, or claw my bag

for another butt. Then all bells blow at once! I grieve
no more: my lot's to wait, my calling to receive.

In Company

After two years of writhing solitude
I come back to the crude
arena of the living, to take my place
at a front desk, arrange my face
and welcome callers to a fabric
company. Behind me, my pick
of seven beds, each arranged
with the firm's designs: deranged
ferns, bulbous roses,
cats, dogs, in supplicant poses.
On sleazy 32nd Street we show our wares.
In the back room, six artists share
four drawing boards and are forever
quarrelling. Allegiances sever,
complaints are croaked into the tainted
air. And still the hideous patterns are painted.

When the chairman has a heart attack
and the glamorous design chief gets the sack
and the artists finally blacken
one another's eyes, I do not slacken
off as once I might have. Instead
I am alert to bell and phone, wed
to the work as a honeymooning bride
is wed to untiring ecstasy. O I tried
the way of the anchorite, and became
no purer than I'm becoming in this game
of argument and hustle and stale woes!
If my calling be to hawk the garish rose
then I accept my calling. To be
imperfect and of use is all I ask: to be
                         in company.

Floyd Skloot

I Am Getting a Mountain View

The men have come again to move partitions.
They are working their way back and toward
my present work station and should be ready for me
by Thursday. I am getting a mountain view,
a station by the eastern windows and far enough
north to see around the stair tube and smoke tower balcony.

My phone already rings over there. When people call me,
I get While You Were Out messages within the hour
and can return their calls from the phone that used to be mine,
still on the credenza I have labeled with my name.
Everything goes and is labeled. You can never tell.
They moved Wayne when he was on break
and he still can't find his map of the state.

The old way to the copy room and the coffee pot
has been blocked by file cabinets but there are worse hazards,
like raised outlets exposed, holes where phone cables were,
chairs in aisles, desks on dollies and movers lunging
blindly behind a load of shelves. I can hardly work
with all the hammering and chatting.

People have been leaving for lunch early
and going home at four. But not me.
I think that's why I am getting a mountain view,
because I have always worked with such concentration.
In fact, I want to be sure to hang my poster of *Le Thermogène*
first thing on the wall behind me because
it depicts so accurately my way of doing business.

A Working Marriage

No hardy phlox or spice pinks in neat rows.
Ragged lawn with untrimmed hedge, wasted space,
no garden. One more sultry spring. No time
for rest, day and night thick with choice. Nothing
on the wind but must, nothing in the way
of movement. The one truth is urgency.

Up at five, worksheets still spread. Urgency
wafting like smoke wakes the spouse. Two rows
of claret stains trickling down the stairway
mark their path to bed. Coffee brews. No space
for cups, no hunger or chitchat. Nothing
to be gained by touching; there may be time

later. They work in separate rooms, time
showers around toast and the urgency
of soft-boiled eggs. Outside, jays with nothing
to stop them seize the backyard, their harsh row
almost distracting. Squirrels sprint through space
a phone cable makes in elm leaves. The way

one's tail twitches before she runs away
makes her mate move through leaves like wind. No time
to lose, nothing on paper yet but space,
nothing quite as clear as the urgency
to look back from the window, start a row
of words down another sheet with nothing

on it. There are needs to project. Nothing
adds up. Footsteps of their child are the way
they know morning is relative. His row
of days leads mark by mark toward summertime,
weeks squandered, play the only urgency.
He eats toast and cheese in a cleared space

among flowcharts, ignoring the tense space
before the rush to scatter. Now nothing
can wait. Lights and locks. All is urgency.
Briefcase and thermos, hugs on the driveway,
all words becoming a matter of time.

They use sidestreets to bypass docile rows
of cars in their way, quick turns to make time.
Nothing can compete with the urgency
of desks without free space, stacks in long rows.

Five Paintings of the New Japan

Steven Heighton

A National Gallery

I. Sunflowers

I WAS THE first foreigner to wait tables in the *Yume no ato*. Summer enrollment was down at the English school where I taught so I needed to earn some extra money, and since I'd been eating at the restaurant on and off for months it was the first place I thought of applying. It was a small establishment built just after the war in a bombed-out section of the city, but when I saw it the area was studded with bank towers, slick boutiques, coffee shops and flourishing bars and the *Yume no ato* was one of the oldest and most venerable places around. I was there most of the summer and I wish I could go back. I heard the other day from Nori, the dishwasher, who works part-time now in a camera store, that our ex-boss Mr Onishi has just fought and lost a battle with cancer.

"We have problems here every summer," Mr Onishi sighed during my interview, "with a foreign tourist people." He peered up at me from behind his desk, two shadowy half-moons drooping under his eyes. "Especially the Americans. If I hire you, you can deal to them."

"With them," I said automatically.

"You have experienced waitering?"

"A little," I lied.

"You understand Japanese?"

"I took a course."

"Say something to me in Japanese."

I froze for a moment, then was ambushed by a phrase from my primer.

"*Niwa ni wa furu-ike ga arimasu.*"

"In the garden," translated Mr Onishi, "there is an old pond."

I stared abjectly at his bald patch.

"You cannot say a sentence more difficult than that?"

I told Mr Onishi it was a beginner's course. He glanced up at me and ran his fingers through a greying Vandyke beard.

"How well do you know the Japanese cuisine?"

"Not so well," I answered in a light bantering tone that I hoped would disarm him, "but I know what I like."

He frowned and checked his watch, then darted a glance at the bank calendar on the wall.

"Morinaga speaks a little English," he said. "He will be your trainer. Tomorrow at 1600 hours you start."

"You won't be sorry, sir," I told him.

"I shall exploit you," he said, "until someone more qualitied applies."

* * *

Nori Morinaga leaned against the steam table and picked his nose with the languid, luxurious gestures of an epicure enjoying an after-dinner cigar. He was the biggest Japanese I'd ever seen and the coke-bottle glasses perched above his huge nose seemed comically small.

"Ah, *gaijin-san!*" he exclaimed as he saw me, collecting himself and inflating to his full height. "Welcome in! Hail fellow well-hung!"

I wondered if I'd heard him correctly.

"It gives me great pressure!"

I had. I had.

Nori Morinaga offered me his hand at the same moment I tried to bow. Nervously we grinned at each other, then began to laugh. He was a full head taller than I was, burly as a linebacker but prematurely hunched as if stooping in doorways and under low ceilings had already affected his spine. He couldn't have been over twenty-five. His hair was brush-cut like a Marine's and when he spoke English his voice and manner seemed earnest and irreverent at the same time.

"Onishi-San tells me I will help *throw you the ropes,*" he chuckled. "Ah, I like that expression. Do you know it? I study English at the University but the *gaijin-sensei* always says Japanese students must be more idiomatic so I picked up this book"—his giant hand brandished a thick paperback—"and I study it *like a rat out of hell.*"

He grinned enigmatically, then giggled. I couldn't tell if he was serious or making fun of me.

Nori pronounced his idiomatic gleanings with savage enthusiasm, his magnified eyes widening and big shoulders bunching for emphasis as if to ensure his scholarship did not pass unseen. I took the book and examined it: a dog-eared, discount edition of UP-TO-DATE ENGLISH PHRASES FOR JAPANESE STUDENTS—in the 1955 edition.

"We open in an hour," he said. "We are *oppressed for time.* Come on, *I'm going to show you what's what.*"

Situated in a basement, under a popular *karaoke* bar, the *Yume no ato's* two small rooms were dimly lit and the atmosphere under the low ceiling was damp and cool, as in an air-raid shelter or submarine. I wondered if this cramped, covert aura hadn't disturbed some of the earliest patrons, whose memories of the air-raids would still have been fresh—but I didn't ask Nori about that. The place had always been popular, he said, especially in summer, when it was one of the coolest spots in Ōsaka.

A stairway descended from street level directly into the dining room so on summer days, after the heat and bright sunshine of the city, guests would sink into a cool aquatic atmosphere of dim light and swaying shadows. The stairway was flanked on one side by a small bar and on the other by the sushi counter where I'd eaten before. An adjoining room contained a larger, more formal dining space which gave onto the kitchen through a swinging door at the back. Despite the rather western-style seating arrangements (tables and chairs instead of the traditional *zabuton* and *tatami*) the dining area was decorated in authentic Japanese fashion with hanging lanterns, calligraphic scrolls, a *tokonoma* containing an empty *maki-e* vase, *bonsai* and *noren* and several framed, original *sumi-e* prints. The only unindigenous ornament was a large reproduction of Van Gogh's "Sunflowers" hung conspicuously on the wall behind the sushi bar.

"Onishi-San says it's for the behoof of the American tourists," Nori explained, "but I'd *bet my bottom* he put it there for the bankers who come *in the wee-wee hours.* It's the bankers who are really interested in that stuff." He sniffed and gestured contemptuously toward "Sunflowers" and toward the *sumi-e* prints as well, as if wanting me to see he considered all art frivolous and dispensable, no matter where it came from.

I didn't realize till much later the gesture meant something else.

Nori showed me around the kitchen and introduced me to the cooks, who were just arriving. Kenji Komatsu was head chef. Before returning to Japan and starting a family he'd worked for a few years in Vancouver and Montreal and his memories of that time were good, so he was delighted to hear I was Canadian. He insisted I call him Mat. "And don't listen to anything this big whale tells you," he warned me affably, poking Nori in the stomach. "So much sugar and McDonald's the young ones are eating these days . . . . This one should be in the *sumo* ring, not my kitchen."

"*Sumo* is for old folk," Nori said, tightening his gut and ironically saluting a small, aproned man who had just emerged from the walk-in fridge.

"*Time is on the march,*" Nori intoned. "*Nothing can stop it now!*"

Second chef Yukio Miyoshi glared at Nori then at me with frank disgust and muttered to himself in Japanese. He marched toward the back of the kitchen and began gutting a large fish. "Doesn't like the foreigners," Nori grinned indifferently. "So it is. You can't pleasure everybody."

The swinging door burst open and a small dark form hurtled into the kitchen and disappeared behind the steam table. Nori grabbed me by the arm.

"It's Oh-San, the sushi chef—come, we must hurry."

Mr Oh was a jittery middle-aged man who scurried through the restaurant, both hands frantically embracing a mug of fresh coffee. Like all the elder folks, Nori explained, Mr Oh worked too hard . . . .

We finally cornered him by the walk-in fridge and Nori introduced us. Clearly he had not heard of Mr Onishi's latest hiring decision—he flung down his mug and gawked as if I were a health inspector who'd just told him twenty of last night's customers were in the hospital with food poisoning.

The *yukata* which Mr Oh insisted I try on looked all right, and in the changeroom I finally gave in and let him brylcreem and comb back my curly hair into the slick, shining facsimile of a typical Japanese cut. As he worked with the comb, his face close to mine, I could see the tic in his left eye and smell his breath, pungent with coffee.

"You look *marvelous*," Nori laughed on my return, "and you know who you are!" He winked and blew me a kiss.

Mr Onishi entered and snapped some brusque truculent command. When the others had fled to their stations he addressed me in English.

"I hope you are ready for your first shift. We will have many guests tonight. Come—you will have to serve the aliens."

From the corner of my eye I could see Nori clowning behind the grille, two chopsticks pressed to his forehead like antennae.

As I trailed Mr Onishi into the dining room two men and a woman, all young, tall, clad smartly in *yukata*, issued from behind the bar and lined up for inspection. One of the men wore a pearl earring and his hair was unusually long for a Japanese, while the woman had a rich brown, luminous skin and plump attractive features. Mr Onishi introduced the other man as Akiburo. He was a college student and looked the part with his regulation haircut and sly, wisecracking expression.

With patent distaste Mr Onishi billed the long-haired man as "your bartender, who likes to be known as Johnnie Walker." The man fingered his earring and smiled out of the side of his mouth. "And this is Suzuki Michiko, a waitress." She bowed awkwardly and studied her plump brown hands, the pale skin on the underside of her wrists.

My comrades, as Mr Onishi called them, had been expecting me, and now they would show me to my sector of the restaurant—three small tables in the corner of the second room. In this occidental ghetto, it seemed, Mr Onishi thought I would do the least possible damage to the restaurant's ambience and reputation. Michiko explained in simple Japanese that since my tables were right by the kitchen door I could ask Nori for help as soon as I got in trouble.

The *tokonoma*, I now saw, had been decorated with a spray of poppies.

"We open shortly," Mr Onishi declared, striding toward us. His manner was vigorous and forceful but his eyes seemed tired, their light extinguished. "We probably will have some American guests tonight. Your job will be to service them."

"I'll do my best, sir."

"And coffee—you will now take over from Michiko and bring Mr Oh his coffee. He will want a fresh supply every half-hour. Do not forget!"

For the first hour the second room remained empty, as did the tables of the front room, but the sushi bar was overrun within minutes by an army of ravenous, demanding guests. "Coffee," cried Mr Oh, and I brought him cup after cup while the customers gaped at me and hurled at Mr Oh questions I could not understand. The coffee yellowed his tongue and reddened his eyes, which took on a weird, narcotic glaze, while steam mixed with sweat and stood out in bold clear beads on his cheeks and upper lip. Orders were called out as more guests arrived. Mr Oh's small red hands scuttled like sand crabs over the counter, making predatory forays into the display case to seize hapless chunks of smelt or salmon or eel and then wielding above them a fish-silver knife, replacing the knife deftly, swooping down on speckled quail eggs and snapping shells between thumb and forefinger and squeezing the yolk onto bricks of rice the other hand had just formed. Then with fingers dangling the hands would hover above an almost-completed dish, and they would waver slightly like squid or octopi in currents over the ocean floor, then pounce, abrupt and accurate, on an errant grain of rice or any garnish or strip of ginger imperfectly arranged, and an instant later the finished work, irreproachable and beyond time like a still-life or a great sculpture, would appear on the glass above the display case from which it was snatched within seconds by the grateful customers or attentive staff.

The process was dizzying. I was keenly aware of my ignorance and when I was not airlifting coffee to the sushi bar I was busy in my own sector studying the menu and straightening tables.

Around eight o'clock Mr Onishi entered the second room, carrying menus, followed by a man and woman who were both heavyset, tall and fair-haired. The man wore a tailored navy suit and carried a briefcase. The woman's hair was piled high in a steep bun that resembled the nose-cone of a rocket, and her lipstick, like her dress, was a pushy, persistent shade of red.

"Take good care with Mr and Mrs Cruikshank," Onishi-San murmured as he passed me and showed them to their seats. "Mr Cruikshank is a very important man—a diplomat, from America. Bring two dry martinis to begin."

Mr Cruikshank's voice was genteel and collected, his manner smooth as good brandy. "How long have you been working in this place?" he inquired.

"Two hours," I told him, serving the martinis.

"Surprised they'd have an American working here." With one hand he yanked a small plastic sabre from his olive, then pinched the olive and held it aloft like a tiny globe.

"I'm not American," I said.

There was a pause while Mr and Mrs Cruikshank processed this unlooked-for information.

"Well surely you're not Japanese?" Mrs Cruikshank asked, slurring her words a little. "Maybe half?"

Mr Cruikshank swallowed his olive then impaled his wife's with the plastic sword. He turned back to me, inadvertently aiming the harmless tip at my throat.

"*Nihongo wakaru?*" he asked in plain, masculine speech. *"You understand Japanese?"* I recognized his accent as outstanding.

"Only a little," I said.

"I'll bet he's Dutch," Mrs Cruikshank wagered. "The Dutch speak such beautiful English—hardly any accent at all."

"You'll find it hard here without any Japanese," Mr Cruikshank advised me, ignoring his wife, drawing the sword from his teeth so the gleaming olive stayed clenched between them.

"*Coffee,*" Mr Oh called from the sushi bar.

"I'll only be serving the foreign customers, sir."

Mr Cruikshank bit into his olive. "Some of the foreign customers," he said, "prefer being served in Japanese."

"Or maybe German," said Mrs Cruikshank.

"I can speak some German," I said. "Would you like it if—"

"*Coffee,*" cried Mr Oh from the sushi bar.

Mrs Cruikshank was beaming. "I was right," she said, lifting her martini glass in a kind of toast. *"Wie geht's?"*

"We'd like some sushi," Mr Cruikshank interrupted his wife, who was now grimacing at her drink as if trying to recall another German phrase.

I fumbled with my pad.

"An order each of *magura, saba, hamachi,* and—why not?—some sea urchin. Hear it's full of mercury these days, but hell, we've got to eat something."

"Yes, sir."

"And two more martinis." He pointed at his glass with the plastic sword.

"Got it."

"*Danke schön,*" roared Mrs Cruikshank as I hurried from the room.

While waiting for Johnnie Walker to finish the martinis I noticed an older guest rise from the sushi bar and stumble toward the washrooms. As he saw me, his red eyes widened and he lost his footing and crashed into the bar, slamming a frail elbow against the cash register. He righted himself with quick

slapstick dignity and stood blushing. When I moved to help him
he waved me off.

Johnnie Walker smirked and muttered as he shook the
martinis and for a moment the words and the rattling ice took
on a primitive, mocking rhythm, like a chant. The older man
began to swear at him and reached out as if to grab his earring,
his long hair. *Shin jin rui*, the old man muttered—*strange inscrutable
creature!* I'd heard it was a new phrase coined by the old to
describe the young.

"Wake up, old man," Johnnie snapped in plain Japanese
as he poured the martinis. "Watch out where you're going."

The man lurched off.

"Always drunk, or fast asleep in their chairs."

"*Coffee*," cried Mr Oh from the sushi bar.

II. The Dream

"Tell me something about the restaurant," I said to
Nori, sweeping my hand in a half-circle and nodding at the
closed bar. "How old is the place?"

Nori finished his Budweiser and balanced the empty tin
on a growing tower of empties. "It was built after the war ends,"
he belched—and I couldn't help noticing how casually he used
the word *war*. His expression was unchanged, his voice was still
firm, his eyes had not recoiled as if shamed by some unspeakable
profanity. That was how my older students reacted when The
War came up in a lesson. No doubt Mr Onishi would react the
same way. But not Nori. For him the war was history,
fiction—as unreal and insubstantial as a dimly remembered
dream, a dream of jungles, the faded memory of a picture in a
storybook. He wasn't much younger than me.

"What about the name," I said, "*Yume no ato?* I mean, I
can figure out the individual words, but I can't make sense of the
whole thing." *Yume*, I knew, meant "dream," *no* signified
possession, like an apostrophe and án "s," and *ato*, I thought,
meant "after."

Nori lit a cigarette and trained a mischievous gaze on my
hairline. His capacity for drink was larger than average for a
Japanese but now after four tins of beer he was flushed,
theatrical and giddy. He wrinkled his broad nose, as if at a whiff
of something rotten, and spat out, "It's a line from a poem we
had to study in the high school. Ah, Steve-San, University is so
much better, we have fun in the sun, we make whoopee, we live

for the present tense and forget all our yesterdays and tomorrows—I hated high school, so much work. We had to study this famous poem."

He stood and recited the lines with mock gravity:

> *"Natsu kusa ya!*
> *Tsuamono domo ga*
> *Yume no ato."*

"It's a *haiku*," I said.

"Aye, aye, captain." He slumped down and the tower of beer cans wobbled. "Do you watch Star Trek?"

"I'm not sure," I said, "that I understand it."

"Oh, well, it's just a TV show—about the future and the stars."

"I mean the poem, Nori, the *haiku*."

"Ah, the poem—naturally you don't understand. It's old Japanese—old Japanese language, old Japanese mind—not so easy for us to understand either. It's Matsuo Bashō, dead like Shakespeare over three hundred years. Tomorrow and tomorrow and tomorrow. We had to study them both in school. Full fathom five and all that."

"But about that last line . . . ."

"Yume no ato?"

I nodded.

"That's the name of the restaurant. You see, when Mr Onishi's uncle built the place after the war he gave it that name. It's a very strange name for a restaurant! Mr Onishi was just a boy then."

"What does it mean?"

"I don't think Mr Onishi would have called it that, but when his uncle went over the bucket he didn't want to change the name. Out of respect."

I finished my own beer and contributed to the tower of cans. The other staff had gone upstairs to the *karaoke* place but they'd drunk a lot of Bud and Kirin beforehand and the tower was growing high.

"I wonder," I said, "if the words mean 'when the dream is over'?"

Nori took a long drag on his cigarette. "I don't think they do," he finally said. "And besides, the dream had only just begun . . . . The uncle was smart and he built *Yume no ato* to attract foreigners as well as Japanese and it's done really well, as you can see." His eyes brightened. *"We're going great guns."*

Mr Onishi's telephone began to ring from the back of the restaurant, where he was still working. We heard him answer.

"The first line," I said, "is 'Ah! Summer grasses,' right?"

Nori seemed to be weighing this, then blurted out, *"Yume no ato* means . . . it means what's left over after a dream."

Mr Onishi's voice could be heard faintly. I surveyed the shaky tower, the ashtrays, the skeletons of fish beached on the sides of our empty plates.

"Leftovers," I said, ironically.

"There's another word."

"What about vestige? No? Remnant?"

Nori stubbed out his cigarette like a game-show panelist pressing a buzzer. *"Remnant!"* he cried, *"your choice is absolutely correct, for five thousand dollars and a dream home!"* Suddenly he grew calm, thoughtful. "So many foreign words sound alike," he mused. "There's a famous Dutch painter with that name."

"You mean Rembrandt?" I said.

"That's him. A bank here in Umeda just bought a Remnant for nine hundred million yen."

"Yume no ato," I said, "must mean 'the remnant of dreams.'"

Nori furrowed his brow, then nodded.

"Funny name for a restaurant," I said. "You like game shows?"

As if in a fresh wind the paper *noren* in the doorway behind the sushi bar blew open and a haggard phantom came in. Mr Onishi. He seemed to look right through us. Nori suggested we clean up and leave. We began to pile the chopsticks and empty plates onto a tray. I glanced up and saw Mr Onishi beckoning Nori.

"Please go examine the guest toilet," Nori told me.

The guest washroom was immaculate—I'd cleaned it myself two hours before—but I spent a few minutes checking it again so Nori and Mr Onishi would know I was thorough. For the second time that night I was intrigued by a notice in the stall, pencilled on the back of an old menu and taped to the door—

TO ALL FOREIGNERS:
OUR TUBES ARE IN ILL REPAIR, PLEASE
DO NOT THROW YOUR PEEPERS
IN THE TOILET.

When I came out of the washroom Mr Onishi was gone. "The boss looks awful," I whispered to Nori, my smile forced. "When he was on the phone before—maybe a guest was calling to complain about the new waiter, eh?"

"Possibly," Nori said, "but more likely it was a banker."

"What, at this time of night?"

Nori shrugged. "The elder folks, I told you, they're working late. And early, too—there was a banker here first thing this morning to talk at Mr Onishi."

"Bankers," I scoffed, shaking my head. "Not trouble, I hope . . . ."

Nori laughed abruptly. Arm tensed karate-style he approached the tower of cans.

III. The Kermess

KAMPAI!

A month has gone past and the whole staff, *gaijin-san* included, are relaxing after a manic Saturday night in the *Yume no ato*. August in Ōsaka: with other waiters and students and salarymen we sit in a beer garden under the full moon above twenty-two storeys of department store merchandise, imported clothing and cologne and books and records, Japanese-made electronics, wedding supplies, Persian carpets and French cigarettes and aquariums full of swordfish and coral and casino-pink sand from the Arabian Sea, appliances and applique, blue-china chopstick-holders computers patio-furniture coffee-shops chefs and friendly clerks and full-colour reproductions of well-known Western portraits, etchings, sketches, sculptures, landscapes that Japanese banks are buying like real estate and bringing back to Ōsaka, anything, anything at all, SPEND AND IT SHALL BE GIVEN, endless armies of customers and ah, summer tourists billowing like grain through the grounds of Ōsaka's most famous department store. SURELY, quoth the televangelist from the multitudinous screens, SURELY THE PEOPLE IS GRASS.

(For a moment the tables shudder as a tremour ripples through toxic earth under the Bargain Basement, and passes.)

KAMPAI! Western rock and roll music blasts from hidden speakers. In a few minutes the *O-bon* fireworks are due to start and we've got the best seats in the house. The plastic table sags and may soon buckle as another round of draft materializes and is swiftly distributed. A toast to this, a toast to that, *Kampai,*

KAMPAI, every time we lift our steins to take a drink, someone is proposing another toast: in a rare gesture Komatsu toasts the wait-staff (Akiburo and Johnnie and Michiko and me) because (this in English) we were really on the balls tonight and made no errors at all. *Kampai!* Akiburo toasts Komatsu and Mr Oh and second chef Miyoshi in return, presumably for turning out so much good food on such a busy night and making it all look easy. *Kampai!* Mr Oh raises his glass of ice-coffee in thanks while second chef Miyoshi, drunk and expansive, in a rare good mood, toasts Nori for not smacking his head in the storeroom when he went back for extra soy sauce, *KAMPAI*, (this translated by the delighted Nori, who immediately hefts his stein and decrees a toast to Michiko, the waitress, simply because he's mad about her and isn't it lucky she doesn't speak English?)

The blushing Michiko lifts her heavy stein with soft plump hands and meekly suggests, in Japanese, that it might be possible, perhaps, to maybe if it isn't too much trouble drink a toast to our skillful bartender, Johnnie Walker, without whom we would hardly have survived the night, it seems to me, after all, or maybe we might have? *Kampai! Kampai!* The flesh of Johnnie's ear lobe reddens around his pearl stud. He smirks and belts back another slug of whiskey.

"To Onishi-San," he says in English. "To *Yume no ato*." And he quickly adds some other remark in harsh, staccato Japanese.

"*KAMPAI!*" I holler, hoisting my stein triumphantly so that beer froths up and sloshes over the lip of the glass. But no one else has followed suit. They are all gazing without expression at the table or into their drinks. Johnnie Walker's head hangs lowest, his features hidden.

Komatsu glances at his watch and predicts that the fireworks will start in thirty seconds.

I turn to Nori. "Did I do something wrong?"

Miyoshi and Mr Oh both snap something at him. I can't make out a word.

"Well, not at all," says Nori, softly, "I guess people just don't feel like talking about work after a busy night."

I purse my lips. "I have the feeling you're not being completely honest with me."

"Of course I'm not!" Nori protests, and I wonder if we've understood each other.

At that moment the fireworks start. Everyone at our table looks up, relieved. "*O-bon*," Nori says to me, relaxed again.

"Tonight the ancestors return." Flippantly he rolls his eyes, or only seems to—I can't be sure because his coke-bottle lenses reflect the moonlight and the fierce red glare of the first rockets. One after another they arc up out of the dark expanse of Nagai Park, miles to the north, then slow down and pause at their zenith and explode in corollas of violet, emerald, coral, cream, apricot and indigo. *Hanabi*, they call them in Japanese: fire-flowers. The steins are raised again, glasses rammed together, toasts made and spirits drawn skyward by the aerial barrage.

My flat is somewhere down there on the far side of Nagai Park and now I picture a defective missile veering off course and buzzing my neighbourhood, terrifying the old folks, plunging with a shriek like an air-raid siren through the roof of my flat . . . .

Nori grabs my arm with steely fingers. "Steve-san, listen—do you hear what I hear?" I'm still concentrating on the look and sound of the exploding flowers, but suddenly I pick it out: the bouncy unmistakable opening bars of "Like a Virgin."

"It's the Madonna!"

"I hear it, Nori."

He lumbers to his feet. "You want to dance? Hey, get up! Come off it!"

Michiko and Johnnie Walker are already up beside the table, strobe-lit by the fireworks, shaking themselves to the beat, Michiko with a timid, tentative look and Johnnie with self-conscious abandon. The older staff sit motionless and watch the exploding rockets. Nori glances at them, at Michiko, at me, and I can tell he doesn't want to lose her. As she dances her small hands seem to catch and juggle the light.

"Life is so curt," he pleads. "You only lived once!" He gives me a half-smile, a sly wink, and I'm no longer sure he doesn't know exactly what he's saying.

KAMPAI! Nori hauls me to my feet and heaves me from the table in a blind teetering polka, out towards Johnnie and Michiko, his big boorish feet beating a mad tattoo on my toes. Komatsu and Mr Oh, the elders in the crowd, link arms and start keening some old Japanese song. Steins raised they sway together to a stately rhythm much slower than Madonna's, their voices rolling mournfully over the antique minors and archaic words. The rockets keep exploding. Their sound takes on a rhythm which seems to fall between the beats of the opposing songs—then as I watch, one of the rockets fails to burst. Like a falling star it streaks earthward in silence and disappears over the city.

IV. Guernica

I woke early the next morning with a headache and a burning stomach. I'd been dreaming. I dreamed Michiko had come home with me to my flat and we stood together hand-in-hand on the threshold, staring in at a gutted interior. The guilty rocket, however, had not actually exploded—it was resting in perfect condition, very comfortably, on an unburnt, freshly-made *futon* in the centre of the room.

Michiko took me by the hand and led me into the ruin. When the smoke began to drown me she covered my mouth with her own. Her breath was clean and renewing as wind off an early-morning sea and when she pulled away the smell of burning was gone. She removed her flowered kimono and stood naked before me. The nipples of her firm small breasts were now the accusing eyes of a seduced and betrayed woman—then I was naked too, and utterly absolved, and we were lying side by side amid the acrid wreckage by the futon. She climbed atop me and took me inside her, slowly, making small articulate sighs and rolling her head back and forth so her dark bangs rippled like a midnight waterfall across my nipples, and the blue-black hair was curved as space-time and full of sparks like the Milky Way, which in the Japanese tongue is called *ama no gawa*, the river of heaven.

I wanted to come, to fill the gathering space inside her, and I wanted to run my tongue down the soft pale line of hair from her breasts to her belly and on up the wooded mound of Venus and lick the nectar from her tender orchid, as the Japanese poets say, but then it came to me that Nori had meant to tell me something important—about Michiko? About a poem? Or was there something I'd asked him that he hadn't answered?

Summer grasses .... Something left over after dreams ....
What a stupid time to be thinking about poetry.

I woke embarrassed but with a feeling of desperate tenderness for Michiko, to whom I'd hardly ever spoken and who had inspired, I thought, no more than a generic interest on my part. It was like missing a lover who'd slept beside me all night and had just left and gone home before I woke ....

Well, I reflected, a dream like that was better than the waitering nightmares I'd had all the time till recently, and still woke from now and then. Usually I'd enter the restaurant and be told I was two hours late and none of the other wait-staff had shown up and the restaurant was full and we were booked solid till midnight. Other times I would realize I'd forgotten a couple or threesome who'd been seated two hours ago in the back corner of the second room and would they believe now it was just an honest mistake and I'd really been busy and meaning to get to them all along? Sometimes they were the Cruikshanks, and sometimes Mr Sato who (Nori had told me) was a professor at the University in Kyōto but had been demoted and now taught primary kids in Nagai, and that was why he drank so much and was so cold and pedantic when he spoke to you. In fact the unrequited dream-diners could be just about anyone, because the summer had been busy and now I was serving both foreigners and Japanese alike.

It had been the busiest summer in years, Komatsu said, and we were attracting more tourists than ever before—so why the visible anxiety whenever talk after-hours came round to the restaurant? Mr Onishi did not look like a man with a flourishing business. Perhaps he was ill and everyone was worried? I'd been reading articles lately about the soaring incidence of cancer in Japan, the spread of big business and factories into the countryside, toxins in the soil, polluted water, poisonous seafood . . . .

"I think you'd better level with me," I told Nori the night of my dream.

Miyoshi was standing by the walk-in, reading the *Sangyo Keizai*, and Komatsu was behind the steam table chopping onion. But I had the feeling they were listening to us, and so did Nori.

"*Not here,*" he whispered.

"Ah, such good news," growled Miyoshi, lowering his paper with an unpleasant smile. Since he hardly ever spoke English I knew the remark was aimed for me. "Such good news about the yen!"

Nori shook his head. "For some the war has never ended."

"*Nihon ichiban!*" Miyoshi cried. "Japan is number one!"

"And he wasn't even born till after," Nori grumbled. "I don't understand."

"Maybe we should talk somewhere else," I said.

Nori nodded, but Komatsu set down his knife and said quickly, "No. It's all right. Steve-san is part of the restaurant now—we should tell him the truth." Eyes pink and glistening, he walked out from behind the steam table and pulled the newspaper from Miyoshi's hands.

Miyoshi scowled, did an about-face and marched into the fridge.

"Look at this," Komatsu sniffled, handing me the paper.

"You know I can't read Japanese."

"Of course. Don't read, just look—the pictures."

In the lower right-hand corner of the front page several well-known pieces of European art were reproduced in hazy black and white. One was a Rousseau, the second a Gauguin, the third a Brueghel. I couldn't read the caption beneath but I could make out the name of a prominent Ōsaka bank, written in *romaji*.

"And Van Gogh," Komatsu said, frowning. "I hear they have just bought another costly painting by Van Gogh—so many paintings they are buying and bringing to Japan."

We could hear Miyoshi in the fridge, muttering to himself, furiously shifting things around.

"They're buying everything in their sights," Nori said, his usual gusto tangibly absent.

I told them I knew a bit about these purchases, but didn't see what they had to do with us.

"Well," Komatsu started, "they need some place to put these paintings . . . ." His voice tapered off on the last words. I sensed I was being counted on, in customary Japanese fashion, to finish the sentence mentally so that everyone would be spared embarrassment.

"Chagall, too," Komatsu resumed, "and Rembrandt and Picasso." *Big-asshole*, it sounded like, but I knew who he meant. "Costly things . . . they need to find a place to put them all . . . ."

"Like an art gallery," I said.

Komatsu rubbed his eyes with a corner of his apron. "I'm afraid so."

It had been just like Dallas, Nori groaned, describing how the bank had first made polite offers to the dozen businesses operating in the block where they meant to build, and most were politely accepted. But several proprietors (including Mr Onishi and the owner of the Idaho Caffeine Palace, a large coffee shop dating to the late forties) had refused to consider them. Secretly the bank made more attractive offers, then a final offer which the firm's representative begged Mr Onishi to accept, because if a negotiated settlement proved necessary then payment would revert to the level of the initial sum—or, conceivably, somewhat less.

Mr Onishi had ignored the bank's covert threats and a negotiated settlement proved necessary. Unfortunately it did not involve negotiation. The bank produced lawyers who showed that actual title to the land had belonged to the bank till the end of the war and they argued that the transfer of deeds had been improperly handled by the over-worked civil authorities of the time.

The young lawyers (I could just hear them) moved further that since the art gallery would be a public facility of great benefit to all citizens of the prefecture and would attract hundreds of thousands of foreigners to Ōsaka, it was in effect a civic institution, albeit privately owned, and the city should urge Mr Onishi to come to terms.

"The court is asking Mr Onishi to accept," Nori said, "but he just says no."

Nihon ichiban, we heard faintly from the fridge.

Komatsu took the newspaper from me and walked back around the steam table. He began to giggle, like a bad comedian setting up a punchline. "They're going to tear us down," he said, laughing openly. "Soon!"

Nori was chuckling, too, as the Japanese often will when speaking of their own misfortunes. Komatsu was laughing harder than I'd ever seen him, so I knew he really must be upset.

I paused respectfully. "Listen, I'm really sorry to hear this."

Komatsu roared with laughter. Nori continued to cackle. I asked them if they knew when these things were going to happen.

"There's no time like presently," Nori said, slapping me on the shoulder a bit harder than he needed to. "Come on, it's a busy night tonight, we'd better get happening."

"Please take coffee now to Mr Oh-San," Komatsu giggled.

Miyoshi was still marching around in the fridge.

V. The Starry Night

September in Ōsaka is just as hot as July or August and this year it was worse. Though many of the tourists were gone, the *Yume no ato* was busier than ever—Mr Onishi's struggle with the bank was now common knowledge, so old customers came often to show their support and the sushi bar was crowded with curious locals. Meanwhile enrollment was picking up at the school and I had to cut back on my hours as a waiter.

Mr Onishi was upset when I told him, but since I knew now of the epic struggle he was waging each day in the courts (Nori got the details from Komatsu and passed them on to me) I found it hard to feel angry in return. The boss, after all, was showing tremendous pluck. Sure, he was of another generation, a hardy breed of industrious survivors, and as a child he would have absorbed with his mother's milk the bracing formula of *bushido*, but this was valour way beyond the call of duty. He was giving Japan's second biggest bank the fight of its life. Already the original date for demolition was three weeks in arrears . . . .

I heard that after receiving the court's final decision, Mr Onishi sighed and said, "*Yappari, nah*. It is as I expected. They will build a museum and a new country and fill both with foreign things."

The demolition was set for the last of September and the *Yume no ato* was to close a week before.

On the last night, a Saturday, the dining room was booked solid from five till closing with regular customers, both Japanese and foreign. We assembled by the bar a few minutes before five to wait for Mr Onishi and at five sharp he emerged from his office. He marched up to us, a menu tucked under one arm like a swagger stick, then briefed us in a formal and highly nuanced Japanese that I could not follow—though the general tenor of his speech was easy enough to guess. Or was it? Sometimes I wondered if I'd ever done more than misimagine what these people felt and believed.

A current of laughter rippled through the staff and Nori nudged me appreciatively, forgetting for a moment I did not understand.

Mr Onishi dismissed us and we hurried off to complete our preparations as he climbed the stairs and opened the door. A long shaft of dirty sunlight pierced the cool gloom, and a few seconds later our guests began to descend, bringing with them the hot muggy air of the street.

"Meet me in the back," I told Nori.

We stood in the kitchen on either side of the open rice machine, slowly filling it with the contents of two clay cooking pots. Thick billows of steam rose between us and Nori's face was intermittently clouded, his eyes nacreous, indistinct, like a man under a foot of water.

"So what did Onishi-San say," I asked, scooping the soft, sweet-smelling grains into the machine.

"He was apologizing."

"Apologizing," I said.

"Sure. He was apologizing for letting the bank close the *Yume no ato*. He says it's all on his shoulders. He feels responsible for the jobs we will lose. He says he is sorry because he has felled us."

The steam was thinning and I could see Nori clearly. His big face was pink and sweating.

"He says his uncle was a soldier in the old navy and after the war he built this restaurant with his own two hands. So he says that by losing the restaurant he has felled his uncle, too."

"But isn't his uncle dead?"

Nori put down his pot and gave me a faintly disappointed look.

"For many years. But so the old people believe—they can fell the dead as well as the breathing. Like being caught *between the devil and the deep blue sea, neh?*"

I nodded and stared into the rice cooker, its churning steam spectral and hypnotic.

"I feel sorry for him," I said.

"So it is, all the while. The big fish eat the little."

There was a harsh grating sound as he scraped rice from the bottom of his pot.

It was the busiest night of the summer but the customers were gentle and undemanding and the atmosphere, as at a funeral reception, was chastened and sadly festive and thick with solidarity. The foreigners left huge tips and Mr Oh grunted graciously whenever I freshened his coffee. It fell to Michiko to serve the disagreeable Mr Sato for the last time and though he usually deplored the grammar and fashions of her generation, he was tolerant tonight and even remarked at one point on her resemblance to his own daughter. The Cruikshanks were among the last to arrive. When they left, just before closing, Mrs Cruikshank said she trusted I wouldn't have to go home to Germany just yet and surely with my good English I could land another job . . . .

The last guests, our oldest customers, intoxicated and teary-eyed, staggered up the stairs around midnight and we dragged together a few tables and sank down for a last meal. Mat and Nori and second chef Miyoshi filed from the kitchen bearing platters of steaming rice and salmon teriyaki; at Mr Onishi's behest Johnnie Walker opened the bar to all staff. And now, though I'd felt more and more a part of things over the last months, I sensed my saddened colleagues closing ranks, retreating into dialect, resorting to nuance, idiom and silence, a

semaphore of glances and tics and nods. Nori loomed on the far
side of the table with Michiko beside him. They were talking
quietly. In the shadows by their chair-legs I could see two hands
linked, like sinuous sea-creatures, twined and mating in the deep.

Johnnie had finished the last of the Johnnie Walker Red
and was now working on a bottle of Old Granddad. Mr Oh was
not drinking. He sat mutely, his agile hands wrapped around one
beer tin after another, crushing them and laying them to rest
among the plates and ashtrays. Komatsu and second chef
Miyoshi were smoking side by side, eyes half-closed, meditating
on the fumes that rose and spead outward over their heads.

Mr Onishi, I suppose, was in his office. At one-thirty he
came out and told everyone it was time to leave. There were
some last half-hearted toasts and deep bowing and then we all
stumbled upstairs and outside. The night air was cool and fresh.
We looked, I thought, like a beaten rabble. As if wounded, Nori
tottered over and proffered a scrap of paper the size of a cheque
or phone bill. "Here," he said, his speech slurred, "I almost
forgot. That poem they called the restaurant for . . . Remember?"

He and Michiko swayed before me, their features painted
a smooth flawless amber by the gentle light of the doorway.
Behind them the brooding profiles of bank and office towers and
beyond those in long swirling ranks the constellations of early
autumn.

I took the slip of paper and held it to the light:

Ah! summer grass/this group of warriors'/
remnant of dream (this poem by Matsuo
Bashō, lived same time as Shakespeare)

So long and take care of yourself. Nori.

He shrugged when I thanked him. "We had to study it back
then. A real pin in the ass."

"Drop by the school sometime," I said. "Please, both of
you . . . ."

I knew they wouldn't come.

Gradually the rest straggled off alone or in pairs and I
headed for the station. Waves of heat rising from sewers,
smokestacks and vacant pavement set the stars quivering, like the
scales of small fish in dark water. In the late-summer heat of
1945, after the surrender, Japanese armies trudged back through
the remains of Ōsaka and there was little where these buildings

now stood but rubble, refuse, dust and blowing ash. A stubble of fireweed and wildflowers bloomed on the ruins, rippled in the hot wind. There was nothing for the children to eat. I heard these things from a neighbour, a toothless old man who had been a soldier at that time, and I heard other things as well: how faceless Japan had been, how for a while it had been a different place—beaten, levelled and overrun, unable to rise—waiting for the first touch of a foreign hand. For a sea change, into something rich, and strange.

On the train to Nagai I had a half-hour to experiment with the words on Nori's farewell card. By the time I got home I had the translation done, though the line *"yume no ato"* was still troublesome and I found it hard to focus on the page.

> *Ah, summer grass!*
> *All that survives*
> *Of the warrior's dream . . . .*

I keep thinking I should send a copy to Nori.

Nerves

I thought you might be celebrating
something, but it was just that you couldn't
bring yourself to tell me
until the third drink before lunch . . .
This morning it was your turn . . .
Your company employs a shrink. They
give you mandatory, yearly check-ups.
They like to determine how happy you really
are, what your work is doing to you.

No sweat of course. Some guys
like it. It gives them a chance
to test their wits, not really lie,
just prove to themselves they're
healthy, still have control of themselves,
can outwit the sweet smiling little expert.

Lately though, things haven't
been going well for you. You're not
sure, but you think they don't like
you downtown, aren't really satisfied.
The new bunch, you think, sort of feels
you might not have what it takes after all.
So all this doctor crap is painful. Dangerous.
Of course, you shouldn't be telling
all this to an outsider, a client. Your
company feels that its medical program
is a positive benefit, something that
helps them recruit . . . It's embarrassing.
Ridiculous.

So we forget about it.
Tucked into your slope shouldered suit, you
give the ruffled waitress with the little cap
your most fragile, intelligent smile. We
order Burgundy, prime rib, fall into
the mood of the brassplated, oak
panelled room, find ourselves pretending
we're dining in the nineteenth century.

Oasis

In gray toned suits
At their separate tables
One sits hunched
Turning the local paper
Inside out.
One with dark eyes
Stares into the dark outside.
One peels open
A spreadsheet
And eats.

The Guided Tour of 7th Avenue

Leonard S. Bernstein

I HAVE AGREED to take you to the garment center, and we begin at 7th Avenue and 38th Street where the cutters are milling around at lunchtime. I approach one of the cutters who has been here a few hundred years and say, "How's business, Benny?"

"Terrible," he answers. "Never in my entire life have I seen it as bad as this."

That means business is O.K.

You ask me how terrible can mean O.K. and I consider sending you to Berlitz for a course in a foreign language.

Clack-clacking down the street come the dress racks and the dollies pushed by the blacks and Hispanics. And you ask, "How come only blacks and Hispanics—thirty years ago there were only blacks and Hispanics!—where are the whites?" And I answer that thirty years is not much time in the garment center.

And then you notice that the street signs read FASHION AVENUE, and you ask, "Why is it still called 7th Avenue when that is no longer its name?" And I answer that yes, the name was changed but change does not take hold easily here.

You don't believe me. You ask *why* is there no change? You mention Park Avenue and Madison Avenue—the breathtaking skyscrapers, the dazzling shop windows. "And here, pushcarts?" you ask.

I consider how to explain. It is difficult to explain 7th Avenue to an outsider. How to explain civilization standing still?

What the hell, I try. "You want to know why there is no change? Because it takes imaginative people to effect change, and all of them have left for the South. Do you know how long it takes to get twelve cartons of fabric up to the fifteenth floor of a garment center loft? In that amount of time a manufacturer in Georgia can sew enough dresses to clothe a medium-sized city."

You are astounded. You've heard of Bill Blass and Halston. You thought they were here. Where are they? Yes they are here, as the Taj Mahal is in India, but India is not the Taj Mahal.

You are incredulous. I don't know what to do with you. I decide to show you one of our modern industrial achievements, and we enter 257 West 36th Street where Meyer Kaufman runs forty machines making children's underwear.

I tell you that Meyer runs a pretty smart operation and you tell me that everybody smart is in Georgia. I tell you it's good that you are listening, but there remain two reasons why anyone could be left: because they make highly intricate handsewn operations and must hire the old-time workers who still remember how to stitch a buttonhole or turn a collar, or because they themselves are too old to move to Atlanta. Meyer is sixty-three.

How does Meyer compete, you want to know. I am pleased that you are asking intelligent questions, or at least questions that I am able to answer.

"On price and value Meyer cannot compete against the conveyer belts and automation of the South, but there remains customer service. There are a lot of retail stores in New York like Korvettes and Alexander's, and sometimes these stores can't wait for a shipment of underwear from Alabama. Meyer can get fifty dozen over to them on a handtruck within a few hours."

I tell Meyer I am showing my friend the garment center and he smiles, "So what are you doing *here*? This is ancient history."

Meyer is a small man with a narrow, pointed face and thin wisps of brown-grey hair wandering over his forehead. He is nervous, and makes quick, mouse-like movements, as though he fences jewelry and the cops are closing in. He welcomes us but says he only has a half hour. The union agent is coming up at 3:30—they have a labor dispute to settle. Meyer laughs. "A half million garment workers in Alabama and Georgia. No unions and no labor disputes. Only conveyer belts and laser beams."

We walk out into the shop. There are two long rows of sewing machines with operators facing each other, mostly Hispanic in bright flowered dresses, their hands and fingers fluttering over the garments.

"Piece work," Meyer says for the benefit of our guest. "They get paid for how much they produce."

Alongside the rows of sewing machines, is a long wooden cutting table with about nine inches of fabric piled up. The cutter says hello and we shake hands. The index finger is missing—not uncommon. Left-handed cutter, I think. The cutters don't lose fingers from the hand that guides the machine. It's the other hand; the one that holds the fabric in place in front of the spinning blade. The hand that guides the machine grips a wooden handle *behind* the machine, always out of danger. The other hand is brought around in front of the blade and presses down the nine inches of fabric. The blade spins forward into the V-shaped opening formed by the thumb and index finger. In an accident it is usually the index finger. There's an old joke that if you went to visit Local 12—the cutter's local, and didn't know where you were, you could find out quickly just by shaking hands.

There's a scissors on the table and I grip it just to confirm my notion. It's a left-handed scissors and I think back twenty years to when I first arrived in the garment center and didn't believe there were left-handed scissors.

Meyer says to the cutter, "Kroloff is coming up at 3:30. I'll send Mary in to let you know when he arrives. Then I'll walk out here with him, both of us together."

The cutter returns to work and Meyer starts to explain—stops—starts again. Is clearly pained. "We have to set things up when Kroloff arrives. Sam can't see ten feet in front of him. Take a look at his glasses. Madame Curie didn't have lenses like that when she discovered radium. Sam can see up close; he can see the pencil marks that guide the cutting knife, but he can't see far. If Kroloff finds out, Sam is retired on the spot. So we have a warning system. We identify Kroloff before he gets close enough to notice the problem. That way Sam gives him a big hello and Kroloff doesn't realize that Sam can't see who he is saying hello to. Today I'll walk in with Kroloff. Sam will vaguely make out two figures and right away he'll shout hello Kroloff. When we get closer he'll know because Kroloff is six inches taller than me and Sam can make that out, so he'll reach out to shake hands with the right person."

"But the cutting blade . . . surely. And he's lost one finger already."

Meyer sighs, as though why am I bothering him with something he already knows. "Sam lost his finger thirty years ago when he could see perfectly. Thank God it didn't happen here. You know, they don't lose fingers because they can't see. They lose them because they think they're hot-shots and don't need to drop the guard in front of the blade."

We're back in Meyer's office. The phone rings. We turn to leave. Meyer raises his hand to say wait. Kroloff is delayed. "Sit down," Meyer says, "we can talk a while."

Meyer is tired. His eyes are bloodshot from the dust of threads and cotton shavings. He slumps in his high-backed chair, behind him a window, framed with the thin silver tape of an alarm system.

"Just as well. It's about Sam. I can't pay him the standard cutter's hourly wage any longer. Kroloff says I have to. The union contract . . . something like that. What do I care? The thing is, Sam is good but of course he can't see. I have to give him a helper for anything over ten feet. The helper always has to be around, and of course he gets paid. If you add the helper to Sam their combined wages make Sam the best paid cutter in New York."

"Why can't you explain this to Kroloff?"

"Because if Kroloff suspects anything about Sam's eyesight he'll stop him from working. Maybe he's right—how do I know? The union has too much at stake. If it would ever be discovered that the union had a cutter on the job with 200/200 vision it would make the newspapers. And can you imagine what they would say about the finger? Kroloff would get indicted. I would get indicted. There would be a whole investigation. You know how those things are. The newspapers get it, it will sound like the garment center uses only blind cutters."

"What does Sam say?" I ask.

"Sam says pay him less and don't let Kroloff near him. What else is Sam going to say? This is the only company on the face of the earth where he could work."

"It's you and Sam against Kroloff," I mutter, thinking this defies any labor problem I've ever heard of. "What about letting Sam go and hiring a competent cutter? Sam's old . . . he can't see . . . ."

Meyer nods, conceding the sense of that. "Sam's old—he can't see. I'm old—I can't see so good either. A new cutter? What will I say to him after all these years?"

At that moment a young lady—slightly agitated—rushes into Meyer's office. "Kroloff is in the shop, talking to Sam," she says.

"How did he get in?" asks Meyer, but he doesn't wait for an answer.

We sit there quietly, not knowing whether to stay or to leave. In five minutes Meyer is back in the office. "Kroloff is walking around the shop, talking to the operators. He'll stop in my office in a little while and I'll introduce you."

"Shouldn't we leave now?" I ask.

"You wanted to show your friend the garment center—this is the garment center. Wouldn't you like to meet a business agent?"

Within fifteen minutes Kroloff walks into the office, a large bear of a man, enormous hands—meat-packing hands. Could have been a wrestler, maybe.

Nice smile though—hellos all around.

"So how do things look, Kroloff? You think I'm ready for IBM?"

"Not bad Meyer; you run a good shop."

"So maybe one year I'll make a profit?"

"A few things, Meyer," and Kroloff turns toward us.

"Friends," Meyer says. "Say whatever you want."

"Josie claims that you have her sewing bottom ruffles and she can't make out. She says you took her off hemstitched sleeves and put her on ruffles, and she wants to know when she can go back on sleeves."

"She can go back when the stores want hemstitched sleeves. Right now they want ruffles. Am I responsible for the style changes in America?"

"What can I tell her, Meyer?"

"Tell her as soon as we have hemstitched sleeves again she will be the first one to get them. I don't know what else to tell her."

Kroloff jots something down.

"You remember, Kroloff, in the old days we argued over the minimum wage. We argued over piece work prices and Saturday work and time-and-a-half for overtime. We argued over *something*. Now we argue over hemstitched sleeves which went out of style five years ago. You remember you used to holler about the price of groceries and how could workers survive on what we were paying? We argued that the Southern factories were paying half as much as we were, and how could we compete with that.

"Two o'clock in the morning—we fought till two o'clock in the morning! Name calling. Everything. No time-outs. You once marched out of this office and said the shop was on strike. We said go ahead, we're closing down the business anyway."

"That was a long time ago," Kroloff says.

"Now we fight over whether Josie works on bottom ruffles. In the South nobody works on bottom ruffles—they do it with an automatic machine. The automatic machine doesn't know the difference between bottom ruffles and hemstitched sleeves. In the South they have machines that cut automatically. A laser beam follows the pencil marks. Here we fight over whether Sam should have an assistant."

Kroloff smiles and nods. He stands, and I think, "The Man with the Hoe." *Bowed by the weight of centuries.*

"What about Sam," he asks. "You think maybe he'll retire?"

"I think maybe I'll retire," says Meyer.

Kroloff says goodbye, turns toward the door. "You know, Meyer," he says, "we are taking a terrible chance."

It is four o'clock in the afternoon and we are standing at 7th Avenue and 36th Street. The operators are emptying out of the buildings, chattering and laughing, speaking rapidly with their hands. The cutters follow, moving more slowly—a caravan of grey cardigan sweaters—each one complaining that nowhere in the world is there a job as bad as his.

I ask if you know what that means, and you answer that means his job is O.K.

We look for Bill Blass—he's not here. He must be uptown having cocktails at The Four Seasons. We look for Yves St. Laurent. He must be in Paris, negotiating to embroider his initials on a new line of scarves. We look for the fashion models, but this is 7th Avenue and 36th Street—there are no fashion models here.

I turn to see if you are disappointed, and think maybe I should have done this differently.

"This is the garment center," I tell you, not knowing what else to say.

We walk another block or two. The sun is setting, casting shadows over the buildings and making them frown, the same way they have for as many years as anyone can remember.

Merrill Lynch

Young scion
of a food chain family
collar and feet too large
sits in a meeting about a new stock offering
Mauna Loa Macadamia Nuts
He raises his hand:
"Shouldn't we be concerned about the amount of cholesterol
        in each nut?"
Everyone laughs.

I am in a meeting
more sales training for young brokers.
A manager without an office
is visiting ours.
He is speaking about motivation:
"Unless you know what you want and go for it,
        you might as well blow your brains out."
He has no office to manage
and his wife has left him.

I am walking down the hall
thinking about lunch and how much I hate nylons.
My big ticket has been noticed
My manager's been friendly toward me all morning
He's visiting the two big hitters in a corner office
Some male bonding, I think.

He motions for me to drop by
this is quite an honor.
I walk in and say hello.
(The usual greeting is more casual)
Four smiling white men turn to me
nails polished, hair trim

The manager without an office
bares his teeth
"Hey Emily, nice ticket. Where are your knee pads?"
Judging from the laughter
this is quite funny.

I am on hold
watching the quotron blink, office babel buffeting me.
A lull, then cries of disbelief
Someone runs heavily past my cubicle
The quotron news service explains in one line
"The space shuttle Challenger exploded 71 seconds after takeoff."
Then some news about coffee prices.

I hang up. Find an office with a television
Usually it scrolls numbers in black and white
now showing, over and over
an arcing smoke trail
then a lopsided chrysanthemum.
The sound is an announcer's grim voice I can't understand
Above the drone, in the tiny dark room, several brokers
        are already trying to outdo each other.
"I'll bet it was the teacher! Pushed the wrong button!"
I can't hear the announcer so I tell them to shut up.

One turns to me:
"Lighten up, Emily."

Lindsay Hill

Taking Up Serpents (Chicago Board of Trade)

The frenzy has the heat of religious faith
But not in the name of Christ as the darkly blessed
Hold the mouths of snakes to their bare chests
Not as the dry hot flicking tongues are prayers
This laying on of hands pretends no healing
This speaking in tongues no dialogue with Grace
Without ritual without faith
This is the spiralling center where coils lock closed
And the numbing ethers of dailiness flow pure to the heart

Matins

The night you didn't know me
was otherwise like other nights;
no lack of car lights, sirens, horns,
singles and couples homing from bars.
In the hospital hallways voices narrowed and widened,
like regions of deluge and drought.
I thought you'd always know me, like birds know south.
Not your eyes with nothing in them.
Not your words gone off their broken strands like beads.
The sky just after dawn was the simple color of paper.
Walking out I couldn't help but think,
how the morning was like countless mornings
when after doughnuts and coffee,
we watched the bond markets open.
But the morning was altered, as if time had somehow
turned away, like a planet tilting on its axis toward winter.
I went forward. I thought how the markets
were opening as I walked. How the private life empties
as the common life continues. I went forward because
the hours were still waiting. I spoke your name
into their long silence. I spoke your name and went forward
into their country of secrets.

M. *Dana Gioia*

The Man in the Open Doorway

This is the world in which he lives:
Four walls, a desk, a swivel chair,
A doorway with no door to close,
Vents to bring in air.

There are two well-marked calendars,
Some pencils, and a telephone
The women at the front desk answer
Leaving him alone.

There is a clock he hardly sees
Beside the window on the wall.
It moves in only one direction,
Never stops at all.

Outside the February wind
Scrapes up against the windowpane,
And a blue-green land is fading,
Scarred by streaks of rain.

The phones go off. The files are locked.
But the doorway still is lit at night
Like the tall window of a church
Bleached in winter light.

Sometimes the shadow of his hand
Falls from his desk onto the wall
And is the only thing that moves
Anywhere at all.

Or else he will drive back at night
To walk along the corridor
And, thinking of the day's success,
Trace his steps once more,

Then pause in a darkened stairway
Until the sounds of his steps have ceased
And stroke the wall as if it were
Some attendant beast.

Eastern Standard Time

Yesterday the clocks went back an hour,
and now, leaving work a little late,

I walk across the parking lot
where it's already dark and empty,

empty on a scale only the suburbs
could afford—thirty acres of smooth,

black asphalt, lined symmetrically by rows
of identical, bare-branched trees—tonight

more of an idea than a landscape,
a vast blueprint vandalized by autumn.

Shades of Callimachus, Coan ghosts of Philetas,
It is in your grove I would walk!

Instead I cross this familiar, stone-paved lot
feeling out of place, a Californian,

a stranger to the darker seasons,
walking through the end of an Eastern fall.

I have learned to tell
the changes that prefigure storms:

the heavy air, the circling wind
and graduate darkness, but still

each time the air goes through even these
accustomed changes, I grow uneasy.

Sudden storms, shifts in temperature, even snow
in midwinter still surprise me,

unable to feel at home in a landscape
so suddenly transformed.

Anxiety in Autumn! O Suburbs of Despair
where nothing but the weather ever changes!

Sometimes the saddest places in the world
are just the ordinary ones seen after hours.

Picture a department store at night
with the doors locked and lights turned off

or a beachhouse in the winter
dark and shuttered by the sea.

Walk through a stadium after the game
or even a parking lot everyone has left.

It's cold. The wind is blowing.
As far as I can see, there are leaves—

dry, brown, curling on themselves,
ankle-deep in places, and everywhere

sweeping across the numbered rows,
arranging and rearranging themselves,

some only to swirl up and fly away,
others to scratch along the asphalt.

They are alive! Swarming in movements
only they can understand.

And suddenly I realize the obvious:
that even this parking lot

was once a field. A field
sloping to the valley where now

the Interstate is running.
How much older they are, the leaves

just fallen
tracing out these shapes from memory.

Money

Money is a kind of poetry.
                                    —WALLACE STEVENS

Money, the long green,
cash, stash, rhino, jack
or just plain dough.

Chock it up, fork it over,
shell it out. Watch it
burn holes through pockets.

To be made of it! To have it
to burn! Greenbacks, double eagles,
megabucks and Ginnie Maes.

It greases the palm, feathers a nest,
holds heads above water,
makes both ends meet.

Money breeds money.
Gathering interest, compounding daily.
Always in circulation.

Money. You don't know where it's been,
but you put it where your mouth is.
And it talks.

When Money Doesn't Talk: Reflections on Business, Poetry, and Audience

M. Dana Gioia

PEOPLE SOMETIMES ASK me why I haven't written more poems about the business world. Confronted by this intimidatingly literal question, I am always a little uneasy. I try to answer in good faith, usually by muttering something about my conviction that while poetry is unavoidably rooted in autobiography, it must transcend the merely documentary or confessional. But surely there is another reason for my poetic reticence, a reason I find it uncomfortable to share with these curious interlocutors—most of them students or professors—because they might think me arrogant or judgmental.

If I have found it difficult to be frank in conversation, however, let me make my confession here in print. I have not written directly out of my experience as a businessman because the serious literary audience in America knows virtually nothing about the subject. This otherwise highly educated audience of writers, academics, and students, which constitute the only dependable readership left for contemporary poetry, is not only ignorant of business and finance but even of basic economics. This ignorance puts all imaginative writers who want to handle this subject at a grave disadvantage, but to the poet, it proves fatal.

Unlike a novelist or playwright, the poet cannot spend the necessary time and space to explain the rules, assumptions, indeed the very language of the commercial subculture he wishes to explore. For instance, in Louis Auchincloss' *The Embezzler*, the best novel I know about high finance, the author carefully sets up the background of his story by describing both the private and public codes of behavior on pre-Depression Wall Street. Only then can the uninitiated reader follow the complex psychological and moral narrative that unfolds. Likewise in David Mamet's Pulitzer Prize winning play, *Glengarry Glen Ross*, which examines the shady operations of a Chicago real estate boiler room, the dramatist spends most of his first act training the audience to understand the language and methods of his characters. (Even here I hesitated before using the term *boiler room*, since most literary readers will not know that it means a high-pressure, low-ethic sales scam.) Only after soaking the audience in this fast, vulgar speech can Mamet speed up the action to its violent climax. The poet trying to deal with similar material, however, has a nearly impossible task. The sheer weight of exposition threatens to sink his verse. Since his audience will probably not understand his subject without lengthy explanations, he must either reduce it to a vaguely atmospheric background or abstract it to a symbolic level so removed from the specifics that it loses all force and immediacy.

Here let me inject a personal experience. Several years ago a well known literary critic asked me what I did in business. I replied that I currently worked in mergers and acquisitions. He looked puzzled, and so I explained in simple terms what my job involved. He still appeared mystified, and so on a hunch I asked him if he knew what a corporate acquisition was. No, he confessed, he did not. I thought at first it was the particular term *acquisition* which confused him. Since there had been front-page articles in the press on various mergers and takeovers almost continually over the previous few years, I tried to use some of those famous cases as points of reference. But, no, he had never heard of *any* of them. In fact, this man of strong political opinions then remarked that on principle he never read any articles about business or the economy. His ignorance not only didn't bother him. He was visibly proud of it—as if this innocence of commercial and financial affairs signified a certain spiritual and ideological purity. That part of American life associated with business seemed either so unimportant or repulsive to him that he could safely dismiss it without investigation. Knowing about the world of money had nothing to do with his intellectual mission.

Not all literary people share this professor's deliberate insularity, but his position is not altogether unusual. It reflects an unfortunately common set of intellectual prejudices. These ingrained biases raise a further barrier to any poet who would write about the business world. Although the literary audience may not know much about business, it does have strong political preconceptions about the subject. Businesses, especially large corporations, are assumed to be sterile, repressive and morally suspect—if not actively evil. They represent the antithesis of the values serious literature is supposed to convey. Therefore, the only permissible attitudes for a poet are either sharp satire or prophetic denunciation—both of which must be conveyed in general or stereotypical terms since the audience lacks familiarity with any of the particulars. One sees these cardboard scenarios used almost interchangeably in both popular and high culture. The same assumptions appear on TV series like *Dallas* and *Dynasty* as in the poetry of Ferlinghetti or Ginsberg. Ignorance combines with political prejudice to produce poetry on the intellectual level of a soap opera.

If poetry's audience ignores business, certainly business professionals pay equally little attention to literature. A friend told me about one of her English composition students at Baruch College, a Russian-born accounting major who carried a copy of Pushkin in his coat pocket. "Pushkin is *my* poet," he told her forcefully. One certainly can tell he isn't a native New Yorker. The true American attitude was summed up recently by Robert McDowell in his essay, "Poetry and Audience." McDowell recounts talking with a land surveyor about the problems of the American poet in reaching an audience. Suddenly the man cut him off. "Yes," he said, "but poetry isn't what this country is about. Our thing is to make money. That's what we do."

Faced with these obstacles, is it any wonder that the American poets who worked in business usually wrote nothing about it? Wallace Stevens, T.S. Eliot, Richard Eberhart, James Dickey, A.R. Ammons, Richard Hugo, L.E. Sissman, David Ignatow, William Bronk and the others who spent all or part of their professional lives in business left virtually no record of their experiences.

Surely their collective silence is not entirely coincidental. Not all of them were as temperamentally reticent as Stevens or Eliot. There have been persistent forces in American intellectual life which make the subject an almost impossible one for poets to treat seriously. Such an assertion is not meant to imply there has ever been a *conscious* program to ignore or demean this area of the American experience in imaginative literature, but it does suggest that this silence is the inevitable result of ignorance and prejudice. As recent feminist and minority scholarship has demonstrated, censorship need not be conscious to be effective.

Unconscious self-censorship is the most potent means of all. Finally, it is important to state that the authors' disinclination to discuss their business experience in poetry does not invalidate the authenticity of what they did choose to write about. One only wishes they had translated more of their life experience into poetry and not less.

Years ago, as I puzzled over my own silence, I was shocked to discover that I had several predecessors—poets with whom I felt little else in common except an unwillingness to write directly about business life. I realized then that not only can one *write* in a tradition, one can also be *silent* in a tradition. I suppose feminists noticed this paradox long ago. In this respect, businessmen are slower learners.

This observation gradually changed my notion of poetic inspiration. Half of what a poet writes may be destiny, but surely the other half is choice. While a poet may not control the act of inspiration, he can select which inspirations are developed into finished work. The process of accepting, rejecting or reshaping the involuntary inspiration to fit the voluntary intentions of the artist may ultimately be so private that it appears unfathomable to an outsider. But certainly a crucial element is each author's set of assumptions about what his audience will understand or accept—intellectually, aesthetically, politically, morally, and eventually, if the author writes for publication, commercially.

The dialectic between the private moment of inspiration and the actual creation of art is too complex to be reduced to a predictive theory, but recognizing the existence of this subjective process is important to understanding the literature of any period, genre, or subculture. An adequate theory, however, must be dialectic and not simplistically deterministic. No genuine artist works passively before his audience. But there is a mutual influence between artist and audience—not all of it conscious. The author's assumptions about that audience's values and expectations help shape the tone, language, style, and subjects of even the most serious and non-commercial literature in ways of which the writer is not always aware.

While the distinction between inspiration and creation has broader implications for the poetic act—on the writing of political poetry, for instance—it does have specific relevance to a poet who works in a non-literary profession like business which the established audience for high culture views as either experientially alien or politically unacceptable. Faced with this dilemma, the businessman-poet must either direct most of his creative energy into bridging the gap between his personal experience and the audience's assumptions or else write about only those areas of his experience which authentically overlap with those of his audience. If he chooses the first course, he must systematically remythologize his world in a way which a skeptical audience can accept. (To give an example from a different milieu, notice how Constantine Cavafy consciously shaped his entire *oeuvre* into a secular mythology for the homosexual *demi-monde* of Alexandria and thereby made it universal.) In American poetry, however, every businessman-poet has taken the second course. None has been willing to choose the business world as the primary subject matter and transform it into something "rich and strange." At best, it has been touched around the edges. And why should it be otherwise? If the poet can do genuine work in another more acceptable vein, why should he struggle to write seriously about business when he knows that half his audience is indifferent, the other half hostile, and all of it uninformed?

I have written specifically about business life on only a few occasions, but I know that in ways I would never have initially expected my professional career has shaped the concerns of my poetry. Having spent much of my adult life working in a variety of business jobs from sales clerk to executive, I have written directly or indirectly about the people I have met—their hopes, fears, and values. As a poet, I have tried never to simplify or belittle these individuals, just as I have resisted romanticizing them. Finding the language and forms to manage this task has been difficult, since contemporary poetry provides few models. Searching out an effective style has been an on-going experiment.

I have tried to write truthfully about the actual daily lives people lead in America—even when the resulting subjects were ones that poets were not supposed to celebrate: suburban towns, airports, commuter trains, parking lots, even money. This decision—or was it, to use my own distinction, simply destiny?—has upset some reviewers. They have felt it was not only improper but immoral for me to approve of middle-class suburban life. I plead guilty to the charge of killing a stereotype. All I can offer in defense is the conviction that poetry must continually enlarge its sympathies and concerns. Subjects, which one generation considers unpoetic, sometimes become central to the next. It took a century for the city to become an accepted setting for lyric poetry—from Whitman and Baudelaire through

Eliot and Auden—with Georgians and other aesthetic conservatives fixated in rural romanticism complaining all the way. Some people resist change in the arts because it violates their sense of beauty and order. But an art grows by finding beauty where it has been overlooked, by transforming the ordinary places in which we live and work—like suburbs and offices—into the poetic. I don't know if I will ever be able to accomplish this transformation in my own poetry, but I would like to be free to try.

A Lateral Move

Floyd Skloot

SKOWRON DIDN'T NEED the company handbook to figure out he was in trouble. A note from his boss in the morning mail said there'd be a meeting in her office Friday at five. Carbon copy to Personnel.

He'd have sworn she'd be a first-thing-Monday-morning firer. And have a nice week. The kind who made you show up for work every day while you ran out your string and wear an I WAS FIRED button on your jacket. He wouldn't be shocked to see a Memo to Staff RE: Gordon L. Skowron's Termination.

But a pink slip at mid-week? So the little artichoke could still surprise him. He crumpled the note and lobbed it into the trash.

"WHAT GIVES? "

Shouting in the empty office made him feel better. It was lunch time, only Myra was around to answer the phones and she'd never hear him, earplugs in place and body rocking to the music from her silenced ghetto-blaster. The only time she unplugged was when the lights on her phone bank blinked.

Skowron stretched to his full six-two and buffed each boot in turn across the back of a cuff. None of this made any sense. Here he was, a degree in History from Bradley, minor in Philosophy, an MBA from Chicago, and five good years with ALEMCO. He was thin despite the Slovak frame, sociable, just this side of a matinee idol if you wanted the truth. Hair in a loose perm, nails and cuticles intact, suits from Brittany. He had considered, as recently as six months ago, a career in commercials. Now they were going to fire him.

"Thanks to the bimbo with three names."

Skowron's office had no door. It didn't have walls either, just orange felt-covered partitions no one had moved in years. He slumped back into his orange desk-chair and stared, through the break in his partition, at the copier machine nuzzled against a wall that was stippled with outlets. The machine's whir was silenced now too. What would be so bad about losing a job like this?

There was a time when a five o'clock meeting with the boss would have been Skowron's idea of successful maneuvering. It would have been something to let slip to the boys over java, something to sell his tickets to the DePaul-Marquette game for.

But that was back before she began talking to him about Productivity Shortfalls and the Peter Principle. He knew what Peter Principle she needed. Skowron couldn't believe it was only ten months ago, when this ogre in a Barbie Doll's body moved into her office, that he was calling her Suzie. He'd admit the familiarity was an error, but nobody told him she went by Ms. Kemper-Elias.

Those first months she was at ALEMCO, buying Susan Kemper-Elias dinner was Skowron's fantasy. He'd slapped an ERA YES bumper-sticker on his new blue Audi and bought some Dior ties because he noticed all her scarves had signatures. He'd added chin-ups, 10% a week until he was at 75, for the muscle definition.

He remembered those months vividly. With her corner office, two sides all window and a view of the lake, she was establishing control. Her door not only closed, it locked, and the jingle of her keys in the morning was a symphony of power.

She had art everywhere. A stretched cotton fabric with cloudbursts and rainbows in alternating panels was above her desk. There was a poster of the Sangre de Cristo Mountains at dawn near the bookcase, a jug sprouting dried weeds on her credenza beside a miniature typewriter that was really a pencil sharpener. Where a bulletin board had been there was a painting of a flower that was so vaginal it made Skowron's palms sweat.

But no family photos. Rumor was she'd been divorced in Pennsylvania, her previous port-of-call. Skowron imagined her ex, probably some toy poodle of a Harvard lawyer, now the happiest man in all Philadelphia.

She kept her office lights off, preferring the natural light, and the temperature cooler than in the other offices. She never took off her suit jackets. Skowron used to think that was a shame since he'd have liked to see her in those creamy silk blouses. There was always a pot of decaffeinated coffee in her Pour-O-Matic and a canister of dry-roasted, unsalted peanuts on her table. No smoking.

Now Skowron hadn't been in her office in four months. Enough of memories. He slipped on his jacket and headed for the escalator. So much had gone wrong in ten months. At least his favorite restaurant, the Sub Culture, wouldn't be crowded since lunch hour was nearly over.

* * *

Wednesdays Skowron ate mortadella. On white with poupon, hold the tomato and onion. He liked onion, but not its smell on his fingertips all afternoon. The sandwich and a side of slaw restored his spirits.

He knew that Friday would not be pleasant. What would she do for openers at a termination meeting? Probably quote unemployment statistics.

Susan Kemper-Elias didn't even start friendly meetings with small talk. The weather was not an issue. Corporate profits were.

"What's up?" she'd ask.

"Strike of sheet meal workers," he'd say. "DuPage County."

You didn't speak in full sentences. Took too long.

"Robbins know?"

"Since nine."

"Wasn't he in at 8:30?"

Yet Skowron was looking forward to the meeting. In a way he didn't understand, she was still stunning to him. Although there wasn't any hint of allure in her manner, every move seemed to exude sex. Her awkward walk suggested to him inner rhythms. Her dark coloration and the moisture in her pelt-brown eyes seemed animal.

His sandwich finished, Skowron began on the gherkins. He was sure that his state of confusion had caused him to misread the woman so badly. One conversation in particular came to mind as the scene that had been his ruin.

It had been six p.m. on a Thursday in June. From her windows, he could watch workers set up a stage for some kind of festival in the morning. It was still a day for sailboats, their colors visible beyond the trees of Grant's Park. He had felt quite comfortable strolling into her office after hours.

"What's up?"

"Molybdenum. We'll feel it in steel prices come fall."

"I read the papers, Mr. Skowron."

"You really could call me Gordon, you know." He flashed his Lothario leer. "Or Moose, like everybody else."

She rested her chin in her palm, looking at Skowron as if trying to bring him into focus. She studied his lean frame, her grin shifting toward smile.

"You said Moose?"

"Or Gordon, at least."

"Not Gord?" She leaned back. "Or maybe Gordo?"

"After this ballplayer, Moose Skowron. He was a New York Yankee."

"Oh," she shrugged. "I was always a Giants fan."

Skowron leaned an arm on her bookcase and studied the spider plants. Six lush growths hung from the drop ceiling at different heights, filling the upper half of her windows. He thought he detected an edge to her conversation and decided to shift tone.

"They need water," he said.

"No." She didn't look up. "Repotting."

"Well, if they don't need a drink, maybe you do. How about letting me buy you one?"

"Not yet," she answered without missing a beat or looking at him. He couldn't decipher her meaning.

"Later, then?"

"I've got to get through my in-box. If you want a drink, there's some in the credenza." She lifted a voucher from her pile, read it quickly, initialed the top and tossed it in her out-box.

Skowron squatted in front of the credenza, finding the bottles and glasses, elated at his success. Just when he thought she was losing interest in him. He thought he might turn back and find her in a negligee.

"Where's ice?"

"Dryden's refrigerator. He doesn't even charge me for the space."

When he returned with their drinks, she had her feet resting on an opened desk drawer. Her shoes were off and Skowron could see that she had very long toes. She was reading a report Skowron had sent the day before about a shopping center proposal for the North Loop.

"You write this?" she asked.

"Edited it. Eric Joose did the draft."

"Listen: 'As regards the proposed proposal to refurbish within the existing building shell itself versus the total demolishment and subsequential redevelopmentation of the site area . . .' You sent this to me?"

"I must have missed that part."

No alarm sounded in Skowron's head. No warning signal demanded heed. He noticed, instead, that she had these freckles, great clusters of them over her cheeks and forehead. It would be nice to lick them off.

"Don't you get paid not to miss parts like that?"

He heard her growing anger as desire, perhaps because her voice grew softer and her color deepened. He'd have to turn on the charm.

"Now that wasn't very diplomatic."

"I didn't mean it to be."

He waved his hand. "My apologies. I'll get you a revised version tomorrow."

"By ten."

He leaned across her desk and covered the report she had picked up, forcing it down to the blotter. He bent close enough to see that her eyes were beginning to redden. Too much strain, he thought.

"You look tired," he whispered. "These can wait, but can we?"

"Mr. Skowron," she said, leaning closer. "Gordon. Moosey. If you can't hold your liquor better, don't drink."

She moved even closer, so that he could feel her breath in his ear. He broke out in goose bumps along the right side of his body.

"Let's not kid," he said. "It's after hours."

"I'm neither flattered by your advances nor the least bit interested in feeling your antlers."

"Wait. You're serious."

"Outraged is closer."

"I thought. I mean, you know?"

"I know."

Skowron stood up and squared his shoulders. The windows had filled with darkness.

She sat back, stretching until her chair squeaked. Then she picked up her report and folded back its clear plastic cover.

"What happens now?" he asked.

"You work on your report. I see you tomorrow at ten."

* * *

Walking to his condo after work Wednesday, Skowron made resolutions. Get fit again. Learn COBOL. No more of the old smockage at work—court elsewhere. Update the resume. Eat more fruit. He reached home jangled.

He dragged his exercise bicycle out of the closet and set it up by the TV. In his Puma sweats and jogging shoes, he oiled the machine, set the timer for 15 minutes, and climbed on board.

Sitting back on the seat, which was as wide as a tractor's, he folded the newspaper in fourths and read the sports while warming up. Soon he threw the paper aside and concentrated on the TV news, keeping the speedometer at 20.

This was the way. The anchorwoman looked like a blond version of Susan Kemper-Elias when she concentrated on the camera. Damn, that upset his rhythm.

He adjusted the tension calipers, pressed down harder with his toes, and brought it up to 25. A rill of sweat worked down his spine.

"Aledo, Bethalto, Cairo, Chicago, Cicero, De Soto, Dupo, Eldorado, Geneseo, Hillsboro."

When he was younger, Skowron could get all the way to Winnebago on one breath. He dismounted, swore to do twenty minutes the next night.

* * *

The city police don't like you to walk on the beach at night. A patrol car comes along the concrete walkway broadcasting the threat of arrest through a bullhorn.

Neither lovers on blankets nor strollers like Skowron pay any attention. Kids smoking dope scatter and the man walking his Lhasa apso heads for the crosswalk.

Thursday Skowron had called in sick. He spent the day downtown picking up things he thought he'd need to get through the weekend. A pale blue shirt with white collar to wear for Friday's meeting. No use getting fired in a plain shirt. He checked out some books on job hunting and even bought a guide to resume writing. A bottle of Wild Turkey for the wee hours of Saturday.

No matter where he walked, including underneath the pandemonium of the el at rush hour, his mind replayed that awful confrontation with Susan Kemper-Elias. He planned at least to be in control on Friday, to determine the conversation's flow rather than let her do it. But then he'd think of her freckles.

Now it was dark, there was nothing good on TV, and he'd felt the need to walk. Where the lakeshore curved out toward the water and the Drake Hotel sign disappeared from sight, Skowron had the compelling urge to walk straight out. He thought this must be what it was like to be at the edge of a cliff or the top of an open stairwell. For a moment, giving up had such fine logic.

He settled for tossing a few rocks in the lake while imagining how cold the water would be on his skin. He saw himself swimming out until he was exhausted, turning over, and trying to count the stars. He imagined the furor when his corpse washed ashore during peak bathing time.

Back at his condo, Skowron poured three fingers of bourbon with just enough water to start patterns in his glass. He wanted enough sleep to be sound tomorrow.

He sat in his favorite butterfly chair to watch a movie. When it ended, and he struggled to get out of the awkward position the chair had forced him into, Skowron sloshed a little of his drink onto the brown material.

He stood watching the dark stain, which took the shape of the flower in the painting on Susan Kemper-Elias' office wall. Then he refreshed his drink, omitting water this time, and raised the glass in a toast to the chair, then the cabinet behind it with his classical record collection, then the TV showing a commercial for Ford trucks.

* * *

He thought they'd be alone. He thought she'd hand him an envelope and say, "I don't suppose this is a surprise."

He was ready for that, had gotten himself geared up all day. He planned to stuff the envelope in his pocket and ask, "That all?" It would be over in forty seconds.

But there was a goddamn quorum. Skowron strode into her office and was surrounded.

She was standing by the windows shooting spray from a mister at her spider plants. At the round table, as though ready for a hank of gin rummy, sat men from Legal, Personnel, and Operations.

It didn't look good. Skowron thought they were ready to throw him in jail.

"Have a seat," someone said.

The only vacant seat was behind her desk. Skowron backed over to the bookcase and rested an elbow on its top.

"Rather stand, thanks."

"Susan and I have been talking," said Operations. Five o'clock, but he looked like he'd put on a fresh suit for the meeting, showered and powdered.

Skowron nodded. The sound of the mister was like a soft sneeze as Susan Kemper-Elias methodically drenched each plant.

"We felt you might not be happy with your present position."

"There may be a reason for that," Skowron said. He hadn't any idea what his next sentence would be.

"We don't want to lose you," said Personnel. "Your file is exemplary."

"So we've pulled together some of your old papers and reports. Susan spent a lot of time going through things and packaged them for Legal to go over."

"What it amounts to is a reassignment, a lateral move. It was Susan's idea and a good one. Think it over, Gordon, and let us know."

She had yet to say anything. Skowron stared at her, afraid to take his arm from the bookcase because he might fall over.

"I could see sitting down now," he said.

"Here," Operations rose, gestured to Legal, and moved toward the door. Legal handed Skowron a file labeled 'Potential Assignments.'

"Read it. I'll talk to you Monday morning about your new office."

The men left and Skowron was alone with his boss. She was working on the last plant, her back to him, her body lifted onto her toes like a ballerina.

Skowron pictured himself running into her like a linebacker, tackling her and taking them both through the windows and down the 22 stories. He bet that'd get a rise out of her.

"Why don't you go home?" she asked. "Take yourself out, eat some couscous at the place near you. Something new."

"I don't eat that stuff."

"Try."

She turned and pointed the mister at him. Skowron wondered if she was going to squirt him.

"I did eat sushi once," he said.

She sat opposite him, landing hard on the chair that Legal had occupied. She looked around her office, checking to see if everything was in order, and Skowron couldn't help but notice the two fine lines etched across her throat. It wasn't hard to imagine kissing her there.

"Mr. Skowron, I don't know if you'll understand this or not." She opened the mister's nozzle and held the bottle up to the light to check its fullness.

"Try me."

"Right: you've got good years left with ALEMCO. It wouldn't make sense, in fact it would be too messy, simply to get rid of you for what went on here this year. Management science says keep you."

"That's all?"

"That's all. Why else?"

He couldn't stop himself from saying, "Because of my sweet smile."

She inhaled deeply and held her breath a long time. Skowron again saw that she sure had some nice buffers.

"Just go over to Legal and do good work," she sighed, sounding sleepy.

Clasped as if for prayer, Skowron's hands supported his chin while he replayed what she said. It wasn't easy. He'd been distracted by the way she worked her tongue against her lower lip between sentences.

He reached his right hand across the table. She accepted his, squeezing it firmly with a quick shake, beginning to stand. Although he was tempted to bring it up to his lips, Skowron pumped her hand a few times and let it go.

* * *

Couscous at The Casbah wasn't as bad as it sounded, chased by two Araks. Skowron would have preferred more meat and fewer garbanzo beans, but he'd done what the boss said, tried something new.

How did she know where he lived, that a Middle Eastern restaurant was nearby, that he'd never eaten there? Maybe she had more interest in him than she let on. He walked home slowly, hardly feeling the wind as he considered her motives.

Settled by the TV at nine, Skowron scanned the documents from Legal but couldn't concentrate on them. He laid them on the coffee table like a hand of solitaire, related topics in piles, to deal with in the morning.

He was tired. The strain of the day, the full meal and liquor, the lack of hard exercise. He slept in his butterfly chair, legs spraddled and hands tucked under his thighs for warmth, back of the neck raw from the new collar he hadn't loosened.

In the morning, stiff as a runner after a marathon, Skowron changed into his Pumas, drank coffee, and mounted the exercise bicycle. Ten minutes without tension, eight with the calipers tight as brakes, and no thoughts of the office. He slowed in the last minute, stopping before the timer bell sounded, and listened to his raspy breath.

Then he began to peddle backwards, easily at first just to see if it could be done, if the machine would work in reverse. Pumping harder, he watched the speedometer drop below zero. If it had negative calibration, he'd be at minus fifteen.

Skowron backpedalled then in earnest and enjoyed the changing stress in his legs. He worked at it hard, speeding backwards, seeing his way past all that had happened in the past months, imagining that he would soon arrive at a logical place to stop, from which to begin going forward again.

*

David Alpaugh

A California Ad Man Celebrates His Art

For those of you
who come here
out of spite
expecting to hear
a con man apologize—
prepare to gnash your teeth.

I am here to celebrate
the TV commercial—
the authentic poetry of our time:
lovingly produced,
widely received,
technically dazzling—
It really changes lives.

My title? "Tubular Poetics."

We deal in time and space:
thirty seconds of sound and light
rolling from earth to sky,
sky to earth,
kitchen to bedroom.

Our spirit is democratic.
We have made a pact
with Walt Whitman
to celebrate fecund America,
embracing all creeds, all colors:
men and women, young and old,

the runt as well as the athlete.
We praise hearth and home
in a manner that Beowulf
would understand.
Our art is tribal, mnemonic . . .
designed to be sung into the heart
by families gathered round the fire—
not warehoused in a public library
or read in private on a printed page.

Our words are deeds.
Like iron weapons
warriors carry into battle
to brandish at the foe
they must contribute to the victory.
If they don't sell cars or condoms
Grendel comes out of the fen
people lose food, status, power—
and like a singer of unwanted songs
under the castle wall
we are not allowed to get on the elevator
and rise to the thirty-eighth floor.

Like Bert Brecht, we believe that art
is an instrument for social progress.
We are concerned about the sick,
the homeless, those denied justice.
Much of our best work is in praise
of cold tablets, real estate chains
and motorcycle lawyers—
and every afternoon when school lets out
we suffer the little children to come unto us.

Like all great craftsmen
we find the material reality imposes
only partly on our purpose.
Our task is to build a world elsewhere,
with porcelain teeth, perfect complexions,
fully rounded bosoms and bottoms:
a pastoral living room . . .
an electronic bower of bliss . . .

Into this world creep many dragons:
zits, dandruff, athlete's foot,
bras that sag or ride up,
bad breath, fatal to love—
relentless fiends called
"Ring Around the Collar,"
"Hemorrhoidal Tissue,"
and surly appliances
that snap, snarl
and refuse to work.

In the cataclysms that ensue
we let good have its way with evil,
demonstrating the wisdom
shown a hundred times each day
by our hero with a thousand faces,
The Consumer.

Finally, like Milton
we have the highest moral purpose,
calling upon our Muse to justify
the ways of any product our agency assigns
to whatever target market is specified.

In doing so we've stumbled on free will
and with it a whole new tragic vision:
the knowledge that despite triumphal odes,
hymns, eclogues, paeans, songs of love,
and Juvenalian satire at its bitterest—
millions ignore the good and choose Brand X
dropping down to darkness and perdition.

These are just a few of the qualities
that link us to The Great Tradition.

They Shoot Copywriters, Don't They?

Jill C. Wheeler

MARTIN SURVEYED THE wreckage of his copy for Hollister Corporation's 1990 Annual Report and realized why most suicides occur early in the week.

He saw his carefully crafted prose had been transformed into an incomprehensible script of Hollisterese, and he heard each wrongfully capitalized Company and decapitated action verb cry out for vengeance against it's corporate executioners. He also questioned whether the corporate editors would recognize a *Chicago Manual of Style* if it were dropped on them from a ninth-story window.

Too much carnage for a Monday morning, he decided. It was bad enough when the corporate lawyers drained the life out of his ad copy, but this was a throat-parching annual report from a company that made industrial ovens. He swiveled away from his desk to gaze out the window. Better to think about something positive in his life. Like his dog. Or maybe his chair.

He liked his chair. The high back and boxy arms reminded him of Captain Kirk's post on the Enterprise. He liked to pretend he was Captain Kirk, kicking the butts of Klingons and Romulans and embarking upon an intergalactic trollop hunt.

He leaned toward the window to see the parking ramp entrance. It was 8:28, and the agency president was a stickler about time. It didn't matter if an employee stayed until midnight, he still had to be at his post by 8:30 each morning. Martin saw his boss, Bruce, drive into the garage in his gray BMW.

"Better hurry, old boy," Martin said as the car disappeared beneath him. "T minus two and counting."

Martin swiveled back to his desk. "Computer," he said in his best Mr. Spock imitation, switching the disk drives into life. He waited for the screen to brighten and the smiling icon to greet him. He grinned back. He enjoyed being assured of at least one friendly interaction each day.

He pulled up the Hollister annual report file from his hard drive and began to input the client's changes. On the fourth page, his entire paragraph on the firm's financial performance had been annihilated with a giant red X. There was a handwritten epitaph next to it.

It's critical to retain shareholder confidence at this important juncture in the restructuring process, he read. *Please reword to incorporate Hollister's tradition of strong returns and sound fiscal performance.*

Martin slid open his file drawer and pulled out the Hollister folder. He scanned the dot matrix figures until he found the bottom line on the company's 1990 balance sheet. Negative $2.3 million.

He turned back to the computer screen, highlighted the condemned paragraph and hit the backspace. Instantly the paragraph vanished, and he began to type.

Hollister Corporation continued its proud tradition of delivering a solid fiscal performance in 1990 despite losing its butt to the tune of $2.3 big ones.

"Oh Martin," he heard the administrative assistant say over the telephone intercom.

"Yes?"

"Call on line seven."

"Thank you, Eunice."

"I think it's Calvin from Petco, Martin."

"Thank you, Eunice."

"I think he's calling about their new kitty litter. He probably wants to ask you—"

Martin hit the flashing button, picked up the phone and wedged his face into his professional smile.

"Martin Worthington. How may I help you?"

"Martin, how ya doing," came the voice on the line. Martin cringed.

"I'm fine, Cal, and how is everyone at Petco?"

"We're fine as usual, just enjoying some gorgeous Texas weather."

"Wonderful," Martin said. "What's it doing down there today?" He picked up his pen and began doodling on his note pad. He wondered again why no one took him seriously when he said one of his occupational perks was getting the Houston forecast five times a day.

"So what can I do for you, Cal?" he said.

"We're fixing to introduce this new kitty litter. I'm sure you've heard about it."

"Right, we're having a brainstorming session on the name this morning."

"Wonderful. I wanted to pass on the results of the naming contest we've been holding here."

"Great. Let me get a pen."

Martin reached into his drawer and rattled the contents. After what seemed a suitable time, he picked up his pen and grinned into the receiver. "Fire away!"

"My secretary came up with some good ones. Wondercat, Supercat and Premium Kitty Litter."

"Sounds great, Cal, I'll make sure we add those to the session."

"I'm not done. I had some ideas, too. What do you think of King Cat or Tabby Toity?"

"I'll put 'em down, Cal."

"Wonderful. Talk to you later."

"I'm sure you will," Martin said. He replaced the receiver and looked up to see Bruce in the doorway, his balding dome already covered with a sheen of perspiration.

"You cut it pretty close this morning," Martin said.

"The folks who live the closest are always the last to arrive," Bruce said, leaning over to jab Martin in the shoulder.

"I see," Martin said as the first wave of post-vodka halitosis hit him. It usually took Bruce's breath until noon to clear up. Eleven o'clock with breath mints.

"So what's on the docket of the world's greatest copywriter today?" Bruce said, his eyeballs looking ready to pop from their sockets.

Martin waited for the air to clear before inhaling. "Revisions on the Hollister annual report. Guess they didn't like the way I said they showed a loss."

"Martin, Martin, haven't you learned?" Bruce said in an intoxicating blast. "Our clients never show a loss, although they may report negative earnings." He chuckled, then licked his finger and sat on Martin's desk to scrub off a spot on his wingtip.

"Bruce, they ate over $2 million. The Environmental Protection Agency fined them $700,000 for hazardous waste disposal violations, and they cut 35% of their work force. Am I supposed to gloss over all of that?"

"Of course not," Bruce said, rising to his feet and adjusting his tie. "You tell the shareholders Hollister began making capital investments with an eye toward greater stewardship of our natural resources, and the company also began streamlining operations for improved cost effectiveness."

Martin paused. "How long have you been in this business?"

"Nearly 25 years. Remind me to tell you about the time I had a client that got caught cheating on defense contracts," Bruce said, his face screwing up into it's customary grin.

"We did this huge national campaign talking about all the little old ladies they helped feed and all the little black kids that went to camp because of them," he said, his dome bobbing in glee. "It was brilliant. We got an award for it, too. After it was over, we took the client to the Oak Room and we all got plastered.

"But, hey buddy, don't let me interrupt you. See me later if you need any help." He winked and disappeared into the hall.

Martin turned back to his computer and attacked the keyboard once more.

Hollister Corporation faced a challenging year in 1990 due in part to a declining industrial oven market and rapidly increasing competition from foreign interests. Of course, we also had the EPA shut down one of our plants when they discovered all the local women had three nipples.

He pushed back from the computer and surveyed his bridge from his command post. His eyes fell on his sole poster. 'Man's greatest weakness is neither love nor hate', it read. 'It is the overwhelming desire to edit another's copy.'

He pressed an imaginary button on the arm of his chair and spoke authoritatively.

"Uhura, get met some coffee, dammit."

When nothing happened, he grabbed his mug and headed for the lunch room, hoping he could still catch a caffeine buzz before the spineless staffers made the mid-morning switch to decaf.

"Martin! I've been looking for you!"

He turned to see Eunice and realized too late she had him cornered between the coffee maker and the photocopier.

"You haven't filled out your order for our company jackets!" she said, the flab on her upper arms wagging as she spoke. "How do you expect to have yours by softball season if you don't return your form?"

"Guess it slipped my mind," Martin said, filling his mug and sprinkling in non-dairy creamer. He glanced at her skirt, the same kind of flowered J.C. Penney creation she always wore. He decided he must be psychologically allergic to J.C. Penney.

"Now Martin, we're a team, remember?" she said, handing him a slip of paper. "We've got to act like a team and we've got to look like a team. The form's not long, just give us your size and the name you want on the front and give it to me by the end of the day."

He watched her floral bulk wiggle down the hall, then walked back to his desk and read the slip she'd handed him.

It's time to order our Olson, Garcia, Yamamoto & Rubenstein Softball Jackets! Be a team player by filling in the blanks below and returning it to Eunice by five p.m. Monday. Size: XS, SM, M, L, XL, XXL. Also, please write the nickname you would like on the front of your jacket.

Martin debated, then took a red marker and scrawled MMXL over the size. He added "Siddhartha" at the bottom and tossed the paper into the garbage. Turning back to his computer, he began typing.

Our shareholders have come to rely upon us for sound, strategic financial management of all our assets. That's exactly why we gave the axe to half our work force last year and put 53 of our geezers out to early retirement pasture.

Martin grabbed his style manual and page through it. As he had thought, work force was two words.

He caught site of the media arts institute catalog as he put the stylebook back in the drawer. Seeing no one in the hallway, he grabbed it and flipped to a dog-eared page. He picked up his highlighter and began making out his wish list. Introduction to Video Production. Basic Scriptwriting. He realized there was an informational meeting that evening for prospective students.

"Attention everybody," Eunice announced over the intercom. "The Petco kitty litter name generation brainstorming session will be starting in the conference room in three minutes and twenty seconds. Don't be late."

Reluctantly, Martin put the catalogue away. He was the second person in the conference room, arriving just after Don, the creative director.

Martin liked Don, but he suspected the man had done a few too many drugs in his counter-culture days. Talking to him was like speaking through an interpreter.

"Morning, Don. How long do you think this will take?"

Don looked at him silently for several seconds, then his eyes opened slightly.

"Hi," he said.

Martin took a seat in one of the overstuffed chairs. All of these chairs had low backs. Definitely not Star Fleet material. He spun around several times, imagining warp speed.

"I think we should be able to have four or five good names within an hour," Don said.

Martin stopped spinning and smiled at him briefly.

"Well, all right!" came a voice from the hall. "Let's get started, people!"

Bruce stormed into the room and stopped short, his pop eyes surveying the meager crowd. In his hand was a plastic gallon jug of what looked like light brown sand.

"Where is everybody?" he said. "I thought Eunice paged everyone to the conference room."

He set the jug on the conference table and scooped up the telephone.

"Brainstorming on Petco's new kitty litter is starting now," he shouted into the intercom. "Move it or lose it!"

He slammed the receiver down and laughed quickly. "That's one way to get 'em!" he said, elbowing Don in the shoulder. Don was unresponsive.

The remaining brainstormers streamed in over the next 10 minutes. When everyone was seated, Bruce set up a flip chart and took position with a magic marker.

Martin enjoyed brainstorming sessions. The concept was that no idea was too stupid (a sentiment he'd argued at times) and people were meant to build upon one another's ideas. He sat back and made notes as suggestions began spewing forth.

"Cat's Delight."

"Litter Pride."

"Fantasticat."

Martin surveyed his notepad. *Shitty Kitty. Litter Rip. Feline Groovy.*

"Well all right! We're really getting somewhere now," Bruce said, pulling a starched white handkerchief from his pocket to mop his dome. "Martin, what's your take on this?"

"What's the difference?" Martin said quietly. "It's kitty litter. People are going to buy it regardless, unless they want shit all over their house."

The room was silent for a moment. Bruce chewed on his marker, then leaned toward Martin.

"But this is *premium* kitty litter, Martin," he said, clapping a hand on Martin's back. "It balls up when the cat pisses in it, so all the cat owner has to do is scoop out the balls. They don't have to empty the whole litter box every week. You know how much time that saves? This product can improve the quality of life of every cat owner in this nation!"

"Sorry, sir, I must have lost my head."

"Apology accepted," Bruce said, adding his trademark chuckle. "Now, people, give me some more ideas. We're going to make kitty litter a household word."

After lunch, Martin stopped by Bruce's office. The door was half closed, as usual, and he heard the sounds of "Dungeon of Doom" beeping from the computer.

He knocked lightly and poked his head inside.

"Come on in and have a seat," Bruce said. Martin saw his hand flick to the keyboard to pull up a spreadsheet on the screen. "What's up?"

"I'd like some advice," Martin said, sitting down in the spare chair. "I've been doing a lot of thinking lately about professional development."

"Very admirable, it's important we all continue to build our skills," Bruce said, whipping on the horn rims he used in client meetings. Martin had looked through them once. The lenses were clear glass.

"What were you thinking of?" he said.

"Actually, I've been looking into—"

"Say, that's not a *real* Rolex, is it?" Bruce said.

"No, it's a fake. But I thought it looked nice."

"My wife bought me a Seiko for my last birthday. I told her it was a waste because I didn't want anything until I could have a real Rolex."

"Wonderful," Martin said smiling.

"You were saying?"

"Oh, it's nothing really," Martin said, standing and moving toward the door. "I was going to ask if you had any advice about what things I could do to improve my work. I know it's not time for my formal review, but I'm always open to suggestions."

Bruce removed the horn rims and assumed his serious client meeting pose.

"Martin, you've got a lot of talent. I've seen a lot of copywriters in my day, but you've got a certain flair the clients seem to love. Really, the only thing I can think of is to starch your shirts."

"Starch my shirts?"

"I find medium starch is best. Of course it's a little more uncomfortable in the morning, but by the end of the day you'll appreciate the stamina."

Martin was silent a moment, then the smile crept back on his face.

"Thanks, Bruce. I'll remember that."

"Good. Oh, Martin? Would you mind closing the door on your way out?" he said, pulling a lint brush out of his drawer and whisking it over his trousers. "I like the silence to concentrate."

If you looked in the dictionary under the word 'insolvent', you'd find a photo of Hollister Corporation.

"Oh Martin?"

"Yes, Eunice."

"Martin, there's a call for you on line two. I think it's Mrs. Worthington."

"Thank you, Eunice."

"She's probably calling about your dinner party tonight. Personally, I think the Oak Room is highly over-rated. They use instant potatoes, you know."

"Eunice, what color underwear am I wearing?"

"My God, Martin. I'm a married woman!"

Martin picked up the line and turned on his smile.

"Hi, this is Martin."

"Martin, this is Tricia."

"My God, you're right, it is Tricia."

"Martin, I don't have time for that now. Did you forget about tonight?"

"No. What's tonight?"

"I knew it, I just knew you'd forget. We're meeting the Powers for dinner at seven sharp."

"But I wanted to go to that informational meeting at the media arts institute tonight."

"Good God, that again? I thought we'd put that behind us. Listen, it's very important to my business that you be there tonight. And wear something nice. This is a formal dinner."

"You mean the Mardi Gras penis tie is out?"

"Why do you always have to be so *gross*? Yes, it's definitely out. Wear your blue suit, your white shirt with the French cuffs and that new red tie I bought you. And watch your mouth. I don't want to be embarrassed again. Don't you forget if it weren't for my business, we'd still be in that crackerbox apartment."

Martin stared at the dead receiver in his hand, remembering the last time Tricia had orchestrated one of her networking dinners. He had made the mistake of trying to engage one of her client prospects in a conversation about business travel. It had seemed innocent enough, considering Tricia owned a travel agency. In fact, Martin hadn't noticed anything wrong and would have forgotten the entire episode had Tricia not pounced on him afterward.

"Why the hell were you telling Mr. Oines that business travel is a thinly veiled opportunity for extramarital affairs?" she'd said.

"You mean it's not?"

"My God, Martin. I can't put you in front of anyone without embarrassing both of us. Why can't you talk about sports, or the weather, or the economy?"

"Boring."

"I don't care if it's boring, it's called polite dinner conversation and you'd better learn how to do it before you drive all my prospects away."

"Actually, Mr. Oines was coming around to seeing my point," Martin had told her. "Maybe if he comes on board you should see that he and his secretary get adjoining rooms."

Martin glanced at his watch. Two more hours to go. He forced his eyes back to the computer screen. He fantasized about beginning his memoirs. Beginning the screenplay for Star Trek VI. He even considered putting some time in on the play he was writing for his local theater group. Anything but Hollister.

"Oh Martin!" Eunice's voice screeched over the intercom.

"Martin died in a car crash over lunch. Memorials are being taken by his wife."

"Martin, you haven't turned in your form for our company jackets! How can you be a team player without a jacket?"

"I thought I'd been doing pretty well as it was," he said, fishing through his garbage can.

"I'm coming to your office right now and I want you to have that ready for me by the time I get there."

"Yes, sir."

Martin smoothed the paper on his desk and waited. He looked up when a floral mass blocked the light from the hallway.

"Ah, there it is. Good. See how easy it can be if you'd just cooperate?"

Eunice whisked the paper from his desk and deposited it within her botanical bulk. "They should be in in about two weeks. Aren't you excited?"

Martin smiled at her, like he smiled at his computer each morning. "Eunice, I'm very happy for you."

Eunice looked at him, puzzled. Shaking her head, she turned toward the door.

"You creatives just crack me up sometimes," she said. "By the way, when were you at Mardi Gras?"

Had Hollister Corp. bothered to look beyond the end of its industrial nose, it would have noted long-term trends within the industrial oven market and begun preparing before its own goose wound up in one of its quality AL-500 ovens.

Martin swiveled to the window and watched one of the grounds maintenance workers cleaning leaves out of the mum bushes lining the visitors' entrance. He was reminded of Jack Conrad, a college classmate who was a gardener at a condominium complex. Jack had told Martin he felt his menial career was still more respectable than most professions. Martin had to agree.

"Oh Martin?"

"Were you expecting someone else, Eunice?" he said into the intercom speaker.

"I believe Cal is on line five for you."

"Really. What does he want?"

"I imagine he wants to know how the naming session went."

"What do you think I should tell him?"

"That's your job, Martin, not mine."

Martin fished his notes from the session out of the file folder on his desk and picked up the receiver.

Martin, how ya doing? Did the naming session go well?

"Great, Cal. We'll be presenting five names next week." He turned back to the Hollister report on his computer, half-listening to Cal as he scrolled down to the management letter.

"Are they any good?"

"Of course. We had a very successful session. I'm sure you'll find one to put the perfect spin on your product positioning."

"It's really kind of futile, isn't it?"

"What?" Martin said, turning away from the computer.

"Naming a kitty litter, for God's sake. I couldn't believe it when they gave me the assignment. And they're so damn serious about it, too. Hell, I'd rather be out playing golf. Do you play golf?"

"No, not yet."

"You oughta try it. Makes about as much sense as the marketing business, only with golf you play your games outdoors. So you'll be getting names to me next week?"

"Yes," Martin said, still digesting the conversation.

"I'll look forward to seeing 'em. You have a good afternoon buckaroo, and keep up the good work."

Martin's eyes strayed to the window, and he watched the gardeners at their work for several minutes. Turning back to his desk, he retrieved the catalog from the bottom of his drawer. He filled out the registration form, then dialed Tricia's office.

"I'm sorry Mr. Worthington, your wife is in a meeting," the secretary said. "May I take a message?"

"Yes. Tell her she can rub shoulders with Klingons but tonight I'm seeking out some more intelligent life forms."

"Excuse me?"

"Kirk out."

He picked up his briefcase and hit the light switch, leaving the flickering screen of the computer reflected in the window.

Hollister Corporation continued its proud tradition of delivering a solid fiscal performance in 1990 despite recording negative earnings of $2.3 million. Fourth quarter sales gains, coupled with a new emphasis on cost containment and environmental stewardship, promises additional gains in 1991 and beyond.

Miriam Goodman

Happy Endings

1

Anybody see that open-heart thing on TV last night? They
shut down the heart for a couple of hours while they work on
it. I wanted to watch the hockey game but I got interested.

2

I'd like to read these dialing instructions with you.
Transferring a call is the simplest to do: one plunge and it's
transferred. If you can't do it, you may as well throw this card
away. Dial the extension, and say, 'Joe, this is Mary. I'm
transferring a call to you.' When you transfer within the
house, you can say anything you want because the other
person is excluded. You can say, 'This is that jerk who's
always bothering us,' but, when you transfer to the operator,
be careful because the person calling in can hear you. And
speak up if a call has been transferred to you; say, 'Yes, may I
help you?'

3

This is basically the cash cow of the company. As
manufacturing comes on-line we'll be making more and more
of them. As you see, we're continuing to grow. Between June,
July and August, we've added 6 to 8 people. We are expanding,
we are augmenting, we are hiring!

4

Today, the company is sponsoring a buffet lunch for our employees. What is this all about? A year ago we started on our product. The prototype took shape last fall and with the snows of winter, the orders started coming. Our customers in the industry showed deep interest. And so today we're thinking bigger. We elevate our sights. This year, every time you turn around, you'll bump your neighbor with your elbow, but we know you will put up with it for three more months. As President, I want to personally express our thanks. We appreciate your contribution to the product. It's a fine product. Our shipping rate is up. September was our best month ever. And now, besides the lunch, I'm pleased to announce another roving holiday. Enjoy your lunch.

5

When the Company feeds you, you know you're going to hear some unpalatable news.

6

This change is just a commitment away from that market as a *specific* thrust. It's difficult for you technical people to go with management on this. You've put two to three years of your lives into the product. To those of you who've put the time in, we say: well done! Now we ask you, like good soldiers, to support this decision and go marching on with other Company efforts.

Job Hunting

A sign at the end of the street says STOP, so should I?
A truck draws a sound from the road: day overcoming
its inertia. The air is a light shawl, fragrant
with clover. Someone in every house has cut
the weeds along the curb. Someone in every house
is sleeping. I rise, subside indecisive, as if
I hadn't known this city.

It's a settled life I seek to move back into: behind desks,
behind dashboards, carried by the wheel of habit.
The sun in the wheel of the sky and the horizon make
a different axis, set the thaw streaming,
warmth from rocks. I fall quickly to despair,
a mired stone. Who knows if I may return, or when?
Whether these stones litter, or take the sun?

Loophole

Don't talk. I'm chasing something I see
and believe in: a hole in a gauzy black
curtain, the night sky full of snow.
Rising from the hassock to the dinner table,
serving the meal: a crack opens. Who rises?
Who serves? I want to hide an unseemly
interest in pleasure. At the office,
we must not make nothing. Behind
the scrim of day, events fall randomly,
and I see there's much beyond
the life that's sharply circumscribed.

Computer Lab

How do the programmers look when they work?
Some sit for hours and the room is full of noise.
Keyboards clack. Behind concentric grillwork—
whirring fans. Hammers knock the print heads
on the teletypes. And under the assault, the programmers
slide down in their chairs like paper in the platen.
Chins on chests. A desultory finger lifts and strikes
a key. The image on the cathode-ray-tube changes.
Bluish light. The disconnected dots construct a message.
Dry and steady, thought pays out like rope.
They breathe, they shift their weight, they tilt
their heads, they flex their feet. So silent
are the programmers, sitting under fountains
of white noise.

A Foot in the Door

Henry Slesar

Hardin used to be big with the receptionists. They'd giggle as soon as he stepped off the elevator, swinging a soft gray glove in his left hand, his homburg tipped at a rakish angle. But that had been at least three years ago. Maybe the girls were different now, or maybe the old sparkle was gone. Or maybe it was because he was on the other side of the desk now, a seller—not a buyer—a man who knew how to cry for a piece of business. The girls didn't like you to cry; they wanted laughs, and off-color jokes, and maybe a little gift at Christmas. Hardin couldn't afford all that any more.

As he stepped inch-deep into the beige carpet of the Imperial Dress Company lobby, the girl looked up with a frozen smile that thawed into a frown the moment she recognized him.

"Hello, Miss Frances." He was trying hard, but she wouldn't even lift her finger from the rental-library book on her desk.

"Oh, hello, Mr. Hardin." Ice, pure ice they made them these days.

"How's my boy Manny? Still honest?"

"I really don't know if he's in, Mr. Hardin. Did you have an appointment?"

Hardin touched the thin hair on his head. It used to be a dignified iron-gray, but now it was muddy and soiled, like a city snowfall after feet had trodden it.

"Look, dear. Since when do I need an appointment to see Manny? I'm a little more than a salesman, you know that? I'm an old friend."

She picked up the telephone, languidly. "I'll tell Mr. Wright you're here."

"You're a good girl."

With an over-exaggerated nonchalance, Hardin strolled to the grass-textured wall of the lobby, and peered with professional interest at the framed color advertisement.

Advertising! He shook his head, in respectful wonderment. Little Manny Wright, his name in 12-point type, right there at the bottom of the page: A Manuel Wright Original. Advertising! Who would have dreamed this about Manny, three short years ago?

"Mr. Hardin?"

He whirled. "Yes?"

"Mr. Wright is really terribly busy. He wants me to apologize, but—"

"Did you tell him what I wanted?"

"Why, no. You didn't tell *me*."

Hardin leaned on the desk top, and tried to make his tired eyes twinkle. "Listen, darling—What is it, Carol?"

"No. Dierdre."

"Lovely name. Listen, Dierdre, darling. How long have you been with Imperial? Two, three months?"

"Three," the girl said.

"All right, there's your excuse. You don't even know who I am. I'm just another pest to you, is that correct?"

"Oh, Mr. Hardin, I never—"

He waved his hands. "S'all right. How could you know? So let me tell you. For your information, Mr. Wright and I used to be *partners*. You hear that? Academy Fabrics. Hardin and Wright. Sounds familiar?"

"Oh, I didn't know." She looked at him with vague new interest, but her young eyes were shrewd, and she detected that there had been a change in his status. "But I only take orders, Mr. Hardin. If Mr. Wright says he's busy . . ."

"Well, that's easy to fix, too. You just pick up your little Ameche again, and you tell him that *Jerry* Hardin is outside, and wants to see *Manny* Wright on something of a *personal* nature."

She looked doubtful, but she lifted the receiver again. She gave Manny the message, and then covered the mouthpiece with a graceful white hand. "Okay," she said. "But he's only got a minute."

"There," Hardin beamed. "And I'll bet you thought I was giving you baloney. See?" He twirled the shabby homburg on his hand, and walked past the girl's desk, whistling thinly.

His face changed when he turned the corner, and sweat broke out on his forehead as if it had been magically contained until this moment. He was getting to be like the man in that Broadway play, he told himself, that salesman. Hardin had seen the production years ago, when the problems of its characters seemed unable to touch him, and he had shed fashionable tears of sympathy for Willy Loman's plight. Now he could cry tears of identification and self-pity.

Imperial was bustling. It was two years since he had been here last, and in that time it had amassed a fortune. A fortune! Manny was really cleaning up. What was the miracle ingredient? Why couldn't Academy Fabrics have enjoyed such a boom? It hadn't been his fault. He was as good a salesman as the district boasted. Manny was good too, but he was a shop man first.

It was money, he thought bitterly. Uptown money came along and set Manny up in business. And now what was he, Hardin? A little salesman from a small struggling shop, a shop growing smaller every day, a shop that would no longer exist after the first of the month. Unless . . . .

He straightened his spine, and put the old confidence in the steps that led him to Manny's plush office.

There was a model paying court to Manny, a big blonde in a basted suit coat, and a thin designer in shirt-sleeves. Manny looked up, his big flushed face redder and beefier than ever. He was an ugly man, with tiny eyes; he had no charm at all. What was the magic ingredient?

"Manny!" Hardin threw out his arms. "It's been a century, you old boozer!"

He knew it was the wrong speech the moment the words were said. Manny was frowning, and the model looked up from behind tumbled hair as if a shipping clerk had gotten insolent. The designer's actions were even more humiliating. He glanced up, and then returned to his conversation without comment.

"So like I say, Mr. Wright. We can lengthen the collar without altering the drape at the back."

"Yeah, sure, Howie. That sounds fine. Be with you in a minute, Jerry."

"A minute's all I got," the designer said. "I thought I'd have Elaine show you how it looked."

"Yeah, well, it looks okay. I'd like to see the whole suit, though, before you give it to the girls."

"Sure, Mr. Wright."

A cringing serf, Hardin thought. The designer went by him without a look, and the girl swung her hips past him with such disdain that he could have reached out and——

"Well, Jerry? What is it?" The familiar voice was deeper, coarser than ever.

"You look good, Manny." Hardin came up to the desk and put the homburg in the Out box. "A little fatter, maybe. Still crazy about those egg creams?"

"Jerry, no fooling. This is my busy day. We're getting ready for the Fall showing; you should know that."

"Well, my time's valuable, too. But I would think, for and old friend . . . I mean, we used to be partners, Manny. Not so long ago."

The heavy face relaxed a bit. "Yeah, yeah, that's right, Jerry. I don't mean to be this way. They got me going like a fire engine in this place. Believe me, you don't know the headaches——"

"Such headaches," Hardin smiled feebly. "I really wouldn't mind." He leaned forward. "And how's the family?"

"Lil is okay. The boys are at school. Mama's not too good, maybe. Gallstones, I think."

"But business? Business is all right, I gather?"

"Yeah, I guess so. If you call it all right to work sixteen hours a day."

"*Agh.* You always worked hard, Manny." Something tightened in Hardin's stomach; it killed him to flatter this man.

"Sure. Only now it's a little different." Manny tapped two fingers on the soft flesh over his ribs. "You heard what happened to me in Lakeville?"

"Oh, sure. But that wasn't a real *attack*——"

"No, maybe not. I walked into the hospital, all right. But I didn't paint such good pictures on that cardiograph, Jerry."

"If there's anything I could do to help——"

"That's nice of you, Jerry." He was looking at his watch. "Well——"

"Now just a second!" Hardin put a smile on his face and left it there. He walked to the office door and closed it firmly. Then he came back and waggled his finger at the big man behind the desk. "You don't get off *that* easy. Old friend or no old friend. I been trying to see you a whole two weeks about those cottons we talked about."

"Look, Jerry." Manny's voice was soft. "Is this what you meant by personal?"

"Manny-boy!" Hardin cocked his head comically and broadened the smile. "You're a salesman, too, no? You should know the old rules. It doesn't matter *how* you get in the door—as long as you get there!" He slapped his knee triumphantly.

Manny looked angry for a moment, and then chuckled. "Same old Jerry," he said.

"Now that's what I like to see! A big smile! Oh, Manny, you old so-and-so! Maybe you're good and rich, but I'll bet you don't get so many laughs now. Huh?"

"Okay, Jerry. So what is it you want?"

Hardin hoisted his shoulders. "What do you think I want? An order! I'm still in the business, you know. Academy still makes nice cottons."

The pencil tapped again. "Jerry—I'm sorry."

"What do you mean, sorry?"

"I just don't need anything now. That's what I mean."

"Who are you telling that? Your shipping clerk? That fancy tomato who wiggles around here? That delicate designer of yours? Listen, I know better, Manny. I'm in the trade."

"Jerry—"

"No, Manny!" The smile was gone. "No, don't tell me that. I know all about what you need and don't need. All you got to do is go downstairs in the street, and you'll hear all about it. You need cottons. And I got them to sell."

His old partner dropped the pencil with a clatter, and walked to the window.

"I'll tell you the truth, Jerry," he said as he turned slowly. "Academy makes good stuff. But you just don't have the manpower or the cloth for what I need. I do a large-volume business, Jerry. I have to deal with large contractors. For me, your price would be out of line."

"Did I quote prices yet? Do you think I wouldn't come to terms for the sake of an old friend?"

The big man shook his head. "Even so, Jerry, you couldn't produce in time."

"Who couldn't?" Hardin's face was suddenly covered with perspiration. "I'll put on extras. I'll keep the shop open twenty-four hours a day . . . ."

But the head was still shaking. "I couldn't take the chance, Jerry. Believe me. I'd like to do you the favor. But this—this is out of the question."

Hardin stood up. His hands went out as in supplication, and they were trembling. All pretense at charm had vanished; he was pleading now, begging for his life.

"Manny. I don't want small favors. I want this cottons order. I *need* this order. Do you understand? I *need* it, Manny!"

"Jerry, I just can't—"

"What—what do you mean, you can't!" Hardin roared. "Who else makes the decisions? You're the boss here, Manny! Nobody else! If I get turned down, it's *you, you* turning me down!"

"But I already promised the order. Samuelson promised me delivery in three weeks, at the best price. Even you couldn't meet it, Jerry. You'd be cutting your throat."

"What do you think you're doing now? Comes the first of the month, Manny, and there won't *be* any business. You know what I'm saying? I owe money. A lot of money. Twenty thousand dollars, Manny."

The big face reflected Manny's genuine sorrow. "Jerry! Why didn't you tell me before? If I can lend you anything—"

"I don't want charity! I don't want a loan! I want an order, Manny. One big order, to tide me over! I've got to have it!"

Hardin was crying now, the tears rolling smoothly from practiced ducts, slipping down the pale cheeks and dropping to the carpet of Manny Wright's office. He cried easily, unashamedly, glad of the presence of this watery evidence of his unhappiness and need.

But the tears didn't do their job. Manny was moved, but not altered. He returned to his desk.

"I'm sorry, Jerry. I hate to do this, but I'm sorry. If you were my own brother . . ."

"*You dirty, rotten, lousy son of a . . . .*"

Hardin was shrieking the words at him, and his ex-partner was listening to their terrible sound with shock and horror.

"Jerry!" he said pleadingly. "Have a little sense—"

"Sense? I'll give you sense!"

He threw himself across the cluttered desk, and his trembling hands grabbed for the fleshy throat of the man behind it. Manny's little eyes opened wide when the fingers began to squeeze, round orbs of bloodshot white. Manny's mouth dropped open, and the breath that struggled through was rasping and ugly. But still Hardin applied the pressure, two years of bitterness and anger and envy supplying him with strength.

Then he let go.

Manny staggered, reaching out for support. He clutched at the blotter, and slid towards the floor, pulling paper and fabric samples and the telephone to the carpet.

Hardin became frightened. "Manny! Manny, I'm sorry!"

Manny tried to speak, but the effort was too much for him. He flopped like a hooked fish, arching his back against the desk. Then he doubled over, and fell with sickening finality.

Hardin stared, motionless.

He took a hesitant step forward and bent down to touch the bulky figure lying on its face.

"Manny?" he said softly.

He rolled the big man over, and saw his open, sightless eyes. He felt his chest and found nothing, not a hint of the palpitation that indicated life. He hadn't killed Manny. He wasn't a murderer. You aggravate a man and he dies, does that make you a murderer?

Hardin's eyes went to the closed door of the office. He had to do something. He couldn't tell them what had happened. They'd say he was a murderer.

Then he saw the telephone. A thin, reedy voice was coming from the receiver, as it lay half-out of its cradle. He picked the phone up, automatically.

It was a girl's voice. "Mr. Wright? Did you want somebody?"

Hardin looked at the phone. And as the idea came to him, he lifted the instrument. "Yes," he said in a deep voice. "Give me Ross."

"Thank you."

A man's voice. "Yes, Mr. Wright?"

"Bobby?" Hardin said. "About that cottons order. The one I wanted to give to Samuelson."

"What's that?"

"I've changed my mind about it. I want to give the order to Academy Fabrics. Speak to Jerry Hardin about it, he'll quote you the price."

"But Mr. Wright."

"Don't argue with me, Bobby! This is my busy day!"

He hung up the telephone, and breathed a long sigh. He forced himself to wait a full ten minutes. Then he ran to the door of Manny's office and flung it open.

"Help, somebody! Help!" he cried.

Tina Quinn Durham

My Work

Six stories of offices, rising out of the corn field,
and two long buildings that house the assembly lines.
Above one of the assembly lines, by an unpretentious hallway
sits my desk—a tasteful, cream-colored steel thing
with oak laminate and a built-in light.
My desk, between two corn fields. I wonder sometimes
why I come there, and what is real:
the missiles on the assembly line, the intermittent sex
the engineers down the hall talk about,
or the ducks I see when I pour my coffee.
I know the corn is real; the defense contracts are real;
and I have a job because of them, putting together numbers
into elegant stacks of small truth.

In the afternoons, I step into the sun,
stop by the security guards,
show them the contents of my purse,
and I'm free for a little while.
The secrets I take with me are not industrial;
I am not paid by the Soviets to tell you this.

But I do carry music in my head
that follows me everywhere;
the engineers make tools and bombs;
yet come spring, the fallow field
will bear the promise of new corn
and there are already baby ducks
swimming in the pond.

Take Me, I'm Yours

Robert Minkoff

I'M NOT DESPONDENT, alcoholic, nursing phlebitis or howling at the moon. I miss the plush slide of good desk drawers, the purr of office telephones, the design delight of a clever paper clip: but I'm not a baggy-pants with nothing to do. I sold Sandersen's because we got a good price. I walked away with more than twenty million, a lot of consolation. It's not as though I'm useless.

And sometimes I miss the old life so much, it's as though it died inarticulate in my arms.

I was in Vail when I first heard the offer.

"How're we doing?" I asked my ex-wife from a ski lodge telephone. It was morning in Colorado, noon in New York.

"You're calling every day now?" Alice asked. "Can't you leave New York once a year and forget it, just leave it alone?" I could hear her closing the refrigerator door: it echoed loudly in that vast white loft.

"I wanted to know if Karen and Maggie are coming out." I had invited our two daughters to join me over Christmas. They seemed to prefer spending the college vacations seeing their old high school boyfriends.

"I don't know, why don't you ask them," Alice suggested. There was a sudden knock: Alice had put a bottle of orange juice on the kitchen counter. "Leo? Before I put Karen on, there's something I want to ask you," she said. "I'm sorry about this, but the dealers say it really would be better if I could still use your name."

I looked around the lodge. The sunlight glared in a thin white strip of poison through windows reduced to slits by cigarette smoke and distance. I didn't want my name on Alice's canvasses any more. I didn't own her, I didn't own them: I wanted my name to myself, my company. "I don't know, Alice. Let me think about it."

"You mean, 'let me talk it over with my lawyer.' I thought you liked my paintings."

"I love your paintings, I love you, I'm glad they're selling," I said, "but it hurts me, with you insisting on the divorce, you were the one—"

"You don't have to shout," Alice said. "Here's Karen."

I took a deep breath. The brown air felt good. "So how're we doing, how is everybody?"

"Hi, Dad," Karen said. Her voice is lower, smoother, than her mother's. "It's not that we like Mom more, okay? We just would rather be in the City and see our old high school friends."

"I can understand that," I said. Tired already, with a whole day of skiing yet to come.

"This way, you can meet someone new," Karen said, like a mother. "Anyway, aren't your friends there?" She asked. "Wouldn't you rather be with them?"

"Sure, there's Dave Wolf and Andy Gurney, if you call lawyers friends." I said it loudly because Dave Wolf was walking by in a red body suit. He turned, grinned, gave me the finger. There was an awkward pause back in New York.

"Maggie's out shopping, food. Should I give you back to Mom?" Karen asked.

I watched Dave Wolf buy a cup of coffee. I missed the loft, Alice, the miracle of daughters. "No, that's okay," I said, my voice stronger. "Time to hit the slopes."

We went outside and hit the slopes.

I had just caught up to Wolf; Gurney wasn't ready for the expert slopes yet. I'm always better than myself outside the Northeast.

"You're pretty young for an old man," Wolf told me, watching as I clapped the snow off the tops of my skis.

"You're pretty bright for a dope," I said, breathing hard. We grinned, looked out at the clear blue and white of the mountains. A four-foot-tall skier in black whizzed past us, jumped three moguls and disappeared—the kind of thing that makes you hate kids. Wolf turned to speak. I could see bad news in his lips, his breath.

"Some day all this will be yours," I said, sweeping my arms out over the world below. "You want it? Who wants it?"

Wolf looked at his boots. "Downeys is about to announce a tender offer. Thirty-four dollars, plus convertible subordinates yielding 12 or so, per share of Sandersen's."

I waited. Wolf raised his eyes to look out at the mountains. "Well?" I asked.

"Well what?" He didn't take his gaze from the sparkling crystal.

"You haven't told me anything," I said. "What are the junk bonds worth? Can I fight it?"

"Based on current values?" Wolf asked.

"Jesus Christ," I muttered. I took an awkward hop toward him.

"Okay, about forty-nine dollars a share. With whatever's added in negotiations, the institutions will like it. Talk to Sally Wright, she'll tell you. It'll fly."

Another skier passed, taking the moguls like a frog. For a moment I was at an airport, there were so many possible arrivals, departures, divorces. I pulled at my ski pants, straightened out my jacket, adjusted my headband. I was Erroll Flynn in the Norwegian Resistance, about to ski down a slope with my comrades to save the day.

"You're representing Downeys?" I asked Wolf. He nodded. "You couldn't approach me first? Some friend." I turned to begin an angry traverse.

"This is private," Wolf said. "The announcement will be Monday. They didn't even want me to talk to you, you've been so hostile to other attempts. I told them it was a good offer, maybe you'd be reasonable. You can walk away with more money than most people dream of. You float down into any life you want. What's the problem?"

"Ed Downey smokes cigars," I said. "I won't sell to a man who smokes cigars."

"Leo," Wolf said.

"All right," I said, just as Andy Gurney nearly tripped off a mogul, righted himself, and wobbled to a stop thirty feet away. He began walking toward us.

I lowered my voice. "It's my company, even if I only own fifteen percent. I didn't need this on the one vacation I've taken in the past two years." I sucked in sharp, hurting air. "What I need is, I need my company, I need Alice back. And don't tell me you know what's best for me."

"Best for your shareholders," Wolf said softly.

"To hell with the shareholders, I want my company!" I heard the words spread; I saw the sound waves pollute stroke by stroke the clear air, the crisp slopes. I turned, pulled down my goggles, and pointed my skis vaguely downhill.

"He didn't go for it?" I heard Andy Gurney ask, just before the rush of the air past my ears took away all words and left me with the bright yellow of ski goggles and the harsh, angry colors of speed.

"The offer's just too good," Sally Wright was telling me. The Board of Directors would meet in another five minutes, and I still hadn't told her what I'd do. "And a lot of the board members own enough stock to be willing to make some money. The others worry about shareholder lawsuits if they block the offer. We could look for another buyer, but they've done their homework. You won't get anything solid from anyone else."

"What do they see in us?" I asked. "Balloon loans, then they spin us off again?" I ran my hands over my desk, a thick, glass kidney resting on rough chunks of travertine. "What does a perfume manufacturer want with office supplies?"

"They're not just perfume," Sally said. "So far they've bought into beer, art supplies, hardware, insurance, tourist agencies—"

"—and they've sold all of them off at losses," I snapped. "They've changed their M & A lawyers twice, their accountants three times, in the past seven years. A team of 24-year-old consultants couldn't run an acquisition program worse."

I looked out the windows at the East River. I gave other people on our floor the Central Park views: me, I like the buildings along Madison, Park and Third, the U.N., the automobile lights bustling across the Fifty-Ninth Street Bridge every night—then the blue, or grey, or dirty green ribbon, the East River.

Once, visiting Florence on my first buying trip, I had thought that health and happiness would consist of walking over a river twice a day.

"So find someone else," Sally said. "Or tell me to. But white knights are just vultures with makeup."

The desk had been my choice, my design. What would I do without new desks, staplers of dappled metal soft as suede?

"There must be someone else," I said. She had had this conversation many times; clients always look stupid to investment bankers. "If the offer's so good, there's room for a better one. We'll talk employment contracts, threaten to expand the golden parachutes. Meanwhile, we put out some feelers, get something to bargain with."

I looked up from my desk. "Sure we'll sell; it's just a question of how late we stay up." The words owned so much space, ghostly paperweights on the sheet of glass.

"Sure we'll sell," I repeated slowly, tasting the loss, my nudity. I stood. "You'll talk and I'll agree."

Sally nodded.

I took leave of everything as we walked the long way, a scenic route, through the office on the way to the board room: the water fountains, the reception desk, the accounting department. Even the doorknobs, the names by the offices, were gentle to my eyes.

Our principal board members: Ned Lewis, an overweight, innocent banker always voting for cancer research money; Charlie Schwartz, slumming to add our board to the other nine he sat on; Frank Magnusson, eager to spend on the arts. When they and the others saw me, there was a rush for seats, everyone avoiding my eye.

. "Gentlemen, you all know Sally Wright," I said as we walked in. "Sally will offer us some advice." I paused, looked around.

"So how're we doing?" I asked. Such a stupid question, such a dumb way to bleed all over the Mughal rug—I had to turn my head and laugh, a harsh bark.

The next morning Ed Downey and I set up a Monday meeting, with the understanding that Downey wouldn't make his offer public yet. I would spend the weekend shopping for a better offer.

"Would you like me to stay with you?" my daughter Karen asked over the phone that Friday. "Why can't you tell us why you came back so early?"

"It's work, that's all," I said. Would they still love me, would I love myself, without the company? "It's okay, I'd rather be alone. It's good of you to offer. Really, it's just work."

"It's always work," she said. "Why can't you open up? Is it still you and Mom?"

"No, maybe in a few days. But it really—"the memory of Karen playing basketball at a summer camp when she was ten, one of my favorites, caught in my throat—"Thanks, Karen." My voice was weaker. "Thanks anyway. I have to be alone. I just can't talk to anyone yet. It's not Mom."

I didn't have so much work after all. We had Data-Com and some of the others look at our books and guess at prices, but it was cosmetic, for negotiation purposes. Sunday afternoon I took a walk, went a block east to the Whitney and returned to Fifth to walk up to the Metropolitan.

It was one of those days when the sun slaps the buildings with such clarity and good cheer that you wince. A bagpipe player deserved money for shutting up; a Salvation Army band played with savage, sour abandon. I almost stepped on a baby-blue wool blanket, then noticed the paperback books set out in rows and columns against the blue. *The Dialogues of Plato*; Spinoza; complete plays of Aristophanes, Euripides; assorted Shaw, Ibsen, Brecht; *Toward a Poor Theatre* by some Polish name. What bizarre form of saintliness could strive for poverty in the same world as conference rooms, mergers, men with cigars?

I looked up to find the scraggly youth selling the books, and instead found a magazine face born for soft focus. She wore fur leggings; a dark green loden coat with high French collars; gloves with fingers cut off to expose fingers with fingernails, perfect half-moon cuticles. No make-up, no fingernail polish: just the clothes, the short, light brown hair, the wide abstracted gaze. Bundled up so, she was still conspicuously clean, a model with hours and fine creams to give to her skin.

"This is a very good collection." I smiled and tried not to look a rich fool.

She smiled back, with a hint of apology, perhaps shame, but said nothing. Still, it was a sweet smile. I wondered if the books were her own, or if she was selling them for some unworthy boyfriend.

"How much is this one?" I asked, picking up *Oliver Twist*. I had never read much Dickens, never intended to.

She still said nothing, her eyes on the book, her hands fluttering until I imitated them and opened the book. "1—" read the price pencilled in the upper right-hand corner of the first page.

I found a loose dollar bill, gave it to her. "Thank you," I said, speaking with the extra clarity we reserve for the slow or foreign.

She almost bowed as she took the money, offered the same embarrassed smile. My eyes still probed hers, perhaps moved her to move her lips. "Thank you," her lips said, without a voice behind them.

I couldn't walk away from whatever she was, not carrying a book about an orphan, not hungering so for a reason to keep my eyes open. "Are these yours?" I asked. "Really, it's a wonderful collection." I was attacking a field of lilies with a lawnmower; her eyes jerked up to meet mine, then fell back to the solace of the books and blanket.

"You're an actress?" I asked, still fighting, referring to the many theatre books.

She opened her mouth and backed away until she bumped into a shopping cart full of paperbacks.

"Look, would you like something to eat?" I asked.

She had green eyes: I usually don't notice the color of people's eyes. She still said nothing and looked even more embarrassed, afraid for once in her life of being seen.

I ran over to Madison, bought a crabmeat-salad sandwich and herbal tea for her, roast beef and black coffee for myself. She'd be gone by the time I got back, I knew.

"I can't carry on this conversation entirely by myself," I told her as I drew her away from the books to a bench and unwrapped the sandwiches. "I got roast beef for myself and crabmeat for you. I just want to know if I can help. There are some things that money can help, for instance. I'm like money. There are some things I can do. I can offer you a sandwich."

I took out a pen and scrawled a stack of solid squares onto the take-out bag. Windows, then a rectangle at the opening of the bag for a door. "Look," I said, putting the paper bag over my hand and moving it like a puppet. "I can even offer you a building."

A distant edge of her mouth twitched: a smile, almost.

"Roast beef," she said, in such a low whisper I thought I imagined it. She took the sandwich from my hands and left me with the wimpy crabmeat.

I had forgotten about ambition. Leslie had had two years of college, had modelled, had had flings with acting and jet-set drugs. Her life seemed as clear, free and lost as one of my ex-wife's exploratory brushstrokes. That Monday, I went to Dave Wolf's offices accustomed to, hungry for, contact sports.

Dave Wolf spoke a bit, then my own lawyer spoke. At last Downey smiled, leaned back and lit a cigar. "So everyone agrees?" he asked. "Thirty-one per share, plus the bonds, and I go home with this guy in my pocket." The smoke clumped tight and heavy over the dark oak table.

"The hell," I said. I saw the ski slopes before me: all this before me, never again mine. "You've had about half our earnings per share for the past five years. Forget the junk bonds and call it fifty-two dollars a share, cash. We can always find another offer."

Downey's thick face flushed: instant crustacean. "We're here in good faith, you—"

"Hold it, Ed," Wolf interrupted.

I leaned back. "In Vail I heard thirty-four per share, plus the junk. What do you mean, good faith?"

Wolf cleared his throat. "Of course we're serious. But what else is on the table, what—"

"Forget it," Downey told him. "Who cares if he wants to play hard to get. We'll go back to thirty-four, just so we get out of here faster. What do you say, kid?" He glanced over in my direction, then stood to read something over Wolf's shoulder, puffing hard.

"We're on the playground again?" I asked, also standing. I walked over to Downey, smiled as though I owned all fates.

Downey ignored me but let a hand drop, available for shaking.

"I don't really care what you stick in your mouth," I told him. "I just wish you wouldn't stink up everyone's air as you do it."

Dave Wolf sputtered, suppressing a laugh.

Flying down the slopes, rescuing Leslie, the world, myself, I continued. "I'm going to take a walk, and I'll come back when that cigar is out *and* when you're talking something better than convertible debentures. Me, I'd suggest straight debt, maybe with anniversary puts, since who would want your common stock anyway."

Sally Wright sat across the room with her mouth open. Surprises are good for investment bankers.

"Just so my shareholders don't get stuck with a lot of paper and no money. See you in church, Ed," I told Downey, and walked out of the meeting.

"Did you mean that?" Sally asked once she found me in one of the other conference rooms. "You got the Board to okay a deal."

"Within my discretion. I don't want a quarter of the payment to be in their common stock. They haven't paid a dividend in the past three years, and—"

"They're a *growth* company," Sally said.

"Growth," I said. The word aged me. "They divest everything they buy within three years, then they buy more companies to reinflate their earnings, and you call it growth. It's a shell game, and it's disgusting to sell them a real company. My company."

I had driven a station wagon around Manhattan to peddle that first shipment of Italian stationery goods. Now I sat in a bland beige conference room, selling everything my young guts had built.

"We need something close to fifty dollars a share," I continued. "Liquid and after taxes, nothing converting into their stock. That would just screw the shareholders. Even if Downey gave me a separate deal for my stock, it's still no good."

Sally looked at me, puzzled. "The shareholders?"

I shrugged, embarrassed to be so suddenly clean.

Then Sally smiled and looked ten years younger. "You guys are pigs."

"I cooked for Downey's fraternity in college," I said. "We didn't like each other much then."

"It's blossomed nicely. What do you say to short-term junk bonds?"

I sat for three hours, taking calls, making notes, reading back copies of the *Harvard Business Review*: declining industries, Japanese superiority, how to manage start-ups, cash cows, dogs. Good managers learn to cut losses, shoot dogs. The *HBR* would have me get rid of Leslie. I began planning a new desk: cleancut travertine top, rough glass lumps, weepy as lava, for supports.

Sally came back so pleased my life ebbed even as she closed the door. "We've got something," she said. "Thirty-nine dollars a share for 40% of the common, with the remainder taken out by senior debt with puts in years three through five. They must have been ready for something like this."

"How are the puts set?" I asked. Sally's confidence meant we were at the beginning of the end. "Should we have lunch?"

I barely followed Sally's explanation of the pricing of the option. I'd soon be out of it all—the conference rooms, the talk, the lawyers; already I was only a guest, borrowing time. My hands, even my pockets, felt useless.

"No comment," I told my secretary to say to reporters after the announcement. It makes you feel powerful, saying those words.

"I'm fine, I'm doing fine," I told Karen on the telephone from the office.

"No you're not, why can't you admit something hurts you for once?" Karen insisted. "Your family, now your company . . . and who's this woman Mom was talking to you about?" She took a few swigs of something: grapefruit juice, I guessed.

"Leslie," I said. A friend of my ex-wife's had seen me with Leslie in a good Italian restaurant. "She was on a few *Vogue* covers, years ago. She's beautiful, but she needs a lot of help."

"But she's just a little older than I am," Karen said, tears behind her voice. "Didn't you stop to think about that? How do you think I feel?"

"She's almost ten years older than you, it's got nothing to do with you," I protested, sinking. "It's me, this woman." Giving Karen something new to take into therapy had been the last thing on my mind. "Why assume everything's directed at you?"

Karen gave a harsh laugh. "Where do you think I got it, huh? I mean, who—"

"Okay." I closed my eyes, ran my hands over the glass desk. "Me, you got it from me. Leslie helps, just by needing me she helps. Damn it, do you know how many people, good people, I'm trying to find jobs for?"

"Dad, I think maybe—"

"I'm sorry," I said. "Can we go to a museum soon? Let's get together."

We made an appointment for a few days later. Over hamburgers my daughter's wisdom would wash over me, soothe me. Maggie had suddenly left the City for a ski trip with a boy friend, and I wouldn't see her until Spring break.

I like to believe that, in general and on average, this is an efficient world, so that people get the professions they deserve. Just as owners and dogs come to resemble each other, jobs mold people—or else they spit people out, and the people become hollow wrecks, teachers, artists. Saints.

For a while I had nothing to become. When you've got millions and nothing in particular to do, after you've worked ten or twelve or fourteen hours a day for years, it's hard to fit anywhere. Investment offers come in, but you wonder how healthy the addiction is.

I took Leslie up to my old office one night, while we were still waiting for Justice Department approvals. No one worked past seven any more: the office was a ghost town. We drank champagne and watched the cars cross the Fifty-Ninth Street Bridge.

I told Leslie that long ago, I had a cubicle on the top floor of the building I worked in. One day someone jumped from the higher skyscraper next door, "the Metro building, you know the one I mean?"

Leslie was watching the night. From the thick carpet, all the lights off, my office was foreign, a boy's bedroom where familiar objects changed shape in the dark.

"They're tearing it down," Leslie said. Her voice was still barely above a whisper, but at least she spoke. "I met the architect of the Metro building once. We ate very well. I thought I'd always eat in fine restaurants, men paying. They're tearing it down now, the Metro building."

The city lights caught a plane of her face as she pressed the glass of champagne against her lower lip and smiled, one grudge accounted for.

I closed my eyes, the better to remember. "The suicide landed in one of the open water coolers on our roof, with the huge blades sweeping through the water. I was sitting at my desk, giving something to a typist, when she turned white and started whimpering. I turned around to see blood seeping down from the ventilation grid behind me. Blood on the wall, dripping."

Leslie turned from the window and walked uncertainly to where I sat on the floor, my back against one of the travertine slabs supporting the desktop.

"What did that tell you?" she asked, kneeling. "What were you working for?"

I wanted my lips on her mouth, her neck. I took her hand, held it still. "It was having this room," I said. "Or it was going into a room, feeling them look at me as I entered, the same as you. Because having power is like having beauty.

"Or it was saying something, making the decision, and knowing it would happen. There's nothing like it."

Even as I said it, I doubted. The corner of Leslie's lips curled discreetly. A dotted past like hers—I had worked so hard, been so simple; I had lost so much time! And then we had the city at our feet, our lips on each other's lips, lightly.

Leslie pulled away. "But there's nothing like anything," she said in a strong voice.

When she had regained her voice and confidence entirely she would probably give me up, return to acting.

"Why did you tell me that story?" she asked. "What did the blood tell you?"

"Right, there's nothing like anything," I agreed. An oil company had bought one of Alice's paintings and locked it away in a vault. As you looked closer and closer at the painting, your eye would be lost in networks of veins very like its own. I loved Alice, I loved her paintings, yet that hadn't been enough. I wondered how similar we were, Leslie and I, to other couples, the many lonely couples, standing, sitting, waiting together in darkened midtown offices, looking out windows for rescue. "Just that I needed something, or someone," I told Leslie, "if I wanted to keep from jumping, too."

"And you had a family, a company, and now you have a fortune," Leslie said, tracing my lips with an index finger. "Poor little rich boy."

My frown was lost in a minor snort.

"I thought I'd be happier," I complained. But then I snorted again, trying to hold in the laugh.

"You, you spoiled *brat!*" Leslie screeched, louder than I had ever heard her. She too was laughing. "You've had so *much.*" She turned to me, pulled me down. We kissed softly, then long and hard, until we knocked over a champagne glass and began giggling.

"We've *both* had so much," Leslie said quietly. "Everybody. Everybody has so much."

We sat up, finished the champagne in her glass, left the building. We took the bottle, though. Consolations meant much, in the world we shared for just those months.

David Del Bourgo

White Collar

on a side street
amidst the sweatshops
at the outskirts of downtown
only a block from skid row
& the broken men & women

in a wool gabardine suit
holding my briefcase
early for an appointment
huddled with the factory workers
drawn by the sun
to the catering truck

where an overfed illegal
in a tight shimmering shirt
proud of his midriff bulge
thumbs money like a man
handing out life

Severance

Al Sandvik

I'M GOING TO dial the phone any minute now, but when I do it will start wheels that go only in the direction of pain. Baylor has been on my case for eight months to take care of this. This and a few other things I haven't gotten around to because they're his choices, not mine, and in my personal ecosystem they're wrong.

But, when push comes to shove, what Baylor ordains as right is what's right around here; around here is an advertising agency of which he is the CEO. I'm Rich Woford, vice president in charge of the account executives, including one Harold Finney, the man Baylor has told me to fire.

I've never gotten good at firing people and, in these last seconds, I wonder if anyone ever does. Or should. How do you tell a man ten years older than yourself, at an age when it's getting too late for the party in this business, that it's all over? How do you say the fourteen years he's invested in a future here are all canceled out? One hour with me and he's out on the street. Oh, we always give severance pay and extend the benefits for ninety days, but that's giving local anesthesia for an amputation.

The phone rings. It's my secretary Marla.

"You've been cooped up in there so long I thought I'd better remind you about the fire drill."

"When?" I ask, immediately defensive about my time for the rest of the day, not wanting anything to put off the Finney thing again.

"The Building said between four and five and it's ten after four already."

"I'll pass," I say. "Anyway, I remember from junior high school how it goes."

"Baylor won't like that," she says. "After all, you are head of a department, one of his agency role models."

"I know Baylor won't like it," I say and, about to hang up, "Oh, is he around? Finney, I mean."

"He's been around all day. Got here before I did this morning," she says. Marla gets in the office early. Finney's had a long day.

So what will I charge him with: screwing off, not knowing his stuff? No, his crime is not enough compromise, not warping his craft enough to please the agency's second largest client, a computer software company called Mind Matter. Not that they expect him to do undoable things, just unsmart things like creating advertising to please each personal taste in their management team which always begets advertising with borderline anemia. And Finney fights it and fights it until the client has to remind him—and me and Baylor—every once in awhile, who's paying the bills.

I pick up the phone and ask Harold to come in. In his good soldier style, he says, "Be right there, but I have to make one call. *Business Week* has a Mind Matter ad going on the press, and the client just called insisting on changes." Then he follows with a few beats on his drum: "Even when they get the kind of crap they want, somebody over there gets an idea for how to make it worse. Apparently they didn't get around to asking the janitor for his opinion until today."

When he comes in, he sits down looking worried and I wonder if he suspects. But I remember he always looks that way, his eyebrows forever in a knit. For some people this wonderful world of advertising is never a good time, just a steady conveyor belt of antsy situations.

He leans forward in his chair, half smiles, and says, "What can I do for you?" which gives me no segue at all into my act, the act where I begin as his friend, knowing he won't let me stay in that role at the end. But there always needs to be a scenario; I can't just lower the boom on him.

"If you can afford to take a little time here, I'd like to talk some about your professional life," I say, laughing and getting up to close the door. I catch myself laughing and stop it. Not fair. I know what's coming; he doesn't.

I begin the story quite a ways back, Harold's first skirmishes with the client in putting together the Mind Matter advertising plan. Then the escalation to ongoing jungle warfare. I go over the several talks we'd had about his inflexibility and its recent high point when it got so bad I had to step in and handle the development of a new product campaign myself.

I think I've got a good flow going, building the import as I go, brick by brick, when the damn fire alarm goes off.

"It's just a fire drill," I say. "Forget about it. I'd like to keep going on this."

"I know what you're leading up to," Harold says flatly. "I'm getting the ax."

"Wait," I say as a commotion bursts outside in the hall: shouting, the calling out of witty remarks followed by shrill laughter. Sounds of gaiety at a time like this.

Harold stands and walks toward the door. My hand raises like a cop stopping traffic. He faces me, drops his shoulders back against the wall and puts his hands in his pockets, like a guy who wants to talk about baseball or something. His voice is like that, too:

"You keep pounding on the fact that you had to step in for me because I wouldn't budge when budging meant doing work that turned out so crappy the new product doesn't have a chance. Admit it."

"The new product is going to be just fine," I say. "And if it isn't, it won't be the advertising that sinks it." My mouth is pasty from the passage of words I don't believe. The success of the product introduction is, in fact, still being argued; Mind Matter's Chairman having had a row with Baylor about it and then Baylor raking me.

Harold pushes away from the wall and reaches for the door. Just then it opens toward him.

"Hey, Chief," one of the account executives says, poking his smiling face in. "We don't want to lose you. We got a roaring fire goin' on out here . . . ." Then he sees Harold behind the door and senses something.

"Oh! Sorry," he says and backs out.

Harold reaches for the doorknob.

"Where are you going?" I ask.

"Aren't we done?"

"If I get a chance to say something, maybe we're done. What a lousy time for fun and games," I say, nodding toward the hall.

"Then I *am* history?" he says.

"You're definitely not making this easy, Harold."

"It's supposed to be easy?" he says, walking out, banging the door closed.

Instinctively, I get up to go after him, but I stop at the closed door and lean my forehead against it. It comes home that he's the one on solid ground, not me. He's the one insisting on good work for his client. And I'm the one who's been preaching,

"If we lose Mind Matter as a client, we also lose any chance to straighten them out as a client." Which sounded pretty good when I began saying it two years ago. But we haven't straightened Mind Matter out so now what it means to people like Harold is let's continue to put up with their shit to get their money.

I sit down and the air smells bad, the overhead light acts sick. My mind steps out of me and is over there somewhere watching this middle-aged middleman curving over his desk. It remembers him in sixties' protest marches and it wonders what he's come to: getting paid to deal out punishment for a man's integrity.

I look at the framed photo of Jan and the girls smiling at me, trusting me, under the green beach umbrella at the resort she wants us to buy and run. I could be a happy man, I tell her, but it would really put us against the wall financially. "Lighten up," she says, "I'll make beds and we'll get a hundred year mortgage."

The fun people are filing back through the hall. No one will poke a head in this time. The word would have already spread that something heavy is going down with Finney. I think about Harold hearing their laughter. I think about Harold in general. He's what's known in the fraternity as a good man, in the old world meaning of that word: not the greedy glad-hander, just unusually capable. He fights dereliction at the typewriter and drawing board every time he smells it, which makes him a five-foot-five, brown-eyed pain in the rear for those who don't like to push themselves. Yes, a good man.

I get up and go to Harold's office, close the door and tell him to forget what just happened, that it had no good reason to happen, that as long as I'm around, he's around. I level with him about Baylor, that he's not a friend of his—he said he knows—but that I would back him up no matter what Baylor says or does.

He stands and thanks me, adding that getting fired would have created a special problem at home. I'm not sure what that means and don't ask.

Back in my office, I stand at the window for I don't know how long, until I sense the quiet. Everyone's cleared out. I start to straighten things up on my desk, get the "must do" pile ready for tomorrow, but then I say the hell with it and grab my coat.

Out of habit, I step down to the end of the hall to say goodnight to Baylor.

He looks up and I can see I've interrupted a thought circuit.

"Oh. Rich. How did it go with Finney?"

"How did you know we talked?"

"*I* went on the fire drill," he says.

"Let's talk about it tomorrow," I say.

Baylor's eyes get deep and tunneled.

"You didn't do it, did you?" he breathes. "Damn it! How many times have we talked? And DeMars is back Monday." Arnold DeMars is Baylor's boss, owner of the agency.

Baylor spins his chair toward the window to let off steam. When he turns back to me, he's different. Someone is near death, maybe him. He never does look in the pink; long hours, cigarettes and fast-food lunches sent in make his skin bone-colored. His eyes seem focused a long way off, looking for a way out of somewhere. I assume now his trouble with DeMars is my not getting Finney fired.

"Sit down," he says to me.

I sit because I hear no choice in the way he says it.

"We need to talk about you and this agency, your part in it. You know how I always see it," he says, his voice softening abruptly, "always do what is best for the agency no matter how much it might hurt someone."

It's a speech I've heard often, but this time it's pointed my way.

"Rich, you have abilities I truly envy. I mean that with all my heart. Such an instinct for marketing. You have imagination. You have . . ."

I'm aware that I haven't moved a muscle since I sat down, not a blink, trying to read where he's going. When Baylor leans forward and tightens his eyes to tell me I would have been great in the creative side of the business, I know the act has begun.

And when he adds, in the past tense, "I think that would have been the best fit, after all," the first thing that comes into me is a final sadness for Harold Finney and the *special problem* he alluded to. As Baylor builds to phrases like *the parting of ways*, I'm able to make out my wife's face in the grey above Baylor's head, watching me as I watch Baylor. She smiles.

Charles Entrekin

Day After the Market Crash
San Francisco, October, 1987

The spare change
saxophone player
at Market and Sansome
holds sway over the pink
gray day, and five o'clock
faces in pin striped suits, and
a young man and his girl, sipping beer
beside the bank's imitation Greek patio,
its concrete columns roofed with glass.

As if in a dream, his sound comes from
inside a cacophony of commuters at day's end,
from all the transients in this corner of the city,
the weaselly newspaper vendor, the birdlike
yelps and yells of bicycle messengers, their
punk red hair, warlike warnings subtly fading
into air, as suddenly from inside it all,
the spare change saxophone player blows, leaning back,
knees bent, eyes closed, into the hollow of the bank's
echoes. A Mississippi melody.
A sound of innocence lost,
echoes.

And at the periphery of being alive, an unfolding
begins, and this random audience stops
inside its life of rushing elsewhere, stops,
steps outside the scheme of things. The newspapers say
the economy is collapsing. But not for now; for now,
even though Rumplestiltskin is working,
spinning straw into gold, it makes no difference.
For they have stopped to listen to dreams

older than their own, and those that can
swim in this tide of sound, listen
to the ebb and flow of things
that have come and gone into the ground,
that now hang suspended,
become the rhythm of one man
in baggy clothes and floppy boots,
and a still urgency of breath,
of neck chords straining
and releasing, bringing the crinkle
of their faces, the sudden patter
of applause, their dollar bills
released in the empty
breeze.

C.B. Follett

From the Warehouse

We stand, side by side,
in rectangular boxes of thick green glass,
peering closely at each other.
Our mouths open and shut;
words swallowed by transparent barriers
built over the years.
Like Snow White, we are encased,
awaiting the kiss.

His life is a warehouse of compartments.
No congress between them.
In one compartment is the source
of today's anguish.
Five years of business problems
teetering on flimsy laths.
We do not talk much of this storm gathering.
He does not like to.
It means seepage from that carton
marked *My Work.*
And why should he risk contamination,
when each forced revelation brings
news worse than before?

In my bell jar, the air grows tight.
I long for the strength of knowing.
I can build from reality.
But I cannot press from him
more public pain. Not even for me
can he let down the barriers.
Not for solutions.
Not for compassion.
Not even to build love.

Return From Oz

Jeffrey Zygmont

So HERE IT all is again, he says to himself. Here are the same beigey walls. The same low-nap carpet. The same gridded, sound-absorbing ceiling overhead. Here are the same low-back swivel chairs, the same green-glowing computer screens, the telephones with banks of extra buttons, the scattered stacks of papers, some in manila file folders, lying helter-skelter everywhere. On the walls hang the same pictures—different pictures really but with the same look of slicked-back sedateness. Funny how offices everywhere always look the same. Strange that he had never before noticed that there is nothing here to invite him.

What do you think of it, she is saying from behind him and he wonders if, standing in the doorway looking at his back, she is able to read his expression.

It's very nice, he says.

Is it bigger than your last office?

No, he says. Then, not wanting to give a bad impression, he adds, but it's plenty big enough.

You must be glad to be getting back.

It's been a while, he says and that's all he can say.

I think you'll like it here, she says. I've got a really good group of workers. Not a slacker in the bunch. We all get along real well together, too. We have a lot of fun. Of course, we get the work done. That's the most important part.

Sensing that it's time for him to speak he adds, that's good. He hasn't quite been listening: his feeling of surprise is too overwhelming. He had expected to be excited, apprehensive at least. So now he is surprised that, the first day on a new job—the first morning even—all he feels is boredom.

That's the most important part, she is saying. We keep a tight ship. My department has actually seen an increase in sales while our competitors are taking a beating. That's why we're hiring while they've been laying off for a good six months now. But of course, you know all about layoffs.

She laughs. He is not offended by the laugh, but he recognizes that it could be interpreted as insensitive. After these last few months he realizes that it is not the sort of teasing he would do at home with his children.

Come on, she says. I'll introduce you to the rest of my team—our team, I should say.

Turning away from the blank desk that is now his desk he sees it again: the big room with the beigey walls and the low-nap carpet. All the desks in here look the same too, even though each is covered with different assortments of papers and books and office paraphernalia, with small-framed pictures of different husbands or wives or children. All he can think of are his feet.

His feet have ached all morning, although he just now realizes that they ache as he follows her along this sort-of corridor that skirts the wall around the big room with all the desks. It's not an aching from fatigue. More a vague pinching feeling, a constriction, a feeling of tightness and confinement as his feet are closed up all around by his leather shoes with their cinched-up laces. When did he last wear shoes? It must have been when they went out to dinner sometime. But what does he wear on his feet at home—never really thought about it before. Sneakers sometimes. And, often, nothing.

I can't believe this, she is saying. Where is everybody? She is looking into the doorways of offices that, like his new office, circle around the outside of the big beigey room. You'd think I'd called a staff meeting or something. She laughs again. He notices that she is wearing low-heeled shoes, but they are low heels that narrow down abruptly to sharp little points, nonetheless (a compromise?), and they look even less stable than stiletto pumps.

But when did he stop wearing shoes? He figures the change must have come over him gradually. Either that or he had stopped wearing them right away but didn't notice because it wasn't important to notice. Now they feel so tight. And hot. Hard to believe he used to wear them every day.

There you all are, she says suddenly, picking up her pace toward a knot of people standing around a coffee maker. They have been watching the coffee stream from the machine into a carafe but they look up at the sound of her voice. He has to walk unnaturally fast to keep up with her as she closes in on them.

I was wondering where all you guys went to, she says.

The machine was broken, one of them replies. We had to form a committee to fix it, says another. A few laugh (nervously) at this.

What's most different about shoes is the grass. He thinks of the feel of it beneath his bare feet, the soft crush of it except for the blades that push up into the hollows of his arches. A million soft brushes. It is a much different feel to walk barefoot on the driveway or sidewalk. There the hard nap of asphalt and concrete, unyielding, leaves a sensation of grittiness on his soles. When he comes back to the house after a walk down the driveway to the box for the newspaper or mail, he always sits on the front stoop and wipes his hands briskly across the bottoms of his feet. It wouldn't do to track grit into the house, especially not now, after he has taken charge of the cleaning. He runs the vacuum at least twice a week. He takes special pride in the floor, particularly now that he's grown to notice the plushy, brushed-up look of the just-cleaned carpet. He likes the way it looks so much that he feels reluctant to let the children in to trample it all down again, though of course he never prevents them.

The children are with the sitter now, he thinks, his mind still distracted as he hears his boss say: I'm glad you're all together at least. This way I can introduce you all at once. This is Paul, the newest addition to our team.

There are four of them facing himself and the boss. They have inched away from the coffee machine to form an attentive little arc around the two of them. He notices their shoes. Two of the men wear wing tips that look nearly identical, except one pair is more highly buffed. The third man wears Rockports. The one woman in the group has on sneakers, or rather running shoes. Her white socks are turned down at the ankles, disguising whether her ankles are tidy or thick.

Paul will get to know you a lot better on his own—he's a real team player, the boss says. But just to get things started, let's see. This is Frank. He covers California. That's our biggest sales region, so we figure it deserves its own full-time manager.

Good to meet you. The better-buffed wing tips step forward, Frank's hand outstretched above them. The two men shake hands, Frank taking a firm grip, then releasing after one quick upward then downward snap. It is an idiosyncratic handshake that also seems affected.

Jerry here has everything west of the Rockies except for California, she continues. That's a lot when you consider the boom in Portland and Seattle. Seattle is going like nothing I've even seen before.

Jerry is the Rockports. These are called walking shoes, which seems to be an excuse for the many seams sewn all around them. He wonders if they're comfortable. The wing tips, he figures, must be dying.

Alice handles the Northeast, she says next. That's New England and as far west as Pennsylvania, and down to Washington. Oh, and Virginia too.

I hear you have some little ones at home, says Alice as they shake hands. I've got two myself. We'll have to trade notes. I've been lobbying to get some child care in here. But so far, it's the ol' brick wall.

The others chuckle at this, but their laughs are nervous, more to break the tension. It's clear that this is a sore spot between Alice and the boss.

And this is Candy, the boss says quickly. He's the South. That's mostly Atlanta, New Orleans, Phoenix and Houston.

And Tuscaloosa, cuts in Frank of California. The others laugh, this time more heartily, a note of relief after the day-care laugh.

Maybe together we can do something about these wise guys, says Candy. His are the unpolished wing tips. The laces are frayed in spots too. One lace may even be broken and tied together in a thick knot (he can't be sure, not wanting to stare too intensely at Candy's shoes). He notices too that the thick-welt soles that run like platforms around Candy's shoes are all scudded up, especially at the toes, which must catch on curbs and steps. These, he thinks, might be comfortable shoes.

After the introductions a silence follows, during which he forces himself to look up. They are watching him, their faces filled with expectation. He realizes that he hasn't yet spoken.

How old are your children, he says to Alice.

Eight and six. How 'bout you?

My sons are eleven and eight, and my little girl is seven.

A seven *and* an eight year old, exclaims Alice. They're close. I feel sorry for your poor wife.

Actually, I've been watching them lately while my wife works.

He realizes suddenly that the others are looking at him awkwardly, because they are excluded from the conversation. A silence: he can think of nothing to say to them.

So you'll be covering the Midwest, Frank says to him at last.

That's right.

Chicago will keep you the busiest, resumes the boss. Detroit's not bad because of the auto industry, but they're in a slump right now.

Too bad Japan's not in the Midwest, says Frank. I bet you wouldn't mind having Toyota and Honda.

Or Sony, Jerry says.

Sony don't make cars, Jerry.

Well, I know. But it's still a big company.

He tries to chuckle at their banter.

Then, back in his office where he is left alone to settle in, he tries all the empty drawers in the empty desk. He didn't bring anything to put in them. Way back in the top drawer a paper clip is stuck in the corner in a gap where the wooden sides don't quite join up. Earlier this morning someone said something to him about getting supplies from one of the clerks, or secretaries, or assistants, or whatever the people in the big room are called. He'll ask later.

He gets up and looks behind his office door. A wooden coat hanger hangs on a hook that's screwed into the back of the door. He takes down the hanger. In its center, the name *Sheraton* is emblazoned in gold ink beneath a gold-printed laurel wreath. It seems to be the only ornament in the room. He'll leave his jacket on for now.

Walking back to the desk he feels for the first time another tightness—not the shoes this time, although when he thinks about it, the constriction of his feet is still there. (Is he growing used to it already?) This other pinching is in his bladder, and like his shoes, it has been there a while before he just now becomes aware of it, creeping up on him almost from his subconscious. It too is an alien feeling, or rather it is the return of a long-forgotten feeling he has grown unaccustomed to. He thinks about how at home it is the easiest thing to urinate whenever the smallest tingling begins. At home he can make innumerable trips to the toilet without them seeming like interruptions to whatever it is he is doing. Sometimes he doesn't even close the bathroom door if he knows the kids are out in the yard or in another part of the house. And if he's working outside himself he uses the toilet right off the back door, so that he doesn't have to worry about tracking dirt onto the floor.

But here . . . he tries to remember where the bathroom is . . . where the men's room is. Earlier this morning someone said something about it being down by the main door then just to the left. Or was it right? He'll find it later. After all, he just got here.

Sitting down (the tightness—tingling in his bladder sends a jolt as he bends), he looks at the top of the desk. He'll have to bring pictures. After all, everyone else has pictures. He looks for a spot to put them. The entire top of the desk is blank, but when he can't decide on a spot, he realizes that he doesn't want pictures of his family here. He would rather keep them separate. He closes his eyes and tries to imagine what his children must be doing right now. It's easy enough because he knows their routine so well, but when he brings them to mind he feels his absence from them. It's a backward sort of thing, a turned-around sense of being: he doesn't so much feel like a presence here as he feels like an absence there, a shimmering hole in the presence of his children that they can't see because it's not of the same substance as they. He opens his eyes and sees Candy standing in the doorway, Candy from Tuscaloosa with the bruised wing tips.

How ya doin', Candy says. There is an unmistakable tone of apology in his voice.

Just getting used to the place, he answers.

I know. It takes a bit of getting used to. 'Specially with a group of crazies like us. Candy chuckles. (But is there a hint of warning in his voice too, or prophecy?)

So far, he says to Candy, everyone's been real nice.

Well, if there's anything you need or any questions you want answered, you just be sure to ask.

I'll do that.

Then a pause, a bit awkward between them, during which he wonders why Candy has come here.

The thing is, starts Candy suddenly, I figured I better let you know that it's time to get ready for lunch. It's a little bit early for lunch, I know. But the thing of it is, we have this little tradition here that, whenever someone new signs on, Cathy takes the whole crew out and buys 'em lunch. It's sort of like a little welcome-and-get-acquainted deal.

Today?

That's right. Today. We don't waste any time around here.

But I was planning to go home for lunch today.

Home?

Sure. To check on the kids. It's not far. Outside of rush hour it's only a twenty minute drive from here. I figure twenty minutes to get home, twenty minutes for lunch, then twenty to get back.

Well, yeah, I guess you could do that. I mean, if your family's expecting you and everything . . . .

It's not so much that they're expecting me. I just thought I'd surprise them. You know, first day away from home and all.

Sure. Hey, you don't have to explain to me.

Another pause, this one more awkward because Candy is so obviously uncomfortable.

The thing of it is, Candy says at last, shifting his weight from one bruised wing tip to the other, grimacing almost, lifting his hands to gesture apology, the thing of it is, I think Cathy has already gone ahead and booked reservations and all. She really likes to do this up, ya see. She makes a little speech and everything. Then she gives you your first-tier sales goals.

Sales goals? Really? In front of everybody?

That's right—right there in front of everybody. She does it to make us more competitive, I think.

Candy leans toward him now and says more quietly: In fact, I'm not even supposed to be telling you this. She likes to keep it a surprise. But the thing is, I think she'd be real disappointed if you were to back out now.

I see what you mean. It's just that, well, their first day with the sitter and everything, I just wanted to get home to see them to make sure everything is all right. I figured I could be there and back in an hour.

Truth is, he doubts if he can really make it in an hour. Traffic is never as easy as a person would like. And even if it is, will he really be ready to return after only a twenty-minute visit? Still, would it matter that much if he's a little late getting back? Even on his first day? After all, how much can be expected of a person on his first day?

I know exactly what you mean, Candy says. Babysitters are hell. After a while my wife couldn't take it any more. She up and quit her job so she could be at home with the kids.

Well, he says, I can't do that. Obviously not. But I thought that, just for today, because it's their first day alone with the sitter . . . .

Suddenly Frank appears in the doorway looking over Candy's shoulder. Candy steps inside the office to make room but actually it seems that he shrinks back in Frank's presence, as if he actually grows smaller.

You two plotting to overthrow the company, says Frank. If you do, make sure I come out of it with a fat severance check, would ya. Frank laughs at this but the other two are silent—he looking out from his desk a little bit bewilderedly at the two of them, Candy with a face that looks a little bit too much like the face of a conspirator who's been caught with evidence.

Anyway, says Frank, Cathy sent me to tell you two that it's time to go to lunch.

He wants to go home for lunch today, Candy says.

Home?

I just want to check on the kids. I figure I can make it in an hour.

Frank's laugh sounds derisive. Sure, he says, but if you have lunch with the boss you get to take two hours. Besides, how can you give up shrimp cocktail for peanut butter and jelly?

It's just that his kids are a wee bit jittery about this being their first day without him, replies Candy.

Hey, don't argue with me, says Frank as he raises his hands and leans back, a gesture of disassociation. I've got nothing to do with this.

I don't think it's that big a deal, says Candy. I don't see why we can't just postpone the lunch for a day.

Tell that to Cathy, says Frank.

As he listens to their exchange his mind wanders to a million simultaneous recollections. He remembers his children sitting in the apple tree in the lot next door with the neighbor kids, together yelling children's obscenities at a rival group of kids from further down the street, fearing the unknown. He remembers how he embarrassed his oldest son when he walked unexpectedly into the boy's room and found him talking to himself as he fantasized a game with spaceman figures. How the boy had tried to suddenly disassociate himself from the play by asking irrelevant questions: Dad, how old are those sneakers? (aha, so he had been wearing sneakers then!) He remembers the mad scramble to get them to the dentist one morning, the three of them with consecutive appointments, and he remembers how long the wait seemed, having nothing to keep him occupied but frayed-edged issues of *People* magazine, which he read to distract himself from the fact that, outside of himself, there were only mothers waiting there. He remembers standing bewildered in the breakfast-cereal aisle of the grocery store. He remembers trying to frost cupcakes without smearing frosting on the paper wrapping. He remembers eggs. He remembers the weariness fuzzing his head as he sat on his daughter's bed reading a story to her, and how when he dozed, she kicked down on the bed, impatient for him to finish. He remembers the sound of the door closing, a definitive thud that followed his son into the house the time he fell off of his bicycle and came looking for consolation, how the boy had so bravely held back the crying until, finding his father at last in an inner room, he held up his bloodied elbow and then tried to back away in fright from his own arm. The antiseptic sting of peroxide. A cinder 'neath the skin. He remembers even his own childhood, reusing the bath water, not minding or even noticing the dirt and soap scum but disliking the clammy feel of the too cool water. He remembers the brown filmy stuff left on chicken meat where his mother pulled it from the bone. He remembers bathroom smells. He remembers finding stones and bottle caps in his sons' pockets before putting their pants through the wash. He remembers a certain toy car with a nick in the yellow paint on its roof. He remembers how muffled their voices sound when his children play in the basement. He remembers a certain flower, in a vase on a table someplace he doesn't know where. It seems he's had his eyes closed for a long time but they have been open throughout.

Then he hears Frank say: All I know is I'm not going to be the one to tell Cathy to cancel lunch because you want to go home on your first day.

He looks up at the two of them. They're standing shoulder to shoulder now just inside his doorway. Frank with the high-buffed shoes has California, the prize territory. Candy sells in the South wearing comfortable shoes.

I never really made definite plans to go home, he says. It was just an idea.

That's good. Because Cathy's got definite plans about this lunch.

But if we postpone it just a day . . . Candy begins.

He says: Besides, that part about the shrimp cocktail sounds pretty good. His attempt to be light doesn't quite come off.

As he rises to go he wonders if it is a change in lighting that suddenly makes Candy's face so lined and weary looking. Then he is stabbed by his full bladder. It ripples shock waves through him like an electric current centered in the pit of his abdomen. Walking out with them, he wonders if it would be better form to excuse himself now to use the bathroom, or if he should wait until they get to the restaurant.

Constance Alexander

Outplacement Blues

1.

Welcome to world
headquarters, the command
and control center
of the corporation.
My name is Hal Fulmer
and you'll have to
pardon my appearance.
I think I'm having
a nervous breakdown,
even though they don't
call it that any more.
It's stress.
Workplace-induced anxiety.
Job misery.
Employment uncertainty.
Career panic.
Vocational anomie.
The corporation,
you see,
is in the midst of
downsizing
resizing
right-sizing
redesigning
restructuring
reshaping
reapproximating
reorganizing
retrofitting
reshuffling the boxes

playing the blue chip version
of three card monte
sketching the new
infrastructure
on the back of a
cocktail napkin
so we can be
lean and mean.
Like assassins.
Wild dogs.
A marathon runner
with PMS.

2.

As we get ready
to meet the challenges
of the future
we are determined
to hit the ground running.
Sharpen the edge
of our competitive advantage.
Strive for excellence.
Thrive on chaos.
Swim with the sharks.
Play games our mothers
never taught us.
Learn what they don't teach
at the Harvard Business School.
Pull our own strings.
Be our own best friends.
Get to yes.
Take the less traveled road.
Mistake our wives for our hats.
This is what happens
when you hit the ground running.
Sorry.
It's just too much for me.

3.

My name is Hal Fulmer
and I'm going to kill myself
with this gun I bought so my wife,
ex-wife, excuse me,
could protect herself
while I was away on
business trips, working
on corporate strategy
so the company could take
an aggressive stance
in an increasingly competitive
worldwide marketplace.
My name is Hal
and I've been designated
for outplacement.
Early retirement.
VIPP—the voluntary incentive
placement program—
sounds like a laxative.
Or is it MOPP—
management outsizing protection plan?

No matter.
Officially, I'm dead meat.
Day old bread.
Surplus.
Like the cheese they give
welfare mothers.
An unmarked box of greasy Velveeta
you're supposed to be grateful for.
Think of me as excess protein,
a little fat to be trimmed
from the corporate gut.

I'm taking it well,
don't you think?
Had the gun all day
and didn't kill anyone.
Aimed at a few
when no one was looking
but managed to restrain myself.

Could've had a VP of marketing
on the jogging path,
a division manager of
transmission systems
at the urinal.
But I decided to
hold off. Or hold on.
Until I thought it through.
If I play my cards right,
my story'll get on Oprah
or Donahue. God! I'd
love to see Phil leaping through
the audience, railing against
the cold corporate heart.
Can't you hear him?

"Do you mean to tell me,
Mr. High-and-Mighty Executive,
that you can actually sleep at night
when you're laying off thousands
of loyal employees with a limp handshake
and a couple of months' pay?"
God! I love that silver hair, the self-righteousness,
the rage of a fallen Catholic who still believes
in purgatory. Phil could do a nice job
with my case.
He'll interview some personnel types,
who will swear that the company's
E.A.P.—excuse me, Employee Assistance Program—
was fully equipped to deal with depression
and the other aftermath of—ahem—restructuring.
Phil'll shove that microphone right into their faces
and give that cross-eyed stare that says, "You've got to
be outta your mind."

But instead he'll whisper to the guy,
probably spitting a little,
still smelling of last night's Scotch and Marlo:
"You mean to say that no one, not one single person
in that well educated group of—
of masters of the universe—
anticipated that Hal Fulmer
might blow out his brains at sunrise on the morning

his so-called outplacement took effect?"
By now, Phil's quivering.
His upper lip glistens with sweat.
He's on a roll.
"Not one of your hot-shot MBA types,
excuse me, masters of business administration geniuses,
predicted that this sensitive, lonely man would—
in a desperate bid to get the attention
of your top level executives—
commit suicide in the very headquarters building
that was really his home for seventeen years?
Why, in his note he said he spent more time in the office
than he ever spent in the house he bought for himself
and his lovely wife, excuse me, ex-wife, Brenda."

Yeah. That's how it'd go.
I wonder if—no, Brenda wouldn't consent
to an interview.
She hates Donahue.
Oprah, maybe.
No matter what,
my secretary'll
defend me.
And maybe the janitorial staff.
"Nice guy," they'll say.
"Always wrote 'Don't erase'
in big purple letters
on his whiteboard."
And maybe my cousin Harry'll
say what a regular guy I was.
"Loved the Dodgers. Hated
that they moved outta Brooklyn.
Never got over it."
That's what
he'll say.
That stuff.

Pinstripe Suite

I know a guy called home last week
to say he'd be late for dinner.
I was there in his office when it happened.
"Hi, honey," he said,
and started talking about
his rough day at work.
"Be home around seven.
Don't wait dinner, I'll get something out."
When he stopped talking
and started listening
I could see his face change,
like clouds passing over the sun on windy days.
He was chuckling a little. Apologizing.
"Just a little joke," he said. "Heh-heh."
But he didn't look amused.
Seems he had a new housekeeper
he didn't know about.
She was the one
who answered the phone.
Not his wife of 20 years.
"She sounds just like Betty,"
he said.
"Happens to me all the time," I lie.
That's my job.

I found out my wife left me
one night, I called home and the answering machine
said she'd moved and would be contacting all her friends
within a week.
Go ahead. Laugh. It could happen to you sometime.
We're not so different, though you probably choke
on admitting it.
I should've known. She kept trying to tell me,
but I didn't, you know, catch on.
I was coming home later and later from work.
Sometimes she'd be there. Sometimes not.
She always left a note saying where she was,
but I never bothered reading them.
She had that subscription to the ballet,
and was working on her master's, she said.

After it happened, I remembered the night I woke up
and she was sitting on the bed just staring at me.
It was 5 in the morning,
and I couldn't figure out why
she was up and dressed for work so early.
She'd been out all night,
I finally figured out. Weeks later.
See, she wasn't there when I came home from work
around midnight, but I forgot.

Now I figure she was gonna tell me that night,
about moving out,
but she didn't bother because
I grabbed my cassette recorder and started recording
some ideas I had for the annual report.
I get my best ideas that time of morning,
you know. Before the cold, blue dawn.

The place seems so empty without her,
but Brenda's everywhere.
The outline of her on the sofa cushions
where she used to read and correct papers from school.
Her perfume smell in the bathroom curtains,
tendrils of her hair clogging the drain
weeks after she left.
Her shelf in the medicine cabinet
is still smudged with flakes of blusher,
and slender gold cylinders of unused lipsticks
waiting for her to try them.
She was always buying new lipsticks
and wearing them once.
She liked the names.
Persimmon. Brown Velvet.
Persian Melon.

She never came back
for her lipsticks,
not to mention any
of the furniture.
She made a list,
hired someone to do it for her.

"I learned something from you,"
she said on the phone that last time.
"If you're willing to pay for it, someone else's
always willing to do your dirty work."

Jonathan Price

Waiting

I am here with the ferns, fast gusts
Blowing frond and stem bang into the plate glass. Click
Go the beams as weight shifts, the corporation walks
Above me, and outside, backhoes beep backing up,
Tearing San Jose farm land into condo lots, acres
Of fake villas suddenly replacing corn. This wind
Scratches and rubs the Japanese maple against the window,
Restless, passionate in a small space, invisible
As emotion, fluidly starting to destroy
This block of integrated circuits, this sea of gates,
This array of pins, wires, nets, and property lists.
The company name is Cadence; its beat of logic
Gouges a path for electrons, turns symbol
Into schematic, compressing years of code in one
Thin wafer, with gold prongs. Mozart's a product,
Striking arpeggios out of silicon. I pull the blinds
To block out the view of people entering, and float,
Within my conference room, clean and cold.

River Oaks Parkway, San Jose, June 14, 1991

Body of Work

Judith Small

I AM PREGNANT the first time I'm asked to do a training session on corporations. "And we want it on tape," said Martin. He's a musician, but he works part-time coordinating the firm's training program for paralegals. There are so many of us now—over a hundred—and the new ones need basic stuff (cite-checking, how to use the library), while the old ones like me need enrichment sometimes, skills-sharpening, keeping at the cutting edge. Martin's a busy guy.

Once a month, Martin holds a lunch session called Continuing Paralegal Education, which an attorney comes to, or a senior paralegal, or anyone Martin can charm or flatter or simply pester into giving a talk about some area of specialization. Whoever it is, there's usually a camera rolling so the session can be used again—the tape checked out by people who missed the meeting—or else shown, years later, with a dash of pomp and a witty introduction from Martin, over plates of sandwiches, pasta salad, or whatever the caterers of the future may be dishing up.

The prospect worries me. This is my second child, so I know I tend to worry when I'm pregnant, but the taping would worry me anytime. Not only will I have to be good but I'll have to be good beyond the needs of the moment—articulate, and polished to a high gleam, a beacon for future viewers. I see before me, already, their trusting, upturned faces.

I work hard on my talk. I'll be talking about how to set up a corporation (nothing fancy, just plain vanilla, for-profit) but in addition to the specifics (like the pros and cons of corporate seals, or how to break through the almost constant busy signal at the Secretary of State's office to check the availability of a corporate name) I want to talk, more generally, about stuff I like to think about. How words become things, how the stamping of one document in the Secretary of State's office suddenly makes a whole new entity whose existence is "perpetual." Where words come from, how "corporation," with its armature of laws and cases and precedents, its quasi-mythical status as an "artificial person" with "perpetual" existence, emerged into history naked as any creature, out of "corpus," the body. How "corporation" used to mean, among other things, a protruding stomach, as in Smollett: "Sirrah! My corporation is made up of good wholesome English fat." But, on the other hand, from the sixteenth century drifts a more ethereal music, a word for the fusing of Christian believers into one mystical body of Christ, one "corporation." Tricky business, then—comprehending this word we use, are used by, in the course of earning our livings, living our lives—watching it stagger through a clumsy dialectic between the sacred and the profane, the abstract and the concrete, mysticism and lard.

And I think hard about what I'll wear. Not that there's a lot of choice, between the couple of good maternity dresses I'd bought new for client conferences or lunches and the more seasoned jumpers, skirts, and smocks I'd borrowed from friends and friends of friends. I decide pretty quickly on a dress that is both "nice" and laden with good karma, lent to me by my friend, Beth, who got it from a friend of hers who had won it in a drawing at some fancy department store, I. Magnin, maybe, or Saks. Beth told me when she brought me the dress on a hanger one night that it was her favorite dress when she was pregnant, and it became, immediately, mine. It's made of soft, narrow-wale corduroy, a rich wine color, and it's cut as a roomy shift that seems to swing when you walk—not blatantly, but like a quiet, encouraging tune someone is playing just for you, for your body outside and in. It's a dress that strangers say nice things about, that keeps me company on bad days, and as I imagine it before the video camera I know that my dress, at least, will do fine.

And so do I, as far as I can tell. (Martin is reassuring, as always; it's part of his job.) Also, there's pleasure, after all, in pulling together some of what I know, in defining it, wiping a fogged lens clear. Along the way I get to tell one of my favorite cautionary tales, which I can get away with in my role as a very senior paralegal, thirty-six and with the firm for twelve years. (This is a young profession; that's part of its interest—we shape it as we go.)

I like this story as a teaching tool. I hate it because it's about the death of Katie, whom I loved. Even six years ago, when she started at the firm, she seemed a kid to me, not just because she was in her mid-twenties but because she brought a particular freshness to her work, energy coupled with insouciance. She would work hard on an incorporation, or harder on a closing, days and nights in a conference room stacked high with documents, but you always sensed she was there solely because she chose to be—for the overtime, mainly, or because she liked the other paralegals working on the deal, or simply because she'd decided this was how she was going to spend her evenings for a while. Whereas with me and most of my other friends at the firm there was something else at stake—some key part of our self-respect that turned on doing things right, getting every detail of a project, every comma, precisely in its immutable place.

Katie danced right past that kind of perfectionism—she was a dancer, I found out when I started getting to know her; she took classes in jazz and modern dance several evenings a week. She had a mass of brown hair, and a long, lithe body that always seemed to fit better into turtlenecks, denim skirts, and clogs than into tailored suits; her cheekbones lifted like birds' wings beneath clear gray eyes. She must have looked me over pretty shrewdly, me and my wardrobe that veered crazily from suits and heels for meeting clients to long skirts and flats for days when I planned to hole up in my office, work on a private-offering memo, and pretend to myself I'd never left home. One day, after we'd known each other six months or so, Katie appeared in my office with a dress pattern and sample swatches of fabric. She did a lot of sewing for herself, and she said she wanted to make me a dress as a present, what did I think of this pattern?

I liked it fine. It was simple, pretty, didn't take itself too seriously—a dress that looked like a dress rather than a tool for career building. We didn't talk about a trade, but I wondered if this was Katie's way of thanking me for the help I was starting to give her with her writing. She'd been having trouble with the scrupulous precision the attorneys required in everything we wrote, even apparently simple cover letters, and I'd offered to work with her. I was excited at the chance to spend time at my job talking with a friend about writing, but a little daunted by what I sensed might be a long, difficult task.

Only I never got to try, because one morning Katie got out of bed, slumped to the floor, and died. Just like that, as far as anyone could tell, though a number of experts did their best to say more. There was the usual coroner's report, and then a second, at the family's request; both gave the cause of death as "unknown." Katie lived in an apartment by herself, so there was no one to offer any clues.

When the news reached the office, I went out as soon as I could. Walking with a friend, pacing, looping the downtown streets, we hunted explanations, stunned by the way Katie'd gone, like a door slammed shut. It was somehow consoling, in the shadow of her death, to come face-to-face with a certified mystery.

Of course, most of Katie's story didn't make it into my talk. For this audience, I had to skate quickly onto a firmer surface: the legal dilemma posed by the fact that Katie had vanished not only as a person but as an essential legal implement—the sole incorporator of BZ, Inc. BZ was a corporation formed a few days before Katie's death, when on behalf of a client she had prepared the Articles of Incorporation from one of our standard master forms, signed them, and sent them off to the capital for filing.

A perfectly routine job—the bread and butter of a corporate legal assistant—and the Articles were, routinely, accepted for filing and promptly returned to the office, stamped by the Secretary of State's office. But by the time the documents arrived at our office Katie wasn't there: BZ had begun its life just as Katie had ended hers. Which, I pointed out to my audience, left the corporation stranded, a disembodied "creature of law." Since the Articles had named no directors, the incorporator was the only person of record who could take action to appoint board members, who could then approve bylaws, appoint officers, open a bank account, get down to whatever business BZ was supposed to be doing.

The cleanest solution, it was decided—after considerable pondering by one of the partners—was to get BZ dissolved by a judge acting with the cooperation of Katie's estate. BZ without Katie was nothing, the ghost of a venture, some frail ambition. I never learned what the business was to be, or whether it prospered in a second incarnation. Maybe the entrepreneurial thrust behind BZ was more enduring than the plans for my dress, which I inherited as a stack of petal-weight paper and some pieces of flowered cloth, cut by Katie into shapes ready to sew together. About the time BZ was dissolved I hunted up a dressmaker, since I barely sew, and asked her to complete the work Katie had started. She accepted the assignment grudgingly, with a sour half smile (maybe she disliked taking over somebody else's work), but brought me the dress a week later. I did wear it once or twice, but it never felt or looked quite right—a little tight in the shoulders, a little prim, nothing at all like Katie.

I want him to leave my office right now. He is too young, stands too close to me, looks me too easily in the eye, is too sure—that he needs only one incorporator, that anything more is superfluous. A "baby associate" (what we call the new lawyers), fresh-faced, straight out of Harvard or Stanford, clad in the shining raiment of his irrefutable logic.

So I explain to him, briefly, about Katie, though I don't use her name. This is just a case history from a while back, one of those weird but telling legal anecdotes. He goes on standing in my office. So I simply suggest, in very different words, that if he screws up on this it'll be his ass on the line, because I'll never back him up, and he stops and remembers that I've been around awhile, that people trust me whereas he just walked in the door, and he shrugs and agrees to a second incorporator: "Three's ridiculous, Deborah, for Christ's sake, but I guess I can live with two."

A month later I'm driving through a pouring March rain, past the malls and condos of the suburbs to Tom Heaney's funeral. Heaney the real-estate partner, dead in his fifties of cancer, Heaney the witty, plain-talking, Jesuit-schooled Irishman, balding, a little slack-bellied, but his eyes blue and keen. Heaney was the guy I'd go see when I wanted to find out what was really going on—"This is what the documents say, Tom, right now, but how do things really work in practice?" Then we'd revise, make the words walk slowly on the slippery trail. I was learning to keep my eyes open. Next to the couch where clients sat in Tom's office there was a real parking meter.

Tom himself didn't seem to sit still for long. He came to the firm as a "lateral"—already a partner at another big firm—and from the beginning I thought of him as someone in motion. People said he'd felt hemmed in at his old firm, though I never asked him why he'd left; I only noticed how his eyes darted among the faces gathered at a conference table, how he'd take in, easy as oxygen, what each party brought to the table, what each wanted to take away—all of the talking points, deal points, sticking points, the ones that could kill the deal. At the funeral, person after person stood up in the crowded church to tell their memories of him, but mine was one I couldn't speak: Tom at the Christmas party one year dancing fast, tie loosened, with Rochelle—another paralegal he worked with—to "I Wanna be Sedated" from a friend's collection of new-wave tapes. Even now, the memory moves too quickly, like film escaping through a speeded-up projector, so that Tom and Rochelle are all blurred elbows and knees—no faces, just fast dancing.

A few years ago, Tom helped me with a sentence. It doesn't seem like much: "The terms of this Agreement, and any amendment hereto, may be confirmed by any single Trustee, and each Trustee is authorized and empowered to execute and deliver all certificates or other documents as may from time to time be required to evidence such confirmation." But what I like about this sentence is precisely its modesty, its utility, the way it leaped from Tom's mind to meet a particular need, soothe the uneasiness of a particular title company. I remember going into his office, by luck catching him alone, and how he thought for a moment and then wrote in pencil, in a silvery, clear hand, the sentence we wound up adding to our standard group-trust agreement, so that whenever I prepared one after that and passed by that sentence in the master I would think of Tom. I like the beauty of his sentence, a well-made tool—the way it pivots at the center on the authority of a single person, closing the first clause, opening the second. And I will always see his sentence in pencil, writing itself perpetually as suggestion rather than pronouncement, and engraved in nothing.

I'm watching the videotape of my talk. Martin has lent it to me with apologies; there's something wrong, inexplicably, with the audio, and he feels bad that after all my work the tape isn't good enough to show at future sessions. I tell him that's O.K.—as long as my talk was useful to the people who were there, and anyway I kind of enjoyed it.

So I'm watching now, curious—I've never seen myself on TV—and at first I don't see what Martin means. I'm just relieved that I basically like the person on the screen: she seems to know what she's talking about without getting too heavy-handed about it, smiles a lot (maybe too much?), definitely touches her hair too much, smooths it—a mannerism; I decide right away to stop that.

Then the words begin to fade. I'm talking, and smiling, and then I'm talking very quietly, and then I turn my face to include some other listeners around the conference table and I'm moving my lips around silence. Then I smile again, turn my head another way, and the words come back, surging, receding, as if a wind were blowing through the tape. We are sitting around a table talking about corporations and suddenly we aren't; we are only mouth, hair, eyes, my dress the color of wine, somebody's sleeve, fingers, a smile, a coffee cup lifted, a head nodded. Somebody raises a hand.

Carolyn Hull

Where Does the Money Go

The desk between us
is like a Texas desert.
The woman across from me,
like a scarf tied to a tree.
She is old, frayed, hard
to pin down. She doesn't remember
the names of things,
and she is crying.

I only need the loan till
my social security check comes in,
honey, she is saying as she sobs.
She smells unwashed, like she
is wearing her pajamas. Her face
folds and unfolds as she speaks.
I think I cashed my last check,
she goes on. If I did, I can't find
the money. I lost it. I'm hungry.

There are people outside my office
impatient for me to finish with this person
and get to them. Those people are real
loan customers, here to sign and get
their money. They can qualify. They are young
and know everything. This woman knows nothing,
not even that she was in my office
last month and we found her check,
crumpled in the vast cavern
bottom of her dark purse.

I ask her if we can look together.
She does not move. The wind has died.
The leaves of her memories fall
slowly downward toward the flat
geography of her life. She unclasps
the lock on the black purse and it opens,
full of dollar bills. They unfold and explode
onto the floor, her shoes, my office.
Ones, fives, tens, twenties.

What's this, I ask her, scooping and stuffing back.
She says, I don't remember.

The people who qualify are talking in loud voices.
Yes, I see them. I'm hurrying. Yes, this is a nuisance.

The old woman is smiling down at me.
Oh, honey, you found it. All my money.
I walk her out to the lobby.
Wait here for me. Wait until I can take you home.
She sits stiffly in the armchair.
She is forgetting. She is getting lost again.
I'm hungry, she says.
I know, I'll take you to lunch. Then home.
She is like a child.
She is my customer.

Declining the Loan

The light in the office is strong
enough only to question
the path through the numbers
that accompany this loan request.

I have sat here nearly an hour,
pencil wearing down and down
into the soft sponge of spread sheets
and flower fields of yellow legal pads.

It is like following bread crumbs
into the dark forest where trees are the stumps
of nines and sevens; the stained glass of light
through the leaves as seen in zeros and eights.
Slowly I have discovered a life: house payments,
car payments, credit cards, insurance, tax
returns, miscellaneous truths that stutter
when I ask, how are you going to pay this back?

Is the truth a desperate traveler who never comes to stay.
From his satchel, does truth extract the knife
that later draws blood.

I sense as I question the man that he aches
for that knife. It would be an easier honor
than hearing me say: there are several items
on your credit, your debt to income ratio
is too high. He looks at me as if I speak
a foreign language.

Does that mean I don't get it, he asks.
I'm afraid so, I say. I look directly at him,
protected by the authority of position,
the mythology of bankers.

He deflates as if that knife made an opening
and all the air escaped. He crumples into his clothes.
What am I going to do, his last question.
This truth and mine are dark strangers.
I don't want to talk to him about it anymore.

I want this to be a clean wound that will heal
with no scar. I don't watch him leave.
I go back to my work.

The numbers don't tell about the cold dinner,
left out for him because he's late.
They don't show the pain of pride to humility
as he shakes his head no when she asks about the money.
Those numbers have straight spines and stiff shoulders.
They shine like lasers.

And their light is only bright
enough to see the knife
dropped to the floor.
The handle in the shape of a six.

Buy a Cellular Phone, Sublet Your Soul

Robert Aquinas McNally

Saw ANOTHER ONE this morning. Some guy zipping through an intersection in his Mercedes, leaning way back into the leather in the power posture, calling commands on a cellular phone. Crossing children and animals and LOLs with Safeway shopping carts scattered, and the dust swirled behind his mindless passing. When it settled, I half-expected to see a newly flattened chicken stuck in the road, one upright wing feather quivering in the disturbed air.

Forget safety. Forget status. This is the insanity of the age, and nobody is calling it what it is. Time is slipping away from us, and it's driving us nuts.

We should have started protesting way back in the thirteenth century, when Benedictine monks came up with this new thing called the schedule so they could fit all their religious obligations into the limited span of a single day. Before that, no one had a schedule; you just did things. The sun rose, you got up. It climbed higher, you planted or plowed or hoed. It slipped low, you went home, drank ale and ate bread, crawled under the blankets to get up when the sun did. Simple, direct, and everything that needed doing got done.

The Benedictines wanted to get more done; they were rationalists, very ambitious the way celibates tend to be. Their day had units, obligations, artificial cues outside the pattern of the sun, of light and dark. A bell rang to signal 6 a.m., and you hustled off to the next task, whether it was winter black or summer bright. In their search for heaven, the monks had separated themselves from the earth.

Clocks came next, dividing hours into minutes, thence into seconds. Measurement was oh so precise, and time was slipping away, under the weight of division and abstraction. It's gone on until now there's this quantity called the nanosecond—one billionth of a second, a unit of time so far below the threshold of experience that its existence must be accepted on faith. Yet, despite such exquisite microprecision, we have less time than ever before.

You hear the complaints, no doubt you make them: "Commuting takes up so much of my time . . . ," "I'd love to have children if I could just find the time . . . ," "Some day, when I have the time, I'll learn how to . . . ," "Sure the house needs cleaning, but I just can't find the time . . . ."

The spirit of the age offers a Benedictine solution: do two things at once. Cram each microprecise unit of time as full of productive activity as can be; make every nanosecond count.

Thus, the cellular phone. It lets you drive—a task that, of itself, requires total concentration—and make a phone call—another task requiring total concentration—both at the same time. Problem is, you can't pull it off; we humans are as dedicated as word processors. So you are divided, split between phoning and driving, doing neither truly and feeling only the tension of waffling between them.

Mass schizophrenia; we have perfected the technology to make the divided self tax-deductible. We don't sell our souls anymore; we lease them out and call it a business expense.

There is too little time to do everything because we don't do anything. When nothing receives full attention, everything slips past. The uncompleted agenda grows, and frustration explodes into violence, aggression, psychosis.

Within each of us resides something that yearns for the whole-minded connections of those medieval peasants who lived by the sun, spent half their days celebrating one or another canonical feast, and still got everything done. They felt the sun and moon and earth in their rhythms, and they moved with them, ignorant of the insanity spawning up the hill inside the Benedictine monastery where some unnamed monk inked the lines of the first schedule on parchment. How surprised they would be to discover the life force of that same monk reincarnated seven centuries later, speeding his Mercedes through scattering children, animals, and oldsters, yelling into a cellular phone, and commanding his broker to sell short.

Penelope Karageorge

Office, 3 p.m.

In the quiet, after-lunch reverence of 3 p.m., you bend
      your head over your desk, at an angle to your ecru
telephone, still now, like a person in prayer. In that
      hushed hollow, you sigh and experience the Big Blank,
the whiteness, everything bleached by the sun pouring in
      but not really warming (the air conditioner's going
full blast) but washing out colors, falling harshly
      on made-up faces. The moment demands a priest with
holy water to anoint the penitent, the faithful, the weary,
      the numbed, the troubled, the meek, waiting to inherit
the paycheck. Instead men in shirtsleeves drift silently
      through corridors, hell-bent for meetings, yellow pads
and folders tucked under their arms. They pick at their
      pants and moue at nothing. The coffee wagon bell rings.

You participate in the ritual, stand by a pile of doughnuts,
      wait your turn, order a regular. A crisp woman with
tight curls and lips dispenses coffee from an aluminum urn
      and doles out one napkin to a customer. How did she
get here? What does she do in the evening? Make wax
      effigies and stick pins in them while watching
the TV news? You drink the dark and acrid poison, consume
      it twice a day, uncomplaining, grateful for the bells
that punctuate your hours of intrigue and striving.

You're anxious, and at the same time soothed and lulled.
      You want desperately to leave, and just as badly
to stay. You don't know what's out there other than chaos
      and another office and another. Offices. Scotch tape.
Paper. Desks. Word processors. Expense account forms.
      Coffee wagons stretching out endlessly. Suddenly

rain pelts the window. How cozy here. How safe.
        You check your watch. 3:30 p.m. The crisis over.
Now the lull before the hysteria of 4 p.m., when phones
        clang away and everyone's trying to make the call
that counts or get something going,
        hoping the night will arrive quickly, with
have-a-nice evenings flung out. You poke your head
        up and consider accomplishing something.

Because you've been coasting all day, just looking like
        working, actually in a low-level, Edward Hopper style
funk, rather unattractive, particularly when you
        should love your job. Yes. You have a title,
a secretary, a place, business cards (embossed, not the
        cheap, flat kind), your insurance, your tote bag
with the company logo, your meetings, your office parties,
        the yearly outing, the bi-annual sales conference.
Then why are you crying as you stare into the windows of the
        skyscraper across the street? People bend and
gesticulate, almost like in a movie, people like you.
        You shake your head.
This can't be real, and since it's not real, are you real,
        or an actor selected by central casting for
this part? You've had a bad day.
        Soon you can go home. See. It's getting dark.
A last memo lands on your desk. It's getting late.

Winging It

Ed Packman

Everyone looked happy in the conference room without windows. They all sat on folding chairs around the large metal table. The greenish-white walls were bare, and it could have been any time of the day.

"It's the biggest deal we've had in a long time," said Nolan, one of the two young owners, smiling with relief. He was black-haired and balding, short but athletically built. "Couldn't come at a better time," he added, and chuckled.

"We softened these guys up for months," said Eric, the account executive, shaking his head, "but it was worth it."

"Thank you again, Paula," said Bruce, his fat round face smiling without inhibition, a happy animal, his curly red hair moist and profuse across his forehead, droplets of sweat shining on his cheeks. She smiled briefly, mechanically, at him across the table, cleared her throat and prepared to resume her presentation.

"We'll need to give Paula a new title for this," interjected Bruce before she could start.

"How about a raise?" she said, smiling momentarily again, her blue eyes briefly opening wide and expectant. Her coiffed blond hair sat atop her head like a crown. Standing, she was just above where Bruce and Albert were sitting down.

"Let's not go overboard," said Albert flatly, unsmiling, shooting Bruce a cautionary look. "I know there's plenty of credit to go around." Albert was tall, slender and prematurely grey, with a pale, unhealthy-looking complexion. He looked now like he had just put something round into his mouth but didn't want to swallow it.

"There will, of course," Paula resumed, "remain the—ah—issue of how much expertise we can bring to bear on this, given the resources available."

"Waddaya mean?" asked Albert.

"Well, they've asked us some hard questions, many of which will take real expertise to answer and, as you know, you get only so much expertise for $10 an hour." She smiled grimly at the senior partner and he smiled briefly back.

"I don't know anything of the kind," he noted. "You dressed the resumes up like I said?"

"That's how we beat the competition."

"So no problem. We'll find answers, no question. We always find answers. We're the experts. That's why they're paying us," he concluded, smiling confidentially down the table at Nolan.

"You know honesty's very good in principle, Paula," said Nolan, looking up at her from his papers, "but it just doesn't work in business."

"You ever look at what our competitors put out?" asked Albert and then: "Can we at least get Dale in on this?" He pushed out his lower lip. "She knows a lot about the industry."

"She hasn't agreed to the terms offered," said Paula, looking briefly at him, and then downward.

"Weren't we talking about giving her a job?" Albert asked, in a higher voice.

"She was supposed to start as an employee in July, right?" said Nolan.

Albert raised his hand and shook his head. He looked at Nolan. "We don't want to give a job to anyone who's not there when we need them." He looked at Paula. "You could tell that to her."

"We could always pay her a little more," said Paula.

Albert and Nolan looked at each other again. "You can go out of business really fast paying people more," observed Bruce, popping up from the sidelines behind Albert, smiling broadly in support.

"I'm not sure," Albert resumed, in a low voice, looking down at the table, then moving his eyes across the group, lighting occasionally on Nolan's face, "that we want people around here at all who are only interested in the money."

"She's getting greedy," seconded Nolan.

"Ten dollars an hour only goes so far," said Paula.

"We're not IBM," said Albert, shrugging his thin shoulders, "no question about it." Bruce smiled knowingly at Paula, and then around the room. "Have we paid her yet for that last project?" Albert asked, looking significantly at Nolan.

"Well," Paula resumed again, "our new clients want the kitchen sink. Market sizing and segmentation, forecasting, growth rates, the usual, for ten years out for all major product lines. They want a comprehensive competitive analysis, with market shares to tenth of a percent on units and revenues."

"What does 'comprehensive' mean?" asked Albert, chuckling.

She paused. Just the things I said, that's the way they put it.

Paula pointed to the diagrams on the blackboard as she explained all the elements of the project. Albert whistled through his teeth. "This is for all their current products and for a dozen new services they plan to introduce. They want us to look at three different scenarios based on variations in projected market response times. They want us to provide, again, a 'comprehensive' evaluation of each of their competitors' products, and they want us to make extensive recommendations in terms of timing of their introduction of new products, market focus, strategy, and so forth."

"All in a day's work," said Nolan.

"We can handle it," said Bruce.

"Did we read this proposal before we bid on it?" asked Albert, turning his long waxy face again around the table.

"As much as we had time for," said Eric. "We had to hit the ground running." Albert formed a disgusted expression on his face. Bruce stood up. He looked as if he wanted to get out without being noticed but was too large.

"Where you going?" asked Albert.

"It sounds like you've got your arms tight around this one," Bruce said, unconvincingly. "I need to stop in at that meeting I told you about, for new consultants."

"What's that?" said Albert. "Oh, yeah," he said quietly, as if reminding himself.

"I didn't know about this meeting here till the last minute," he apologized to the larger group, "so I'll get back with you all later." Everyone smiled as Bruce lumbered toward the door.

Outside the conference room, Bruce looked instinctively toward the counter for coffee. The machine had been turned off the previous week because too many drinkers had failed to pay their $3 monthly dues. That shouldn't by rights affect him as vice president, but for him, too, it was an inevitable inconvenience. A weekly memo had warned independent contractors the company would not subsidize their coffee drinking. The company kept a tight lid on costs. It had stopped providing employees with yellow legal pads in favor of reams of advertising forms from its numerous hastily discontinued activities. The office was spartan and disorganized. Instead of mailboxes, the company gave contractors dozens of tubs somehow acquired from the postal service, as well as several disks of pirated software available in every cubicle.

Bruce entered the second conference room, the only one most people knew about, the one with windows, where thirty or forty people sat around another long table, stood in the sun by the long glass panes, or sat on the green carpet behind the chairs. There were men and women, young, middle-aged and older, a few dressed casually, but many in suits, all looking for work or having recently started, along with a few veterans who apparently wanted to hear what he would say this time.

Bruce prepared the rap again in his mind as he walked to the front of the room, smiling but with his face downward. He liked to sit by himself for a few moments first, when he could spare the time, to really get ready, so he could somewhat customize his message. But he could wing it; you had to. He could dominate any meeting. Bruce prided himself quietly on his leadership qualities, attributes the owners did not cultivate. They were short-sighted, callow, almost monomaniacal in their focus on the fast buck. Bruce knew vaguely that some people who had been around the company long enough to form considered opinions felt that he, on the other hand, had a disease that prevented him from ever telling the truth. He didn't experience reality that way, he knew. His reality was quite different; it was holistic and cybernetic.

He went through his routine with the new people again with all the enthusiasm he could muster but it was a hot day and he'd done it too many times before. Like always, he looked toward the center of the crowd, and then away, and then back again. It was an up-and-coming company, an emergent cutting-edge company, a rapid growth company, a comet, on its way to being the biggest publisher of high-technology research in the United States, and the world, too, by the way, what with the new offices in Antwerp and Tokyo. They were doubling their production of reports every year. They would soon top the giants in the field. It was a vigorous, young, dynamic firm perfect for people with a strong positive work ethic. The company wanted a "win-win" relationship with new analysts: It wanted long-term "partners." He dilated on the prosperous future that awaited them in this new role, though then at moments he would turn somber and firm, looking off into the distance toward the highway off-ramp out the window, as he explained the good reasons for company policies, like not paying contractors or reimbursing any part of their considerable expenses, until projects were fully completed.

"We've tried the other way. We've tried it all. We've got these rules because we tried it and it hasn't worked. We always try to be nice guys first. And we're still nice guys."

He wasn't always sure if his timing was off. The main thing was to push on, undeterred, make every performance as seamless as possible. They could make a great deal of money on royalties. You play ball with us, we'll play ball with you. There was plenty of ball to be played. Revenues were growing 50 percent a year, more. Corporations were shelling out for this kind of research like crazy. This wasn't a company for people who don't want to grow, stay stuck in a rut. And it was about much more than money. They'd always have work for good people, hard-working people. The company offered flexibility, too, for its researchers, the opportunity to work where they wanted, according to their own needs, at home or in the office, set their own hours. All that mattered was the quality of the product. The company would be *the* high-quality supermarket for high-technology market research. It was a booming future. Of course there was a turnover, and for ambitious people this meant still more opportunity. They could build vital connections with the companies that were inventing all of their futures. They could be paid on royalties or fees, though they'd make a lot more on royalties. If they could just wait a few months for sales, they could share the wealth. "We can't talk certainties, but we talk probabilities, like the probabilities of the sun coming up tomorrow." They could become experts in their fields. They were going to be the best at what they did. They had competitors, in the Valley as well as back East, but he wouldn't talk about them. Sales were up. The sky was literally the limit.

Bruce always managed to keep his gaze just above the faces of the anxious crowd. He looked relaxed and stressed somehow at the same time. At points, he realized suddenly he was repeating phrases over and over as he waited for the next one to slip effortlessly out. He knew things weren't just as they should be. In the middle of everything, in this pleasant conference room with sun pouring through the windows, in the middle of his usually fluid and well-practiced presentation, his face would turn strangely stern, as he would look down at the desk, or toward the wall, repeating a particularly trenchant phrase for the third or fourth time, like "this work isn't for everybody," as he waited for the next phrase to walk gracefully out of his mouth. He thought he must be tired, and said abruptly: "Can I answer your questions?"

The questions were always the same. Someone always wanted to know how much the average study brought in royalties. Bruce always sighed. It was a tough but perennial question. He didn't want his answer to be misinterpreted. Averages were misleading. Besides, the company didn't have time to compile them; they were too busy producing. "Our *minimum* sales goal for *each* study is forty thousand so, you figure it out, times 30 percent, that's about—what is it—fourteen thousand, twelve. That's our minimum sales goal on every single study. We don't let anything fall through the cracks. Many make lots more. We've had studies sell a hundred copies."

"Do most studies make the goal?"

He nodded and smiled slightly. "If we don't, we're not in business."

He answered more questions, repeated portions of his talk, bantered half-heartedly with them, and left. He went to the bathroom, stopped in to talk to the office manager, into the sales office to look over charts, around to graphics about some brochures, all the while greeting people, chatting, reassuring. By the time he got back to his office it was five-thirty.

Paula was unsmiling as she stepped into his office and glared at him. "I need to talk to you."

"What's up?"

She straightened herself to what seemed to him to be more than her full height, swallowed, and looked directly at him again. "I've recently found out that I—and, I imagine, other people—haven't been paid for overseas sales of my studies."

Bruce said nothing. He still sat back in the chair behind his desk. Then he shook his head in confusion. "What?"

"I need to get my money."

"What are you talking about?"

"The studies I did before I was a manager. There have been sales out of Antwerp of them, over two years. I haven't been paid royalties on them. You should know about this."

"That's all wrong." Bruce was waving his right hand in dismissal. "What's giving you that idea?" He was frowning. His usually ruddy, complexion was turning pale.

"Bruce, I have my ways. I need my money. You know, last year I just about went hungry waiting for it."

"I can show you the sales records!"

"But your sales records don't include Europe."

"Of course they do. I was just so happy when you finally made some sales, after going dry so long," and he started pawing vaguely into a pile of computer printouts.

"When am I going to get paid?"

"You've been paid."

"Bruce, when am I going to be paid?"

"I'll look into it, Paula, I'll look into it, all right?"

"I need my money."

"You know how busy I am, Paula."

"Bruce, I want my money now."

"I've got so much to do," he gestured around the room, "it's unbelievable. I'm just trying to keep this damn company alive."

"How long's it going to take?"

"I'm trying to keep this company going, Paula."

"How long?"

"I don't know," he said, his voice angry now. "You'll have to wait like everybody else."

"I want to get paid, Bruce, and I mean soon," she said, putting her hand on the door.

"Paula," he said, "you'll hear from us."

A Little Number

"A guy comes swinging in the door
Looking for a feature for
His Model 2 P. C.
I take the opportunity
To do a little number on
The Model 3. Expound upon
The many wonders of it. How
It's lighter. How the letters glow
Brighter. How it does ten—
Make that a hundred times again
As many things . . .

                          "He clearly buys
The better part of this—but says
He's worried that the 3 is more
Computer than he's ready for.
After all, a genius you
Could hardly call him on the 2.
I smile—and proceed to play
The card that puts the guy away.
Namely—and you're gonna love
This—that that's the beauty of
The Model 3; a model so
Potent that your basic no
Genius on a 3 can do
What *takes* a genius on a 2."

Gary Grelli

city

in a chicago hotel room the
distillation of my loneliness
condenses on the night walls
At home, a night alone
would be bliss

a potted palm, rootless here
cut off from that which defines
wife and children, home and work
the daily acts which consume
creating me in the consumption
Away from them i feel temporary
poised in a waiting room
held suspended
until
the
machine is available again.

hotel

even in the lux
ury of the Hilton
loneliness shrinks
the room and grays
the lights

looking out the
window, the city
seems a postcard
promise - excitement
adventure
newness -
then you walk out
the door and the
postcard fades.
Reality is all that
awaits, hard-edged
and consistent
like gravity.

The Safe Man

Andrew Schultz

THE CORPORATION IS pervaded not by the sensibility to make profit but by the human contortions of love, love that is selfish, love that is confused, love that is exalted, love that is base, love the inevitable. Like a rain it falls evenly, upon those most high and powerful to those most ordinary and mundane. In every department of every division of every group, within each clique or klatsch or core, love abounds, secret, furtive, dangerous and thrilling. And the one who knows this most of all, the one who was the least ominous and most pleasant of corporate dwellers, the one who was the most patient and understanding of confidants, was the one known as The Safe Man.

I was he.

Some years ago, we had a senior executive who was desperately in love with a young assistant 30 years his junior. She was younger than his youngest daughter and it was not out of some foolish, late-life crisis that he loved her, but sheer and genuine attraction. She was painfully bright, possessing great energy and the smile of youth that he craved. And though the corporation was large, though this executive was able to use the perquisites of his office to pretend to the utmost discretion, still, through the informal reticulum of knowledge that runs spine-like up and down the firm, everyone knew that he had fallen for her and fallen hard.

About this same time, down in the mail room, two clerks had fallen hopelessly for each other. They spent their days roaming the hallways and offices of the headquarters, wading through a stream of broken conversations that wafted over the cubicles and across the open doorways of offices. In delivering and picking up mail, rarely crossing routes in their rounds, surrounded at lunch by the cadre of mail room lifers, there was no moment for consort. You must know how constrained they were: both were married, happily it seemed, with large broods of children. And their time was spread so thinly across the veil of their lives, with work and family and church and softball leagues and volunteering, that it seemed, like the flight of bees, a logical impossibility their affair could happen.

Yet love persisted. On those rare days when their paths crossed and they shared a private elevator to the next floor, they stole a passionate kiss. While the president made love to his protege in the private comfort of an out-of-town suite, our mail room couple had finally and desperately resorted to duplicity. He called in sick; she took a day off; they drove to a far suburb and spent the day in a Comfort Inn, consummating at last their desperate, forbidden love.

The Safe Man was privy to such knowledge; I collected it with a passion. I was, of course, married, with three happy, handsome children. My wife had also worked in the corporation, but she had quit years before, when our first child was born, and had, after the youngest was in pre-school, successfully operated her own retail gift store in the renovated Old Town district.

I was, of course, quite good at my job, rising to senior middle management, in charge of a sizable department in the marketing division. I travelled frequently and spoke at corporate and industry gatherings. I was at a level high enough to be in regular attendance at all the annual bigwig events, the sales meetings, conferences and conventions. I was well-thought of and well-liked and I possessed, proudly and more than any other manager, many women friends. Women at all levels of the firm admired and respected me. I treated them, as I treated the men I worked with, always with kindness, respect, encouragement, openness. Many flocked to me for career advice; I was known for my political insights and corporate diplomatic experience, making me an expert in how to win promotions and plum jobs in the firm.

And at the public events which the corporate membership attended, and the internal functions at which there was entertainment and drinking and recreation off-site, I, who came to be called The Safe Man, never, ever indulged in outward conduct unbecoming a gentleman or a professional businessman. Around me, colleagues behaved foolishly, openly flirting, soliciting strange women or corporate comrades or both, engaging prostitutes, drinking too much, using expense accounts for personal purposes and generally abusing the privileges which attended their station.

Surely such activity is now a thing of the past, I told myself with a light but reproachful tone. For The Safe One's lack of participation in such activities, my unwillingness to wink at the cheat and play along, put me in a position of isolation from the Good Ole Boy groups which, even in this time of women in the workforce and the trickling down of feminism, persisted in the corporate body.

My principled position, though, was held in high esteem not only by those who were morally self-righteous, but more so by those whose personal resolve was not so apparently unimpeachable, in particular by those women, young and old, married and single, plain and beautiful, who sought me out, sought out this Safe Man who was the rarest of a bad breed, someone who was male and yet still could be trusted. I was the one man they knew who could listen with interest, sympathy and insight to their problems and sins.

With my many women friends and my widespread reputation as The Safe Man, some of the other fellows, those who felt a bit indignantly loutish in my presence, accused me behind my back of being a closet homosexual. For a while, I am given to understand, they referred to me as "FH," which stood for "Fag Hag." They dismissed my marriage and children as a mere curtain to hide my aberration, acknowledging, of course, by negation the concept that men and women could be just friends. For I am not a homosexual.

In explaining myself to one friend who had for the first time fallen by the wayside, I was predictably modest. I refused to judge him, relating instead that I was pleased to hear his confession for it was the spectrum of human behavior that fascinated me, not any one person's actions. I, in turn, confessed that while my heart quickened at the passion of a lurid tale, it was the vicarious excitement of the observer, not the participant. "I'm just someone who can say, 'But not for me,'" I finished, singing this last phrase in my pleasing tenor voice, smug in my comfortable position as the eyes and ears of my firm. And because I was father confessor to so many, because I stood at the center of a many-spoked wheel of information, I knew the dirt on everyone. I was an unabashed and shameless repository of gossip, though I attempted to be exquisitely discreet in not being a purveyor of it. Well, only to the extent that it was productive to do so. Knowledge has no currency unless it is shared . . . .

I reflect now that my fate may be likened to that of the physician or psychologist or minister gone awry from his calling.

Was I not the sort of noble fellow whose charm and patience, stability and magnanimity, benign and helpful demeanor, becomes twisted? The self-righteous one is a hypocrite who flirts with danger not to prove his sanctity but to prove his ultimate weakness; the sinner is a fool who knows not moderation. But how difficult it is to be moderate when you discover in yourself the deft act wherein the uses of position and power and the intimate knowledge of a subject's weaknesses allow you to take from them whatever you desire.

✳ ✳ ✳

It began with a friendship, a woman I had known for a number of years, let us call her Sharon. I had never paid her special attention. She was an odd giantess of a woman, over 6 feet tall. Her height and intimidating size obscured most people's ability, my own included at first, to note her pretty face and good figure. Sharon was then in her early 40s, married for over twenty years and with three children; I believe her husband was a former professional football player who'd become a high school coach and was purported to be as out-sized as was she.

Sharon and I had been thrown together, for the first time, to work on a new project. In our many hours toiling on it, I kindled for her what was a new feeling for me, a sense of infatuation. It was against any reason, for Sharon was all-work, a severe, focused woman who dressed plainly and did not laugh easily, at my jokes or anyone else's.

The culmination of the project was its presentation at the annual sales meeting, held at an island resort on the Gulf Coast. The meeting was in winter and the balmy tropical weather released in all of us Rust Belt dwellers a severe case of spring fever. Particularly, me. I drank, I stayed up late, flirting, focusing mostly on Sharon, but alighting upon others as well. The presentation was a success and in congratulating her after, I, the Safe One, gave Sharon a rather familiar smack on the lips. That evening, the last night of the conference, I had what was for me entirely too much to drink. After the banquet I blearily noted that Sharon, who had been at my table earlier, had disappeared, gone up to her room. I waited a bit longer, and then quietly went after her. I was feeling uncharacteristically bold. I knocked at her door and she appeared, wearing a flannel nightgown, her unadorned, pretty face well scrubbed, a toothbrush in her mouth.

She looked down at me, casually, in her dour manner, with the serene look of someone who is not often surprised.

"Sharon," I sputtered, entering her room and watching her while she went back to the sink to complete her brushing. "I have an idea for you, which you can reject, if you feel uncomfortable with it. But for some time I've had this notion that . . ." Before I completed the sentence she was already moving toward me, her mouth still wet and foamy, her eyes intent, metamorphosing as they approached, glowing warm and warmer like the coil of an auto cigarette lighter. Her mouth surrounded mine, devouring me. The sharp flavor of mint toothpaste coated my tongue and it's foam singed my lips. She wrapped me in her long, arms and squeezed. I was stunned at her sudden passion, and at my own, which rose to follow her ardor. She was so big and strong. I felt something other than a man, being possessed by such a creature. We fell sidelong onto the couch.

What a prodigious and remarkable specimen of amazon womanhood was Sharon! Later, when we were in bed, I eyed her with the abashed sense of a daunted explorer. The epic journey began with the long, unexpectedly dainty and painted formations of her toes, I then continued up the ridges of her shins and past the dimpled mesas of her knees daringly toward the tufted veldt above. Across the smooth, unchartable and undulating terrain of her stomach I ascended . . .

In the weeks following this magical night, I tried in vain to feel guilty for my sins. But it had been too wonderful, too easy, too delightful. I would see a flash of pastel and be reminded of the curtains and bedspread and upholstery of her room; I would catch a scent of honeysuckle in the soap they provided in our corporate restrooms, and my mind would go reeling back to that night, for Sharon had showered with the hotel's similarly scented soap. Back within the halls of the firm, Sharon reverted to her aloof workplace self. She behaved as if she barely knew me, much less as one who shared with her a dark and wonderful secret. This was incredible to me for in my experience, those who committed the act appeared to wear the stain of their sin like a scarlet mark.

Sharon, the ice woman in public, revealed nothing. She avoided me—not studiously, but fastidiously enough for me to know it was quite intentional. I began to doubt our tryst had ever transpired at all. Was I mad? When finally I managed to corner her in her office, after hours one evening, she was unrepentant. "Be reasonable," she lectured. "It was just one night."

"But didn't you enjoy it?" I pleaded, relieved she had at least acknowledged our episode and that I was not losing my wits.

"Immensely," she admitted, hardening me instantly with the sudden warmth of her tone. "But what would you like me to do?"

I wanted to see her again. When would such a thing be possible, she demanded. We were both married, both incredibly busy, both living utterly separate lives, both without any intention, or interest, in giving these lives up.

"Would you have us sneak off to some hotel every week and concoct excuses to explain away the unaccountable time, the odd charges on the Master Card bill? Or were you going to charge it on the company account . . . . ?"

I, the Safe One, who, for all intents and purposes could no longer make claim to this appellation, blushed. I had indeed thought exactly of this mundane scenario, even to the point of, yes, I admitted it, hiding the charges of the cost of adultery on my company American Express charge, promising, privately, of course, to pay it back to the firm at a later date.

Sharon came around the desk and stood over me, glowering. She rested her large hand on my shoulder and patted me twice. "We had our night," she said, then added magnanimously, "We shall always have it. And perhaps, if things go well, at next year's conference . . . ."

Ah, I did not want to wait, could not wait so long. But Sharon's eyes turned steely and she asked me to leave.

I went into a funk. I was in love. I wanted nothing more than to spend my days and nights with my loving giantess. This went on for some weeks and then I began to come to my senses. My disposition to my wife floated suspiciously into a state of inattention that was exceedingly unlike me. I got my bearings back, but rather than returning again to that higher moral plane, that level of good behavior to which I had always and successfully aspired, my thinking devolved, spinning down to depths lower still. I had tasted the fruit of another and now, hungry, I wanted more. I became more conscious of my skills, the effects my fine qualities had upon others, and I saw now the ways in which these elements could be used to satisfy my darkest, newfound needs . . . .

This was how I operated: I became the most devious and manipulative of charlatans because in changing my true self into an apparition, a mask of what was once real, I was creating for my unsuspecting women friends, not to mention my wife, a confidant of Iagoish proportion. I lured them with trust, learned their secrets, made them dependent on me, not only as a devoted listener but as someone with whom they could share their every emotion, and then slowly, slowly, with exquisite patience, the spider circled in on the prey, enveloping it with his arms which the unwitting victim by this time was wilfully pulling around her.

I selected my women with the utmost care and precision. I developed three rules which I adhered to with iron intention. My first requirement was that the woman must be, in some way, unusually attractive. I was not after quantity, but quality and variety. For a time I was taken with large breasts, and then, surfeited, I swung the other way. After that came a penchant for firm, young rumps and, still later, tall, leggy women. Finally, as I recall, I got on an ethnic kick, trying out my powers for the first time on a black woman and a Japanese consultant.

My second requirement was that the prey have more to lose from exposure of an affair than I did, or, at least, that the woman perceive she had more to lose. Consequently, all of my women were married or, if not yet wed, engaged or going out with some corporate bigwig. Early on, some of the women were good friends with my wife, and I believed this added another layer of protection against revelation. These friends saw themselves not only jeopardizing a pair of marriages, but more importantly, they risked the valued friendship of The Safe Man's spouse.

My last operating rule was the most important and essential: only do that which one is invited to do. I never made the first move. And I never told them that I loved them . . . And if perchance I was not getting the desired response? Then I told them that I loved them. This was always a killing moment, and occurred only after I knew that, emotionally, my victim had given herself to me and that I could avail myself of the full physical and sexual expression of this devotion at my leisure. My sense of this moment had grown only more acute over the years. It was as if I could read not only their minds, but also intuit their very needs, so finely tuned was my instrument of seduction.

You may perceive that I had become a cynic. An artist is how I thought of myself. But how did I extricate myself from those I told I loved? That is always the trickiest problem, isn't it? In the end, when the affair was finished, I made it seem my lover's decision to terminate it, out of guilt or fear or diminished need. But really I was calling the shots, for perhaps the cleverest of my many skills was the ability to make the whole thing become drenched in a searing sadness. When an affair was over, I mustered bitter tears of regret over our terrible lot, a life in which love was confined by harsh reality, of the responsibilities of a marriage, a career, society.

I possessed friends, most devoted and true friends, who were endlessly critical, even needling of me. At our many and various gatherings over the years, these male compatriots assumed a tone of amused surprise at my antics. In the early years, they demanded more and more explicit details of each union. But then as the conquests mounted, they were more intrigued by the subtle and patient machinations I employed to subdue my victims. And, later still, they were interested only in the specific psyches involved, not in what they looked like or how they performed in bed, or how I had tricked them and lured them there, but of the quirks of temperament which characterized my diverse collection of women.

Not even one with the reputation of The Safe Man could expect to play this game long before some of the women had the opportunity to compare notes and determine what I had become. And yet my history was so pristine, my public demeanor so above reproach and my selection of women so meticulous, that rumors about me seemed short-lived indeed. In ten years, I captured and released fourteen of them; I was not only an artist, I was a connoisseur.

* * *

And then came a change. The insouciance with which I led my double life began to evaporate. It was unlike me to be anything but completely open with my friends yet now I was reticent and depressed. The source of my angst was a new woman who had caught my fancy, an extremely bright, self-possessed young woman working temporarily in my department, on a training program from a subsidiary. She was strikingly beautiful, jet black hair, of mixed heritage. Her name was Lydia.

For the first time since Sharon, I was almost unable to contain my attraction. But Lydia surpassed Sharon, surpassed all of them. Also for the first time, none of my charms seemed to have any affect on her, nor did my extrasensory skill provide insight—I could not read Lydia at all.

I should have left her alone; I could have. But I was proud now, and I dwelled on this new prize, seeing Lydia as the ultimate test. I reassured my friends that although I had to admit to less than my usual detachment, still I would prevail and would do so with strict adherence to my rules of conduct.

Indeed, a short while later I was my happy self again. I admitted to a certain period where my resolve was shaken. My growing attachment weakened my judgment. But then I recouped my powers and submerged all feeling, investing in the repression of my desire so that I could, like the deadly sea urchin, blend anonymously with the sea bottom. And it worked! Soon, circumstances forced Lydia to seek me out, spend time with me, travel with me. In every instance I was thoroughly pleasant and completely a gentleman; it impressed her. She felt secure with me, saw me in an avuncular way, began, ever so slowly to relax, let down her guard, confide in me.

It was only a matter of time, I thought. And yet something about the undertaking remained troubling to me, and in relating my tortoise progress to my friends, I was again warned to take the utmost care. It was quite a different day and age, in the workplace especially. I might press my luck too far and be destroyed in a sudden conflagration of exposure.

But I was still The Safe Man, and I grew ever more confident of success with Lydia. I believed I could read her now, and I was circling ever so slowly for the final attack.

* * *

When next my friends beheld their corporate charmer, they were shocked at my haggard appearance. I was dressed in slovenly fashion and my eyes were red and tired. Ruefully I informed them that I was in a hell of a jam. Seems I was the one who'd been taken in. Lydia, the little viper, had duped me. She had made careful logs and even tape-recorded some of our conversations. Now she was threatening to charge me with sexual harassment. I had scoffed at her, called her bluff. My reputation was clean, if not my conscience, and I dared invite an investigation. I stood by my remarks. I felt there was nothing in them to endanger me.

I did not realize then how big a mistake my honesty was. As I closed in for the kill I naturally took more risks, helping to establish the mood by engaging my prey in conversations laden with personal and suggestive content. They were always theoretical in scope but clear in meaning. In and of themselves, in the context of a gentle, flowing, confessional talk, these comments seemed playful, perhaps mildly flirtatious. But taken out of that context and read in black and white, they looked damning and in clear violation of the letter of the law.

My friends eyed me in sadness as I told the tale. They mocked my contention that this Lydia woman was a plant of the EEOC, an entrapper who was gunning for me, a wild-eyed feminist version of myself, a Jean Valjean seeking to capture the likes of a Safe Man for years.

What had I said to her? What kinds of things? They were nice things, amusing things. Compliments about what she wore, how she looked. Questions about her social life, boyfriends, and so on. Just chat. And if she brushed against me accidently, then excused herself, I might reply, nonsense, it was most pleasant.

And I had touched her, too. You know, a pat on the shoulder, a lingering finger on the wrist as we spoke. Once I took her pulse. We had taken a company fitness class together, a class offered in lieu of lunch. I only joined it to impress her, to be with her. Once, in mid-workout, when the instructor asked us to check our pulses, I was possessed of an idea. I reached out with my right hand to Lydia and delicately placed my fingertips on her pulsating jugular, even as I continued to feel my own fluttering beat under the quivering fingertips of my left hand. In that moment our heartbeats were joined and a dazzling, amused smile brightened her lovely face.

In retrospect, it was perhaps the smile of the spider who has seen her prey stick in the web. I have been on the other side of that smile; I should have recognized it for what it was. But I was smitten. It all seems sweet and innocent now, but the law is designed to protect the offended. I had grown up in a different corporate environment. I did not know how much I risked with such gestures.

* * *

Lydia formally brought the charges. I fought them valiantly. In the end, the corporation could not allow itself to be exposed to the liability I had broached. The last day was a terrible one. With my termination, I felt withered. I was given three hours to clear out. Word spread like wildfire. Dismayed, my many friends, admirers, even my enemies, flocked to my office. I was in no shape to receive them. I babbled bitterly, incoherent. Too late I had reversed myself and denied everything in a last-ditch effort to bring my reputation to bear and discredit my youthful accuser. Too late I had secured counsel. I threatened countersuit. There was no case. I had already confessed convincingly. The rumors and gossip that had lurked about the edges of my reputation for years now lurched to the fore to convict me. Too late I prepared a resume and looked in earnest for a new job.

After I was fired, my friends lost track of me. I moved away. They heard so many things, that my wife had left me and my children had ostracized me; that I was on the verge of a breakdown and was at a complete loss as to how to find new work, given the blot upon my name. Months went by and more stories surfaced: that I was living, alone, in Oregon, teaching history at an all-boy's school, that I had killed myself, that I had gone abroad to work in Bangkok or Buenos Aires or Dublin, that I was a work-a-day sales representative for a competitor's line, that I had gotten back together with my wife, that I was in prison, that I was on the verge of becoming a millionaire investment banker, that I had written a new, bestselling romance novel under a *nom de plume*, that I drove a UPS truck in Cincinnati, that I had been in and out of alcohol rehabilitation and was working with the homeless in New York, that I was a successful real estate agent in Florida, that I was a deckhand on a tramp steamer in the Orient, that I had died of heart failure. As the years have come and gone, I can say that all of these were true and none of them were true. And on and on the rumors multiplied, representing more the dreams of the teller than of any link to the truth of what had become of the Safe One.

But perhaps you are unsettled, perhaps you now feel sullied with possessing knowledge you do not want to own. If the mighty are fallen, then what of the weak? How is one to live a life, where is the order, or even the consolation, if no one, not any one, is ever safe in a corporation, in a world, in a universe, governed ultimately by the senseless, inexorable, juggernaut power of love.

All that remained for my friends was a view of the tragic element, of a loyal and entertaining fellow who by dint of some quirk in his personality chose to apply his remarkable skills to dark purposes; all that was left perhaps for his slayer or the others who may have harbored some resentment at being either taken in or jilted or both, was the cold comfort of the fact that there was no such thing as a Safe Man after all.

Walter G. Sutton, III

Christmas 1987

I knew that it would happen
life was going too well
or seemed to be
but really there were problems everywhere
and I couldn't see them
I was the boy genius
who made up the impossible company
vice presidents in charge of everything
all of them played golf too

Flying to important meetings
with important people
in pinstriped suits
that was my life
there was no time to dig in and
turn over the rocks
to see the bugs crawling around
I was in a dream
a power dream
one which made me think I was seeing clearly

Important papers delivered to my desk
by one of my two secretaries
little yellow tabs sticking out of the stack
so that I will know where to sign
"What is this" I ask
"oh just a five year lease
on two floors of a skyscraper
in Century City"
"Of course," I say
in for a penny in for a pound

or three million pounds as it turned out
Standing up from my desk looking down 25 floors
at all of the little movements
people I think, but here I am
feeling powerful

I signed a lot of paper today
I think I will manage by walking around
so I walk
People greet me in the hallways
from their desks
even in the bathrooms
"Hi Mr. Sutton how are you today?"
"I am great
Colline,
Tim,
Marilyn,
Alex,
Vincent,
Tom,
Roger,
Sam,
Eric,
Tamara,
Joan,
Richard,
Karen
"And how are things going here at the office" I ask
and they all say "great, everything is wonderful"
Of course it is
I have made this business up
I only make up things that are
wonderful
things that work perfectly.
I deserve it

Sitting in a patio looking out at the waves breaking
at Poi Pu beach I receive the message
"I am sorry to interrupt your vacation, but you must get in touch
with the office immediately"
I'm absorbing tropical sun, being cooled by the tradewinds
A Hawaiian Lizard, the big Kahuna Lizard

The tops of the waves rolling in
are white with feathers
trailing a veil of spray behind them
like so many brides rushing to the
beach on a windy day
Then there is something large
rising up in the water
something as wide as the beach
inhuman extra human size
My father dead for ten years
and still stalking me
I look at the telegram again
and know that I've been caught

Calling to the mainland
makes voices echo
So really bad news sounds even worse
And this was really bad
We have lost the big contract
If we don't get another soon we will go under
I knew that we couldn't replace the contract
soon enough

I wrote in my journal that night
scribbling disbelief
Invisible feelings with visible ink
I drew a cartoon of a building falling over
a little stick figure standing on top as it fell
Again I could feel Father behind me
I actually turned around,
I didn't want him to see what I was writing
I knew he would be critical

The next day I stood in front of my wife and
Jessika my 17 year old daughter
Marcel my 16 year old son
Nick my 15 year old son
and said . . . "we have had a huge failure
I am afraid that in the next year or so I may lose the business
and all of our money will be gone
We will all be living a very different life"
Jessika and my wife both looked wide eyed and shocked

the boys asked if we had to go home now or could we stay
until the end of our vacation
Jessika smiled and said
"Aw Dad, you will pull it out . . . ."
"Yes," said my wife, "we know you can
You always have in the past"

Alone again on the beach,
walking towards the sunset
the sand changing from white
to orange
the waves still rushing in
Bright green algae clings to the black lava rocks
which jut through the sand
Water covers my feet each time a wave comes to shore
I am alone except for Dad
And he is laughing
"I told you so," he is saying.

Notes on Contributors

CONSTANCE ALEXANDER is president of INTEX Communications. She is a former AT&T executive. INTEX specializes in providing consulting services in long-range planning and marketing for organizations experiencing major change. She also writes a twice-a-week column for a newspaper and has written three plays which have been produced locally and elsewhere in the state of Kentucky.

DAVID ALPAUGH has his own desktop publishing business in the San Francisco Bay Area. He has been Advertising Director for Central Bank, Heald Colleges of California and National Education Centers. His poems have appeared in *Exquisite Corpse*, *Poets On* and *Byline* and are forthcoming in *Deviance*, *Poultry*, *University Bookman* and *Writer's Journal.*

JAMES A. AUTRY is the president of Meredith Corporation, publisher of *Ladies Home Journal, Better Homes & Gardens, Metropolitan Home*; his most recent publication is *Love and Profit*, a collection of poetry and essays. He lives in Des Moines, Iowa.

ART BECK has worked in corporate middle management all his life. He has published six books, including translations of Rilke and the 6th c. Roman poet, Luxorius, plus a long narrative poem based on memoirs of Casanova. He lives in San Francisco.

LEONARD S. BERNSTEIN is the president of Candlesticks, Inc. in New York and Pennsylvania; a manufacturer of children's clothing. His articles have been published in *Ladies Home Journal, The New York Times, The Wall Street Journal* and *Family Circle.*

KATE BERTRAND is a business writer and editor who works from her home in Pacifica, California. She is currently senior editor for *Business Marketing*. She has published several poems in small literary magazines.

JAY A. BLUMENTHAL is a professional writer and marketing manager. His clients include Barrons, Merrill Lynch, Chase Manhattan and AT&T. His poetry has appeared in *The American Scholar*, *The Carolina Quarterly*, *Northwest Review* and elsewhere. He says he's an emigre from academe—Ph.D. in English, Drew University. He lives in Chatham, New Jersey.

PAULINA BORSOOK was an editor for McGraw Hill for five years and now works as an editorial consultant and technical writer. She is also enrolled in Columbia University's MFA writing program.

LES BRIDGES is president of Lyndawn Corporation in New York. He performs his poetry at various places in New York City and Chicago. His work has appeared in the *The New York Times*, *ABC No Rio Magazine*, *Libido*, *National Poetry Magazine* and *City Rant*, etc.; he has published two chapbooks. He has written, directed and starred in a short play, *Vampire on Flight 8* performed at New York's La Mama theater in 1990.

CRAIG BROWN has been a programmer/analyst for twenty-three years. He lives in Danville, Illinois. He is currently writing a science fiction novel.

DAN BROWN is a systems analyst for IBM (10 years). His poems have appeared or are forthcoming in *Poetry Northwest*, *Cream City Review*, *Tar River Poetry*, and *Poet and Critic*.

ROSS CHICHESTER was president of Stonelight Tile Company from 1954-1980, then vice-president and manager under the new owner until 1986. He has sold freelance television scripts on scientific subjects, and one of his articles was published in *Sports Illustrated*. He lives in Saratoga, California.

LAWRENCE COATES has published stories in *Coydog Review, Alchemy, Berkeley Fiction Review, Missouri Review,* and a non-fiction article in *Chicago Tribune* (1988). He spent eight years with the Coast Guard and Merchant Marine and has lived in Spain, France, Mexico and at present Albany, California.

RICHARD COLE is a technical copywriter in a New York advertising agency.

RON CZERWIEN is a marketing manager for Kemper Insurance and a member of the Wisconsin Fellowship of Poets. His poems have appeared in *WFOP Calendar,* and the *Wisconsin Academy Review.*

DAVID DEL BOURGO has been writing poetry for thirty years. Currently, he sells computers for Hewlett Packard. His poems have been published in *Epos, Hyperion, Electrum, The Northridge Review* and elsewhere. His sixth book of poetry is titled *Composite Things.* He lives in Woodland Hills, California.

JOHN DICKSON spent forty years as a member of the Chicago Board of Trade and had his own futures trading business. Three collections of his poetry have been published. When his first volume of poetry *Victoria Hall* was published, he gave up business for poetry. He has since published a second collection of poetry *Waving At Trains.*

TINA QUINN DURHAM is currently freelancing in desktop publishing and computer training. She has owned and managed a computer store, and has worked as a microcomputer operator. She lives in Mesa, Arizona.

CHARLES ENTREKIN is founder and partner of a computer consulting firm in San Francisco, The Application Group, Inc., which specializes in large mainframe data bases and human resources technologies. He was one of the founders of the Berkeley Poets Cooperative. A Yaddo Colony Fellow, his work has appeared in many small press publications. His fourth book of poems was published this year.

GAVIN EWART is an English poet.

C. B. FOLLETT has been for the past seventeen years the designer and owner of The Peaceable Kingdom, a ceramic company in Sausalito, California specializing in animal/bird/fish related jewelry. Her poems have been printed or accepted by *South Coast Poetry Review, Snowy Egret*, and the *Taos Review*, among others.

JAMES CASTLE FURLONG is managing editor of Dow Jones International News Service and the Capital Market Report. He writes that he does more managing than editing. He lives in Rye, New York.

M. DANA GIOIA is vice president, Marketing Desserts Division, KRAFT GENERAL FOODS and has been with that company since 1977. He holds an MA from Harvard in Comparative Literature and an MBA from Stanford Business School. He has published over 100 essays in magazines (*The Hudson Review, Kenyon Review, Poetry, The Nation, The New Yorker, The Atlantic, The New York Times Book Review*, and others). Two collections of his poems have been issued by Graywolf Press. He is a translator of Italian poetry and is co-editor of two editions of Italian poets. His poetry has appeared in numerous literary journals.

MIRIAM GOODMAN has worked for many years in speech recognition technology at MIT's Lincoln Labs; currently she is at Kurzweil Artificial Intelligence, Inc. She has published a chapbook *Permanent Wave* and a book of poems, *Signal:: Noise*, both published by Alice James Books in Cambridge, Massachusetts. Her poems have appeared recently in *Poetry*, in Paul Ruffin's *Contemporary New England Poetry: A Sampler* (Texas Review Press) in *Word of Mouth* (Crossing Press) and in *Labor in the Post-Industrial Age* (Pig Iron Press).

GARY GRELLI is currently a data base analyst at a large insurance company in San Antonio, Texas. He has published poems in several anthologies—*Poets of The Lake*, and forthcoming, *A Language We Know At Once*.

MARK HALL is currently editor-in-chief of LAN Technology, a monthly computer-related magazine with paid subscriptions of 50,000. He was founding editor and publisher of *Sun World* magazine and continues as contributing editor and columnist. He is co-author of a book on Sun Microsystems—*Sunburst* (eight weeks on *San Francisco Chronicle*'s best-seller list). He has published more than 125 articles in more than 30 magazines, journals and books. Many of his articles have been translated into German, French and Japanese.

EMILY HAWTHORNE was a broker in the San Francisco office of Merrill Lynch for a number of years. A recent graduate of Stanford's Product Design MA program, she is now working at LSI Logic, in Milpitas.

STEVEN HEIGHTON has worked as a waiter in a Japanese restaurant. Currently, he lives in Kingston, Ontario, Canada. He is editor of the literary magazine *Quarry*. "Five Paintings of the New Japan" won *Prism International*'s prize for best story, 1990.

LINDSAY HILL is executive vice president (Director of Sales) at Vining-Sparks IBG, an investment banking firm headquartered in Memphis. He has published two collections of poetry—*Avelaval* (Oyez) and *Archaeology* (St. Luke's Press). His work has appeared in numerous periodicals and in the anthology *The Good People of Gomorrah* (St. Luke's Press). A book-length poem *Kill Series* is forthcoming from Arundel in 1992.

CAROLYN HULL is vice president, branch manager and commercial lender for an independent bank in San Diego, California. Her poetry has appeared in *Talapus, San Diego Poets' Press, Pacific Review* and other literary journals.

PENELOPE KARAGEORGE has moved from publicity manager at *People* magazine to a freelance publicist, journalist and adjunct professor at City College of New York. Her poems have appeared in *Alchemy, Wordsmith,* and *Poetry in Performance*. She has written two novels.

C. ALLAN MAY, JR. was an MIS manager for 20 years at Tektronix, Inc., in Beaverton, Oregon. He was laid off in 1990 and formed his own consulting company that specializes in strategic planning and organizational renewal. He published two literary magazines in college and has written poetry ever since.

ROBERT J. McKENTY is with The Equitable Financial Companies. He provides PC support for executives. In 1972 he updated the psalms for a modern, urban society. (*Psalms for the Pseventies*). His verses have appeared in many periodicals including *The New York Times, Marriage and Family Living, Playboy, The Wall Street Journal, Reader's Digest,* and *The Arizona Republic.* He lives in New York City.

ROBERT AQUINAS McNALLY is a poet and writer. He has published two non-fiction books and is working on a third. Most recently, he was vice president, director, and senior copywriter for Image Group, a Northern California marketing communications company. He lives in Walnut Creek, California.

ROBERT MINKOFF has worked as managing editor of The Fiction Collective, as a paralegal in a corporate law firm in New York, and as manager of internal finance at CBS, Inc.; he is currently a free-lance business writer specializing in speeches and annual reports. His stories have been published in *Epoch, Kansas Quarterly, New England Review/Bread Loaf Quarterly,* and the 1989-90 Pushcart Prize anthology. He has an MBA in finance and accounting from Columbia and a Ph.D. in English from Cornell.

G. E. MURRAY is chairman of Ruder-Finn Public Relations Chicago office and chair of the Midwest branch of PEN American Center. He is poetry critic for the *Chicago Tribune* and *Chicago Magazine.* He has published five books of poems and has appeared in more than sixty magazines. His reviews, criticism, features and interviews appear in numerous journals and newspapers.

WADE NEWMAN was an executive recruiter and now serves as director of personnel for Moishe Shipping, New York City. He has published poems in various literary magazines and journals: *Kenyon Review, Carolina Quarterly, Kansas Quarterly, Nimrod, Croton Review* and elsewhere. He also has appeared in several anthologies of American poetry.

ROBERT ORNDORFF managed software development teams at Microsoft for four years, and is currently working for Microsoft in Tokyo.

ED PACKMAN lives in the San Francisco Bay Area. He has worked as a market research analyst and manager. His short stories have appeared in regional and literary magazines.

JONATHAN PRICE is a computer consultant, creating documentation, interactive demos, and online help for software on personal computers and mainframes. He lives in Albuquerque, New Mexico.

AL SANDVIK has been writing free lance since his retirement in 1987 as Chairman of Kerker & Associates, a Minneapolis advertising agency. He has published in literary magazines, commercial magazines and newspapers.

ANDREW SCHULTZ lives in Des Moines, Iowa and works in magazine circulation for Meredith Corporation, publisher of *Better Homes and Gardens*.

CATHERINE SHAW says she is a "managerial type" (she was an editor at Simon and Schuster for several years). She lives in New York City. Her poetry has appeared in *The Little Magazine, Rhino, The Centennial Review, Thema* and *Pig Iron*. She has been an office temp in over one hundred New York City corporations.

JAMES SHEPARD is proxy supervisor of Georgeson & Company's Pittsburgh office. He has written numerous short stories, business plans and speeches. He was named a winner in *Writer's Digest* 1991 Short Story and Script Competitions.

BETTY SHERWOOD is president of Second Wave Computing, Inc., a business she started in 1983. Her company specializes in computer user documentation, computer applications training, and desktop design. She lives in Chicago.

FLOYD SKLOOT's first novel, *Pilgrim's Harbor*, is forthcoming next year from *Story Line Press*. He has published three poetry collections. His work has appeared in *Harper's*, *Shenandoah*, *Commonwealth*, *Runner's World*, *The American Scholar*, and *Prairie Schooner*. For many years he worked in business and public policy in the states of Washington, Oregon and Illinois. He lives in Portland, Oregon.

HENRY SLESAR is currently a full-time free lance writer but for twenty-three years worked in advertising as copywriter, creative director, and owner. He has also been owner-operator of a cable TV company in Duchess County, New York. He lives in New York.

JUDITH SMALL is a senior legal assistant at Morrison & Foerster, San Francisco. She has published poetry, essays and fiction and has won three awards for her poetry.

WALTER G. SUTTON, III is founder and president of the evidence management and litigation support firm of Logan Pearsall, Inc., located in Los Angeles and Seattle.

JILL C. WHEELER is an account executive with Dunstan & Partners, Inc., a Minneapolis public relations firm. She is author of twenty-one children's books.

JEFFREY ZYGMONT lives in Boston and is president of MESAGO USA Corporation, a Boston subsidiary of an international company, MESAGO Holding, based in Stuttgart, Germany. MESAGO organizes conferences and exhibitions in the high-tech industries.

Credits

The University of Phoenix Press gratefully acknowledges the publications in which the following works first appeared.

Alpaugh, David. "A California Ad Man Celebrates His Art." *The Irreversible Man.* Los Angeles: R. Poetica Press for Pacificus Foundation, 1991.

Autry, James A. "Irreverent Thoughts About Organization Charts," "Lights Flashing at O'Hare," "Listening and Learning," "Recessions," "Romantic Revelations." *Love and Profit: The Art of Caring Leadership.* New York: William Morrow & Co., Inc., 1991.

Beck, Art. "Nerves." *The Discovery of Music.* Ellensburg, Wash.: Vagabond Press, 1977.

Bernstein, Leonard S. "The Guided Tour of 7th Avenue." *Prairie Schooner* (Spring 1980): 68-74.

Bridges, Les. "NW Flight 1482, Seat 6A." *Proceed With Caution.* Baltimore: Apathy Press, 1991.

Coates, Lawrence. "other." *Coydog Review* (1988 Series): 14-23.

Czerwien, Ron. "Oasis." *Wisconsin Poets' Calendar.* Oshkosh: Wisconsin Fellowship of Poets, 1990.

Del Bourgo, David. "White Collar." *Vol. No.* 10 (Fall 1987).

Dickson, John. "Oxygen Tent." *Overtures* (1987): 28.

Dickson, John. "The Retirement of Louie Berman." *Victoria Hotel.* Chicago: Chicago Review Press, 1979.

Entrekin, Charles. "Day after the Market Crash—San Francisco, October, 1987." *In This Hour.* Berkeley, Calif.: Berkeley Poets Workshop and Press, 1989.

Gioia, M. Dana. "Eastern Standard Time," "The Man In The Open Doorway." *Daily Horoscope*. Saint Paul, Minn.: Graywolf Press, 1986.

Gioia, M. Dana. "Money." *The Gods of Winter*. Saint Paul, Minn.: Graywolf Press, 1991.

Gioia, M. Dana. "When Money Doesn't Talk: Reflections on Business, Poetry, and Audience." *Epoch* (1989 Series): 151-154.

Goodman, Miriam. "Computer Lab," "Happy Endings," "Job Hunting." *Signal:: Noise*, Cambridge, Mass.: Alice James Books, 1982.

Hall, Mark. "All The Young Fausts." *The North American Review* (March 1984): 42.

Heighton, Steven. "Five Paintings of the New Japan." *Prism International* (Spring 1991): 7-25. *Stand Magazine* (July 1991): 47-61.

Hill, Lindsay. "Taking Up Serpents (Chicago Board of Trade)." *Archaeology*. Memphis: St. Luke's Press, 1987.

Murray, G.E. "Crossings: November 21-22." *The Ohio Journal* (Fall/Winter 1988-89): 32-35.

Newman, Wade. "Business and Poetry." *Crosscurrents* (January 1989): 39.

Sandvik, Al. "Severance." *Wellspring*. Long Lake, Minn.: Castalia Bookmakers, Inc., 1990.

Skloot, Floyd. "A Lateral Move." *Confrontation* (Fall/Winter 1989): 185-192.

Skloot, Floyd. "A Working Marriage." *Chelsea* (Spring 1985): 138-139.

Skloot, Floyd. "I Am Getting A Mountain View." *Phantasm* (Spring 1979).

Small, Judith. "Body of Work." *The New Yorker* (July 8, 1991): 30-32.